FACES from HISTORY

George Woodcock

FACES from HISTORY

Canadian Profiles & Portraits

Hurtig Publishers

Hurtig Publishers
10560 105 Street
Edmonton, Alberta

Canadian Cataloguing in Publication Data

Woodcock, George, 1912-
    Faces from history

        Includes index.
        ISBN 0-88830-151-0

        1. Canada–Biography.   2. Canada–Biography–
Portraits.   I. Title. FC25.W65   920′.071
C78-002064-2   F1005.W65

Printed and bound in Canada

Contents

Introduction/7

The Colonial Period
William Lyon Mackenzie/*10*
Allan MacNab/*12*
Robert Baldwin/*14*
Francis Hincks/*16*
Louis-Hippolyte La Fontaine/*18*
John Sandfield Macdonald/*20*
Egerton Ryerson/*22*
George Simpson/*24*
William Hamilton Merritt/*26*
Casimir Stanislaus Gzowski/*28*
William Molson/*30*

The Men of Confederation
John Alexander Macdonald/*32*
George-Étienne Cartier/*34*
Joseph Howe/*36*
Alexander Tilloch Galt/*38*
Thomas D'Arcy McGee/*40*
George Brown/*42*
Samuel Leonard Tilley/*44*
Charles Tupper/*46*

From Ocean Unto Ocean
Hugh Allan/*48*
Alexander Mackenzie/*50*
Donald Alexander Smith/*52*
George Stephen/*54*
William Van Horne/*56*
Oliver Mowat/*58*
D'Alton McCarthy/*60*
Edward Blake/*62*
Wilfrid Laurier/*64*
Clifford Sifton/*66*
Richard John Cartwright/*68*
Timothy Eaton/*70*
Margaret Murray/*72*
John Wilson Bengough/*74*
Alexander Graham Bell/*76*

The Fact of Quebec
Louis-Joseph Papineau/*78*
Rodolphe Laflamme/*80*
Antoine-Aimé Dorion/*82*
Ignace Bourget/*84*
Elzéar Alexandre Taschereau/*86*
Honoré Mercier/*88*
Joseph-Israel Tarte/*90*
Henri Bourassa/*92*
Camillien Houde/*94*
Lionel-Adolphe Groulx/*96*
Louis-Honoré Fréchette/*98*
Philippe-Joseph Aubert de Gaspé/*100*
Émile Nelligan/*102*

The Opening of the West
Louis Riel/*104*
Alexandre-Antonin Taché/*106*
Adams George Archibald/*108*
John Norquay/*110*
James Morrow Walsh/*112*
Samuel Benfield Steele/*114*
Albert Lacombe/*116*
Edgar Dewdney/*118*
Gabriel Dumont/*120*
Crowfoot/*122*
Poundmaker/*124*
Big Bear/*126*
William Dillon Otter/*128*
Sandford Fleming/*130*
Piapot/*132*
Nicholas Flood Davin/*134*
Robert Chambers Edwards/*136*
Almighty Voice/*138*
John Ware/*140*
George Mercer Dawson/*142*
Charles Edward Saunders/*144*

Land Beyond the Mountains
James Douglas/*146*
Amor De Cosmos/*148*
John Sebastian Helmcken/*150*
Matthew Baillie Begbie/*152*
John Robson/*154*
William Barker/*156*
William Duncan/*158*
David Oppenheimer/*160*
Kootenay Brown/*162*
Peter Vasil'evich Verigin/*164*
Simon Gun-an-Noot/*166*

The True North
John Rae/*168*
Robert Campbell/*170*
William Carpenter Bompas/*172*

Wilfred Thomason Grenfell/*174*
Joseph-Elzéar Bernier/*176*
Vilhjalmur Stefansson/*178*
Wop May/*180*
Henry Asbjorn Larsen/*182*

Provinces of the Mind
Susanna Moodie/*184*
Catharine Parr Traill/*186*
Charles Mair/*188*
Charles G. D. Roberts/*190*
Archibald Lampman/*192*
Duncan Campbell Scott/*194*
Ralph Connor/*196*
Stephen Leacock/*198*
Lucy Maud Montgomery/*200*
Nellie McClung/*202*
Grey Owl/*204*
Pauline Johnson/*206*
Frederick Philip Grove/*208*
Paul Kane/*210*
Cornelius Krieghoff/*212*
William Notman/*214*
Tom Thomson/*216*
Alexander Young Jackson/*218*
Emily Carr/*220*
George Monro Grant/*222*
Goldwin Smith/*224*
Harold Adams Innis/*226*

Days of Trial
Robert Laird Borden/*228*
Arthur William Currie/*230*
Arthur Meighen/*232*
William Lyon Mackenzie King/*234*
John Wesley Dafoe/*236*
Emily Gowan Murphy/*238*
Thomas Alexander Crerar/*240*
Agnes Macphail/*242*
Richard Bedford Bennett/*244*
James Shaver Woodsworth/*246*
William Aberhart/*248*

Notes/250
Picture Credits/252
Index/253

Introduction

The special feature of this collection of portraits of Canadians is that they are all photographs. In the long history of Canada there have been many portraits made by other means than the camera: by the painter's brush, the craftsman's pencil, the engraver's burin, and–in the case of the splendid portrait masks which Tsimshian and Haida Indians used in their ceremonial dances–by the delicate jade adze of the carver. Some of these portraits have been notable works of art, like Pierre Le Ber's three-centuries-old painting of Marguerite Bourgeoys or the haunting anonymous canvas of Mrs. Charles Morrison, made somewhere about 1800, which hangs in the National Gallery. But all of them belong in a different world from the photograph. They are dominated, as any nonmechanical form of art must always be, by the individual talents of the artist and the aesthetic conventions of his age. They are also the expressions of societies arranged according to degree and class, societies that in their various ways–whether they belonged to the old regime of La Nouvelle France, or to the gentlemanly world of New Brunswick Loyalists or Upper Canadian half-pay officers, or to the complex ranking patterns of Pacific Coast Indians–were essentially aristocratic. Only the wealthy and, by implication, the powerful could employ the painter or the carver to portray them by his slow processes.

Photography is in its essence democratic. In so far as it is an art, it becomes so by the perfection of a rather mechanical and eminently reproducible craft. There are conventions even in photography, and there are artifices that photographers use to enhance the appearance and hence the quality of the people or scenes they portray. But this happens in a limited range, and the camera justifies its reputation for candour by showing–no matter how deceptively the lighting may control the mood–only what is actually there. And as a photograph is taken in a mere fraction of the time that is needed to create in paint or wood what was once called "a speaking likeness," the camera is inexpensive in time and money alike, and hence it is a populist form of portraiture, and all the more so since, somewhere about eighty years ago, it was finally harnessed to the service of the daily press.

The transition from the painter's to the photographer's studio corresponds surprisingly closely to the emergence of Canada out of colonial dependence into national self-consciousness. The earliest portraits made in Canada by any kind of photographic process–the daguerreotypes–began to appear during the late 1840s, but most of the surviving examples date from the early 1850s, after which they were briefly superseded by the ambrotypes–glass negatives produced by the collodion process and seen as positives by being mounted on a black surface. Wet-plate photography quickly brought in the fashion of the *cartes de visite* bearing the portraits of those who presented them, and by the 1860s this innovation had almost ruined the art of miniature painting.

The photographer as artist began to appear in Canada by the late 1850s; it was in 1856 that William Notman–the first internationally known Canadian photographer–established his studio in Montreal and began to produce those extraordinary views adapted for the stereoscope on which his earliest fame was built. But Canada also has a historic place in the development of that most democratic form of representational art, the press photograph. The *Canadian Illustrated News*, our first national news magazine, was founded in 1869, two years after Confederation. The *Illustrated London News* had already made wide use of photography in the preparation of relatively authentic line engravings of interesting events, but the *Canadian Illustrated News* was the first magazine in the world to include half-tone reproductions of photographs; they were produced by a process invented by Augustus Leggo, but they had to be printed lithographically, independently of the letterpress text, and they did not continue to appear after 1872 when Leggo left for New York. It was not until the later nineteenth century, after George Eastman developed in the late 1880s a rapid and practical form of dry-plate photography with his Kodak camera and its celluloid film, that effective ways of combining half-tone photographic reproductions with letterpress resulted in the kind of newspapers we know today, in which portraiture, formerly the privilege of the flattered men of power, has been brought–in often unflattering forms–into everyone's house.

The portraits included in this gallery of notable Canadians are drawn from all the stages of photography I have mentioned, beginning with the carefully posed daguerreotype, which demanded minutes of stillness on the subject's part, and ending with the instant snapshot of the news photographer. They cover almost a century, from the early 1850s to the early 1940s, but the relevance of their subjects to Canadian history is considerably broader in time, covering the whole span of our awareness of ourselves as a distinct collection of peoples inhabiting a distinct territory: in other words, as a nation. Some of the earliest figures in this volume, like W.H. Merritt and Allan MacNab, played their part in the War of 1812 when American invasion first made Canadians in large numbers aware that they had something of their own to defend and made them willing to defend it.

Others were involved on various sides in the Rebellion of 1837 and in the later conflicts of 1869 and 1885 which helped to shape the Canadian West. The later photographs bring us up to the men and events of the 1930s, immediately preceding World War II, the virtual watershed between the largely rural Canada of the century our portraits represent and the very different, mainly urban Canada that emerged after 1945. What we present, in other words, is basic and historic Canada, the age of becoming rather than being a nation.

Not every distinguished or interesting Canadian of the first century of photography is here represented. Some, so far as we know, were never photographed; of others, the surviving photographs are too imperfect to be reproducible. Some, like the governors general, were here too short a time to rank as Canadians; others, like the poet Bliss Carman and the novelist Sara Jeannette Duncan, elected by departure to cease being Canadians. But those that remain represent, in their lives and achievements, a true cross section of the emergent Canadian nation in all its aspects, in all its activities. If the pseudoscience of physiognomy were still fashionable, its practitioners might be inspired by the gallery of faces we present to establish a national psychology. For us, their interest lies in their individuality, just as the narratives which accompany each of them project the immense variety among Canadians, the product of a continuous process of immigration and intermingling which began when the first proto-Indians and proto-Eskimos came over the land bridge that once closed off the Bering Strait, and which has not ended to this day.

When these photographs were brought together and the profiles in prose were written, various possibilities of arrangement were considered. They could have been ordered alphabetically, but that seemed to establish no meaningful relationship at all; they could have been arranged according to the date of the birth or death of the person photographed, but as the successive volumes of the *Dictionary of Canadian Biography* (arranged according to the date of death) have shown, a man can survive long after the period when his actions were significant. The arrangement we finally established may not be an ideal one, but we feel it tells more about Canadian history and the people who made it than any mechanical arrangement by alphabet or calendar.

Canada is a country where distance as well as time is important and where geography and history mingle in differing proportions as motivating factors, and we have observed both factors. There are some people in our collection whose importance is related less to what happened in a particular region than to what happened in a special period in Canadian history. These people we have gathered in period clusters, "The Colonial Period," "The Men of Confederation," "From Ocean unto Ocean" (dealing with the age from Confederation to World War I), and "Days of Trial" (dealing with the period of World War I and the depression). Other clusters embrace people whose lives were related to place perhaps even more than to period, as in "The Fact of Quebec," "The Opening of the West," "Land Beyond the Mountains," and "The True North." And then there is the section – "Provinces of the Mind" – inhabited by those whose region has been mainly the timeless land of the imagination, expressed in the creations of the artist, the speculations of the scholar.

One thing unites the people whose portraits appear in this collection. They are, like all of us, shaped to a degree by the grand old mechanisms of heredity and environment. But in history, as in human lives, there is a saving reciprocity. We in turn shape the times and places that have shaped us. Perhaps more than the people of any other century, those whose portraits are here reproduced created the form of our nation, the aspirations of our people. Without them, Canada would not exist as we know it. If we belonged to a traditionalist society, we would call these men and women "the Ancestors," but as we do not, let us merely claim kinship and regard this book as nothing more portentous than the family album of a country.

We must end by mentioning how much this book owes to the efforts of Hugh Dempsey. He gathered the original collection of photographs from which most of these have been selected; only a few have since been added from other sources. A great deal of basic research for the profiles was also done by him. The writing of them, the form they have taken, and the judgments they sometimes make are entirely my responsibility.

GEORGE WOODCOCK

8

FACES from HISTORY

William Lyon Mackenzie

William Lyon Mackenzie, leader of the only armed rebellion among English-speaking Canadians, was a man of fiery temper and minute stature; in any company he was likely to be the smallest, but also the most dynamic, his nervous and vehement manner emphasized by the fiery red wig he wore on a prematurely bald head.

Mackenzie was born near Dundee in 1795, grandson of a clansman who fought at Culloden, son of an impoverished weaver. After wandering in England and France, abortively attempting various careers, he left for Canada in 1820 on the sailing ship *Psyche*. He engaged in petty retail business in small Upper Canadian towns and then, in 1824, entered journalism by founding in Queenston the *Colonial Advocate*. In the autumn he moved both home and journal to York; his career as the most intransigent Canadian radical of his time was about to begin.

As a journalist, Mackenzie was intemperate and indiscreet, qualities that quickly created a public among the malcontent farmers of Upper Canada, whom he made his special constituency. It was said of Mackenzie that he could be trusted with your life but never with your secrets, and in 1826 his indiscretions while discussing a duel between members of the Family Compact led a band of young Tories to wreck the *Colonial Advocate*'s press. Mackenzie won heavy damages, which saved him from bankruptcy, and became so popular among the discontented that in 1828 he was elected to the Legislative Assembly of Upper Canada. While the Reformers controlled the assembly, Mackenzie was a tolerated radical independent, blaming all economic and political woes on the governor, his officials, and the appointed Executive Council.[1] But when the Tories gained power in the assembly, Mackenzie was expelled for libellous statements. The electors returned him, and he was expelled again–achieving in all five expulsions and as many re-elections. Eventually he was allowed to return to his seat in 1835, the year he became the first mayor–and a highly impractical one–of the newly created city of Toronto.

In the Legislative Assembly of 1835 Mackenzie became chairman of its Select Committee on Grievances and drew up a report of over five hundred pages, which served as an indictment of the whole system of government by delegated authority. He travelled to England to put the case before the British government but realized how unsuccessful he had been when the new governor, Sir Francis Bond Head, manoeuvred an election in which the Reformers were defeated, and Lord Russell in London enunciated in 1837 the Ten Resolutions which maintained the status quo and authorized the governor to appropriate funds if the assembly refused to vote them.

It was once again the issue of "taxation without representation," over which King Charles had lost his head and King George his American colonies. Admiring the American Revolution, Mackenzie decided that armed revolt was the only way out, and he was the most persistent organizer of the rising of December 1837, when rebel farmers gathered north of Toronto and were defeated by the loyalists, Mackenzie fleeing to the United States while many of his followers were imprisoned and some were hanged.

From exile Mackenzie attempted to sustain a provisional government on a speck of Canadian soil called Navy Island in the Niagara River, but the Canadian militia made his position untenable and the Americans imprisoned him for infringing their neutrality. After release he became an American citizen but was so disillusioned by 1847 that he said, "Had I passed nine years in the United States before instead of after the outbreak, I am sure I would have been the last man in America to be engaged in it."

In 1849 Mackenzie was glad to return to Canada under an amnesty. He was re-elected to the Legislative Assembly but gathered no following, agreed with no party, and in 1858 retired–disillusioned–from politics. In 1860 he even ceased to publish his last newspaper, *Mackenzie's Weekly Message*, and in 1861 he died of apoplexy.

The times seemed to have passed Mackenzie by; indeed, perhaps there was only one significant period in his life, between the founding of the *Advocate* in 1824 and the Rebellion of 1837, when he served as a focus for discontent and a catalyst for the events that led, through the Durham Report[2] on the rebellions, to responsible government in the 1840s. Mackenzie was a rebel rather than a statesman, with no positive policies. It was always difficult to say what he stood for but never difficult to say what he stood against: authority in general and its inherent liability to be abused.

Allan MacNab

If any single man became William Lyon Mackenzie's nemesis, it was Allan Napier MacNab, another Highlander by descent. MacNab's father had been an officer in Simcoe's Queen's Rangers during the American Revolution and had settled in Upper Canada, where he remained an impecunious hanger-on of the establishment. Allan Napier MacNab, born in 1798, saw service as a boy in the War of 1812 and was made an ensign at the age of sixteen. After the war he found he must succeed by his wits, since he had no relatives in the inner Tory circle that ruled the province, and he acquired a predatory adaptability that marked the whole of his later career.

Having been called to the bar in 1826, MacNab realized that there was no future for him in York, the stronghold of the established Tory families, and decided to build an independent centre of power elsewhere. Settled in Hamilton, he began to speculate in property and within a decade owned most of the valuable real estate in the town and its vicinity. He went into banking, gaining control of the Gore Bank which was chartered in 1835, and early on realized the importance of steamship and railway promotion, in which he was engaged for the rest of his life.

MacNab was elected to the Legislative Assembly of Upper Canada in 1830, where William Lyon Mackenzie earned his enmity by forcing his suspension for ten days over a breach of privilege. Later MacNab played a leading part in the five expulsions of Mackenzie from the same assembly. When the rebellion broke out in 1837, he hurried as lieutenant-colonel of the Gore militia to the support of the government, and it was he, under the nominal command of Colonel FitzGibbon, who led the main column that marched up Yonge Street to disperse the insurgents. He suppressed a later outbreak in the London area and led the attack on Mackenzie's provisional government on Navy Island, almost causing an international incident by authorizing the destruction of the American ship *Caroline*, which had been supplying the rebels.

MacNab was active in Upper Canadian politics for most of his life and for a brief period was prime minister of United Canada. He had always posed as an independent,

which led to his election as speaker of the assembly in 1837, and he showed a business-oriented pragmatism in his attitude to public affairs, perhaps best expressed in his port-wine inspired remark of 1851: "All my politics are railroads." Whatever was good for business, he held, was good for the country.

This attitude prevented him from becoming a doctrinaire Tory, and although he distrusted responsible government, he was willing to participate when it came into being. It was this flexibility that enabled him to take part – with that other superb pragmatist, Sir John A. Macdonald – in founding the curious coalition of radical Tories and conservative Reformers that became the Liberal–Conservative Party. From 1854 to 1856, as uneasy figurehead of the alliance, MacNab was prime minister of Canada and presided over a series of important reforms, including the abolition of seigniorial tenure in Lower Canada, the final secularization of the Clergy Reserves in Upper Canada, and the transformation of the Legislative Council – the upper house of the government – from an appointed to an elective body. He resigned in 1856, largely because his prime ministership had become involved in the war of interests between rival railway groups.

MacNab departed to England, tried in vain to enter the House of Commons in Westminster, and in 1860 returned to Canada, something of an anachronism, since the Family Compact world of his youth was dead and the business world in whose emergent stages he had been so successful had fallen into the hands of younger, even less scrupulous men. It is true that he joined the Legislative Council in 1860 and was elected speaker in 1862, but his health became too precarious to sustain the office and he withdrew to his seventy-two-room mock castle of Dundurn at Hamilton and treasured the empty triumph of his baronetcy until he died later in 1862.

Robert Baldwin

"The race is not to the swift, nor the battle to the strong," says Ecclesiastes, and the text is appropriate to the situation after the Upper Canadian rebellion of 1837, when political change followed neither the pattern anticipated by the precipitate rebel, Mackenzie, nor that envisioned by the Tories who defeated him, but rather the line laid down by the moderate Reformers, and especially by Robert Baldwin and his father William Warren Baldwin.

William Baldwin came to Canada from Ireland with the double profession of physician and lawyer, and practised both in York. From 1824 to 1830 he was leader of the Reformers in the Legislative Assembly of Upper Canada; in 1836 he became president of the Constitutional Reform Society; and he is said – in a letter to the Duke of Wellington – to have set going the idea of responsible government in Canada: the principle of an administration being answerable to the people's elected representatives and liable to dismissal when it loses their confidence.

Robert Baldwin, born in 1804, followed his father into the legal profession and into politics, being elected briefly to the Legislative Assembly in 1829. Because of his known ability, he was appointed to the Executive Council by Sir Francis Bond Head in 1836 but resigned in a few weeks when it was evident that the governor had no intention of establishing a true responsible government. During the Rebellion of 1837 Baldwin tried unsuccessfully to persuade Mackenzie to abandon his armed struggle; later he impressed Lord Durham and led him to advocate responsible government for the North American colonies in his famous report of 1839.

Until responsible government came into being, Baldwin held office for short periods only and with some reluctance. He was made solicitor general for Upper Canada in 1840, and attorney general for Canada West when the provinces were united in 1841, but he resigned almost immediately when the governor general refused to reform the administration. He took a leading part in the opposition in the Legislative Assembly and introduced resolutions demanding responsible government. In the elections of 1842 the Reformers gained a majority in the assembly and Sir

Charles Bagot, now governor general, made an important step towards full responsible government by inviting them to form an administration, which Baldwin and Louis-Hippolyte La Fontaine jointly led. After just over a year they resigned because Bagot's successor, Sir Charles Metcalfe, refused to allow them to control political appointments.

By 1848, when Baldwin and La Fontaine again took office at the head of their Great Ministry, as it was called, it had become clear that the imperial government, acting through the new governor general, Lord Elgin (Durham's son-in-law), had accepted responsible government as a better choice than irresponsible authority leading possibly to another rebellion. The test came in 1849 when Baldwin and La Fontaine introduced the Rebellion Losses Bill, which aimed to compensate those who had suffered from the rebellion, including former rebels. Lord Elgin sanctioned the bill although personally he found it repugnant, and so the principle of responsible government was vindicated, even though the angry Tories burnt down the Montreal parliament building in protest.

Canadians were not notably grateful for the achievement, at least at the time, and in the elections of 1851 Robert Baldwin suffered personal defeat. He retired into private life under the impression that he had lost the confidence of his countrymen. His conclusion was an expression of the pride that accompanied his reasonableness and moderation as a reformer. Baldwin went into politics to serve an ideal, not to make a career, and he was perhaps less touched than most Canadian leaders by the corruption of power, since he sought nothing for himself, though in the manner of his time he did not neglect the use of patronage to further his policies. He died relatively young, in 1858.

Francis Hincks

If William Lyon Mackenzie represented the activist and Robert Baldwin the constitutionalist reformer, Francis Hincks can perhaps best be described as the adventurist reformer, for he was a talented arranger and compromiser – rarely without an eye to the main chance.

Born in 1807 as heir to a line of Anglo-Irish parsons, Hincks quickly decided that commerce and politics provided better possibilities for a young man in the early nineteenth century than the Church of Ireland, and he started his working life with an apprenticeship to a Belfast banking house. In 1830 he set off to try his fortune in the West Indies but decided instead to settle in Upper Canada, which he visited on his way back to Ireland. He came to York in 1832 and set up a wholesale warehouse in a building belonging to Robert Baldwin. This began his association with the Reformers, among whom he quickly assumed a leading role, managing the People's Bank (an early predecessor of the Credit Unions), which they set up in 1835 in opposition to the establishment-oriented Bank of Upper Canada, and in 1838 founding a newspaper, the *Examiner*, which quickly became recognized as the organ of the Reform cause.

In 1839 and 1840 Hincks showed his negotiating abilities by initiating a correspondence with Louis-Hippolyte La Fontaine, which led to an alliance of the Upper and Lower Canadian Reformers when the two provinces were united in 1841. Though an outspoken advocate of responsible government, Hincks showed his adventurist inclinations in 1842 when he deserted the other Reformers to become receiver general in Sir Charles Bagot's appointed Executive Council. Later, after the elections of 1842 when Bagot invited the Reformers to set up an administration, Hincks retained the same post and in 1843 resigned with the other Reformers.

In 1844 he showed his political talents in a different way, by organizing strong-arm groups in Montreal to combat the hooligan gangs by which the Tories tried to control elections in that city. In 1848 he took his place as inspector general in the second Baldwin–La Fontaine administration, and when both Baldwin and La Fontaine resigned in 1851, it was Hincks who with A. N. Morin headed the new government.

The Hincks–Morin administration, nominally reformist, was in practice reluctant to offend the vested interests of either Upper or Lower Canada and left unsolved such crucial issues as seigniorial tenure and the Clergy Reserves, though it encouraged railway promoters and pleased the mercantile interests by negotiating, with British mediation in 1854, a tariff-lowering reciprocity agreement with the United States. When Hincks became involved in dubious financial transactions connected with the railways, he and Morin gradually lost support and were forced to resign before the end of 1854.

It was the end of Hincks's career as an influential Canadian political figure, but not of his public life, for the former advocate of responsible government now became surprisingly metamorphosed into an authoritarian colonial official. In 1855 he was appointed governor-in-chief of the Barbados and the Windward Islands, and in 1862 he became governor of British Guiana. On his retirement from the colonial service he returned to Canada and in 1869 joined Sir John A. Macdonald's federal cabinet as finance minister. But his political base had withered away, he was out of touch with the ways of the new dominion, and in 1873 he resigned. He attempted to enter the financial world, but even here he seemed to have lost his touch; the City Bank of Montreal which he directed from 1873 to 1879 was a failure, and he ended his career as the uninspired editor of the *Journal of Commerce* in Montreal.

Louis-Hippolyte La Fontaine

Louis-Hippolyte La Fontaine, first Canadian prime minister under the system of responsible government, was born in 1807, the son of a Boucherville carpenter. Like many ambitious Quebecois in his day, he chose law as his profession and was called to the bar in 1828, assuring his financial position by marrying a wealthy Quebec lawyer's daughter. He developed early an interest in politics, wrote in the Patriote newspaper, *La Minerve*, and—elected to the Legislative Assembly of Lower Canada in 1830—fell under the influence of Louis-Joseph Papineau, carrying his partisanship to the extent of dressing in Patriote homespun and writing aggressive denunciations of the British administrators.

As Papineau and his followers moved towards violent action, La Fontaine's enthusiasm cooled, and early in December 1837, aware of the likely course of events, he went to the governor, Lord Gosford, and pleaded with him to convene Parliament; Gosford refused. La Fontaine then boarded a ship for England, remained abroad during the Lower Canada rebellion, and returned in June 1838. This did not save him from being arrested later in the year when rebellion broke out a second time, but he was released without charge and he later mediated between the Patriotes and Lord Durham to secure lenient treatment for the rebels.

La Fontaine had not abandoned his aim of securing self-government for French-speaking Canadians; he had merely concluded that it could only be achieved through a working alliance of Upper and Lower Canadian Reformers. Thus, he welcomed the approaches of Francis Hincks in 1839, and while he began to invest his considerable legal earnings in Montreal real estate, he established a close political relationship with Robert Baldwin. This was cemented into friendship during the elections of 1841; La Fontaine was defeated in his own constituency of Terrebonne, but Baldwin had run in two constituencies, according to the custom of the time, and been elected in both. He resigned his seat in York and secured La Fontaine's election there.

La Fontaine was a man of cold, commanding presence, with a remarkable physical resemblance to Napoleon, and when in 1842 Sir Charles Bagot decided to call on the Reformers to provide a government, it was La Fontaine–

with the rank of attorney general for Canada East–who naturally stepped into the role of virtual prime minister. When his administration resigned in 1843, it was mainly because Governor General Metcalfe's refusal to transfer political appointments to the cabinet cut off the rich stream of patronage by which La Fontaine had hoped to attach his Quebec followers to the alliance with the Upper Canadian Reformers.

La Fontaine was an ideological predecessor of present-day Quebec federalists and he opposed the theory, then current, of the double majority (which envisaged alliances of separate francophone and anglophone groupings) in favour of a unified Reform party. The close mutual trust between him and Robert Baldwin, leader of the Upper Canadian Reformers, enabled him to achieve a modicum of success in this direction and to establish, in 1848, the first truly responsible government of the united Canadas. During the three years of this second Baldwin–La Fontaine administration, he used his position to make vital gains for the Quebecois, such as re-establishing French as an official language and securing the passage of the Rebellion Losses Bill–an achievement not without personal loss, since in 1849 his house was destroyed by the angry Tory mob in Montreal at the same time as they burnt the parliament house.

Office brought its disappointments. La Fontaine fell into disagreement with his own followers, particularly over the question of compensation–which he advocated–to the seigneurs whose feudal tenures were about to be revoked. He suffered from acute rheumatism; he was downhearted when Baldwin resigned in June 1851; he abandoned politics and in 1853 became chief justice of Lower Canada, presiding until his death in 1864 over a legal system he himself had reformed as attorney general. His principal achievement now lay in the past: the creation, with Robert Baldwin, of the Canadian parliamentary system as we know it.

John Sandfield Macdonald

John Sandfield Macdonald often described himself as an Ishmael of politics, and among the leading figures in Canada before Confederation he was perhaps remarkable for his combination of brilliance and a lack of opportunity to use it effectively. Sandfield's father had been one of the crofters from the sheep-invaded valleys of Scotland, who settled in 1786 in the Glengarry district close to the borders of Upper and Lower Canada. The Macdonalds were Highland Catholics, and this fact was later to set Sandfield apart among the leading politicians of his day in Upper Canada.

Born in 1812, Sandfield began work as a store clerk and then in his late teens went to the grammar school founded by John Strachan in Cornwall, where he graduated top of his class. He entered law and was called to the bar in 1840. He decided to take up politics and in 1841 was elected to represent Glengarry in the first Legislative Assembly of United Canada. His first alliance was with the Tories but he soon fell under the influence of Robert Baldwin and became – and remained until the end of his life – a maverick Reformer. Clan loyalties in Glengarry were stronger than party discipline, and despite his change of allegiances, John Sandfield Macdonald was the only man to be elected to all the eight assemblies of United Canada.

During Sandfield's apprenticeship to the law he was chosen on several occasions to act as queen's messenger, carrying documents from the governor of Upper Canada to the British minister in Washington, and on one of these trips he met a French-speaking New Orleans girl, Marie Christine Waggaman, who in 1840 eloped with him from her finishing school in Baltimore; they were married that autumn in New York. A French-speaking wife and the fact that Montreal rather than Toronto was the natural metropolis for Glengarry people made John Sandfield Macdonald unusually sympathetic to the claims of the French Canadians for recognition of their cultural rights. Long ahead of his time he realized that any hope of the French becoming assimilated was fruitless and unjust. The way to achieve a real rather than a mechanical unity – he believed – was to admit the duality of Canadian society, and for this reason he advocated throughout his career a return to the double majority system, by which Canada would be governed by an alliance of the majorities in each section of the country. This, he argued, would prevent either anglophones or francophones from feeling forced into a minority position.

Whether practicable or not, the double majority was not favoured by either French or English political leaders, who sought more stable structures of power, and this was undoubtedly the reason why John Sandfield Macdonald was so often to be found in the political wilderness. He served from 1849 to 1851 as solicitor general for Canada West in the Baldwin–La Fontaine government, but in 1852 he was relegated to the innocuous post of speaker of the assembly, though here ironically he had one of his finest hours in a speech denouncing the governor general, Lord Elgin, for unconstitutional behaviour in dissolving the House without proper cause.

In 1854 Sandfield refused to enter the Liberal–Conservative coalition engineered by his near-namesake, John A. Macdonald, and became the nominal leader of a disunited opposition. When he next gained office it was for less than forty-eight hours as attorney general for Canada West in George Brown's ephemeral government of 1858, which was quickly outmanoeuvred by John A. Macdonald in the famous Double Shuffle.[3] By 1862 the strains within the United Province of Canada had become so acute that it was almost impossible to find a leader who could command a majority; at this point, when nobody else wanted the office, John Sandfield Macdonald became prime minister and navigated an uneasy coalition to its collapse in 1864.

It was the failure of this final attempt at creating a stable administration that precipitated the swing towards a federalist solution and the creation of a coalition later in 1864 to carry it out. John Sandfield Macdonald was an anti-confederationist, like many of his French-speaking friends, but he accepted the dominion once it came into being, abandoning federal politics to become first premier of Ontario. He ruled at the head of a coalition called the Patent Combination until in 1871 he was defeated by the Liberals under Edward Blake. Among other measures, he was responsible for passing Ryerson's School Act in his last year of office. Sandfield died in 1872 of a lung affliction he had borne stoically for many years.

5312   Rotman

Egerton Ryerson

Adolphus Egerton Ryerson began his career by changing religious horses. Born in 1803 into a United Empire Loyalist family of New York Dutch extraction – his father had been a colonel in the British army during the War of Independence – he was converted from Anglicanism to Methodism and in 1825 became a circuit rider, one of the sect's itinerant preachers in Upper Canada. Almost immediately he made a name by ably disputing a sermon in which John Strachan had laid claim, on behalf of the Anglican church, to exclusive enjoyment of the Clergy Reserves, the tracts of public land set aside for the benefit of Protestant clergymen.

As a result of this early prominence, Ryerson became in 1829 the first editor of the Methodist periodical, *Christian Guardian*, in which he continued to defend the equal rights of all sects. This brought him for a while into alliance with extreme political reformers like William Lyon Mackenzie, who also wished to end the alliance of the state and the Anglican church. But Ryerson was never a political radical; as a Loyalist he had always been disturbed by the fashionable tendency to link Methodism – many of whose supporters were American born – with Republicanism. Eventually, on a journey to England in 1833 to seek the imperial government's intervention in the Clergy Reserves dispute, he wrote a series of articles denouncing political radicalism. Mackenzie attacked him as a turncoat, but Ryerson continued in his conservative course, opposed the Rebellion of 1837, and in 1844 gave his support to the anti-Reform administration established by the governor general, Sir Charles Metcalfe.

If Ryerson was changeable in his religious and political allegiances, he remained constant in what became the principal current of his life – the aim of establishing in Upper Canada a system of schools and colleges available to all children, irrespective of creed or social rank. Ryerson was a notable preacher, a gifted polemicist, but it was as an educator that he changed his world.

In the 1830s he was a leading promoter of the plan for a Methodist university, and when it materialized in 1841 as Victoria College in Cobourg, he became first president. Four years later he was appointed first and only superin-

tendent of education for Upper Canada, and set the goal of establishing free universal schooling. In the process he moulded the educational system of the future Ontario into a secularist pattern, basing his innovations on wide journeys of inquiry in Europe and the United States. He won his goal when the Legislative Assembly of Ontario passed the School Act of 1871 and universal education became an accomplished fact. In 1876, when the Department of Education became a ministry, Ryerson retired from the superintendency, his work completed.

In his last years Ryerson turned again to writing. His main work, a history of *The Loyalists of America, and Their Times* (1882), showed where his heart lay. He remained himself too loyalist to reject the monarchy or the British connection; he did not even accept responsible government as a desirable goal. Yet the consequences of his actions – the opening of education to the underprivileged and the creation of a profession for Victorian women through the mass recruitment of teachers into his educational system – were to change the structure of Canadian society and ensure the democracy which he foresaw with such divided feelings.

George Simpson

As Canada moved politically towards Confederation, there were parallel changes to the economic structure. Eighteenth century colonialism had been linked to the mercantile system, based on exports of "staples" (or raw materials) by the colony and the import of manufactured goods. This sustained secondary industry in the imperial mother country and meant that colonial economies remained at the level of exploitative primary industry. As colonial societies took on their own characteristic forms, local secondary industries appeared, and the process of self-determination has continued, though even now in Canada we have still an economy geared to primary industries and the export of resources, and therefore vulnerable to the economic pressures that spell political dependency.

Typical of the primitive colonialism that survived into the nineteenth century was the Hudson's Bay Company. The company did not even willingly colonize in the sense of occupying the land with settlers. It was devoted entirely to making profits by exploiting a single resource – the furs of wild animals – and its charter, granted in 1670 by King Charles II, gave it virtual control over British North America west of Sault Ste. Marie for the sole purpose of reaping its harvests of furs.

In the late 1860s land-hungry Canadians, wishing to turn the prairies into farmlands, would bring an end to the Hudson's Bay hegemony, but the first challengers to the company's monopoly were other fur traders – mainly Highland Scots operating from Montreal – who sought to reap a share of the trade. These Montrealers formed the North West Company. In the years immediately after the Napoleonic wars the rivalry between the fur traders in the rich region around Lake Athabasca reached a pitch of violence that led the British government to intervene, with the result that the two companies united in 1821 in a reconstituted Hudson's Bay Company. The Hudson's Bay Company came out on top in the struggle largely because Andrew Colvile, one of its directing committee in London, recognized the force of personality in a 23-year-old clerk – related to him on the wrong side of the blanket – named George Simpson.

The company's governor in the North West, William Williams, was hard pressed by the end of 1819, since the North-westers had warrants out against him for the arrest of their partners, and a *locum tenens* was needed in case he were arrested. Simpson was chosen and he arrived at Norway House on Lake Winnipeg in June 1820. Williams immediately sent him with a brigade of canoes and voyageurs into the far North West, where this London-trained Scottish bookkeeper handled the brutal and unfamiliar situation with such boldness that the tough traders the North West Company had sent into the region were frustrated in their hopes of driving out the older company.

After the union of the companies, Simpson's ability was recognized by his being made governor of the vital northern department. He achieved a *modus vivendi* with the old North West wintering partners who chose to remain in the company, and at the same time he cut down costs by rationalizing operations. In 1824-25 he undertook a great tour across the West and into the Columbia district on the Pacific coast, and he continued such arduous personal inspections, culminating in his great journey across the world, via Siberia, in 1841-42. In 1839 Simpson was appointed governor-in-chief with virtually dictatorial control over the Hudson's Bay Company operations in North America, which he directed from headquarters established in 1833 at the Lachine Rapids near Montreal. He was a shrewd and rather cold man, and not generous or gentle in his treatment of the women with whom he liked to consort according to the custom of the North West in his day. His ruthless and arrogant rule over the Hudson's Bay Company's empire earned him the title of the Little Emperor, yet more than any other individual, Simpson staved off until the 1860s the final destruction of the company's hegemony over the Canadian West.

Simpson was a devotee of fur trade ceremony; he travelled always with his piper and a flag in the stern of his canoe. When he died in 1860 it was, appropriately, from the excitement of having entertained in a great canoe procession over the waters at Lachine the Prince of Wales, later Edward VII.

William Hamilton Merritt

To the earliest immigrants the rivers became the arteries of Canadian transport. The habitants of Lower Canada used the St. Lawrence that flowed before their strip farms extending back from the water's edge; and the fur traders, with their light birchbark canoes, penetrated as far as the Arctic and Pacific oceans, carrying craft and cargoes over land portages when navigation became impossible. The earliest settlers in Upper Canada also used the lakes and major rivers, and as long as the roads remained mere earth or corduroy trails through marsh or forest, water transport was as essential to the movement of goods as water power was to the mills which provided flour and lumber.

But Canadian rivers in their natural states, with cascades, rapids, and gravel banks, were not ideal channels for transporting heavy bulk goods like grain, nor were they efficient – in times like the War of 1812 – for the transport of troops and military equipment. Thus, during the decades before the railways appeared, Canadians thought in terms of canals, as the English had done in the early decades of the industrial revolution. And among the Canadian canal makers few were more persistent or more visionary than William Hamilton Merritt, whose Loyalist father, like the elder Allan MacNab, had served in Governor Simcoe's Queen's Rangers during the American War of Independence.

Born at Bedford in New York State in 1793, W.H.Merritt came to Canada, where his father finally decided to settle near St. Catharines, Upper Canada, in 1796. He picked up a broken education, including surveyor training, which he later put to good use, and began work rather prosaically in his teens by farming his father's land and opening a general store. He fought in the War of 1812 as a militia lieutenant at Queenston Heights and as a captain at Lundy's Lane, where he was captured and remained a prisoner in Massachusetts until the end of the war.

Returning to Canada, Merritt became involved in a variety of enterprises in the St. Catharines district, such as a chain of retail stores, grist and saw mills, a potashery, a salt spring, a distillery, a land agency – but always on a small scale and never very efficiently, so that he went bankrupt in 1819 and spent years paying off his debts.

It was through the need to supply water to his mills that Merritt became involved in canal construction. He thought first merely of a feeder canal from the Welland River, but as soon as he began to survey the route the idea came to him of a canal, using the course of the Welland, that would unite Lakes Ontario and Erie, by-passing Niagara Falls and providing not only a peacetime means of transporting Upper Canadian produce to Montreal without expensive portages, but also a useful wartime military thoroughfare. Merritt began canvassing interest for the project in 1819, but only in 1824 was he able to found the Welland Canal Company. In 1829 the first two ships sailed through the uncompleted canal, and work was finished in 1833; ten years later its public utility was recognized when the government of Upper Canada bought out the owners and made it provincial property.

Merritt's concern for the improvement of transport did not end with the Welland Canal. As early as 1836 he was involved in railway construction and he promoted the first international suspension bridge over the Niagara gorge, opened in 1849. Entering politics, he was elected to the assemblies of Upper Canada in 1832 and of United Canada in 1841; he became president of the Executive Council in the Baldwin–La Fontaine Great Ministry of 1848, and in 1850 – appropriately – he was appointed chief commissioner of public works. His vision of a comprehensive Great Lakes –St. Lawrence canal system was unfulfilled during his lifetime because of competition from the railways, but it eventually came to fruition when the St. Lawrence Seaway was opened in 1959, almost a century after Merritt's death in 1862.

Casimir Stanislaus Gzowski

Canada has benefited often from receiving the refugees of political upheavals. In our days it has been Hungarians, Czechs, East Indians, Pakistanis, and Tibetans who have contributed to the richness of our culture and the variety of our ways of life. In the 1830s and 1840s the most celebrated political refugees were the Poles, whose kingdom after the Napoleonic wars had been divided between Russia, Prussia, and Austria. In November 1830 the Poles under Russian rule rebelled against the Tsar Nicholas I and his brother, the Grand Duke Constantine, who was at that time the virtual ruler of Poland. The rebellion began among junior officers in the Polish regiments who objected to Nicholas's plan to send them to attack France after the revolution of 1830. It spread quickly to the whole Polish army and was supported by many aristocrats and political leaders. The Sejm, or Polish diet, formally severed links with Russia, and the tsar sent an army to crush the uprising, which came to an end in November 1831.

Among the officers involved in the rebellion was Casimir Stanislaus Gzowski, born in 1813 and trained as a military engineer. Gzowski was wounded and taken prisoner. Many of the Polish rebels were sent into Siberian exile, but Gzowski was more fortunate. After a short time in prison he was allowed to leave for western Europe.

Paris and other western capitals became havens where Polish refugees dreamed nostalgically of their country and divided into mutually hostile political groups, living precariously because of a lack of remunerative occupations. Gzowski, not deeply dedicated to political revolutionism, quickly recognized the futility of such a life and found his way to New York, where he arrived in 1833. For some years he lived by giving lessons in French, drawing, and fencing, and studied law to teach himself English. He passed his lawyer's examinations in 1837 and began to practise in Pennsylvania, but engineering remained his real vocation. Eventually he found employment on a canal project in the northeastern United States.

In 1841 Gzowski arrived in Canada and made the acquaintance of the governor general, Sir Charles Bagot, who was impressed with his intelligence and good manners, and appointed him an engineer in the Department of Public Works. In this position Gzowski began to mingle with the speculators and politicians involved in the growing wave of railway construction. Seven years later, in 1848, he set up in private practice as a consulting engineer and the year afterwards became chief engineer for the St. Lawrence and Atlantic Railroad.

But Gzowski was well aware that the profits to be made from railway construction lay in contracting rather than engineering, and in 1853, in co-operation with politician entrepreneurs like David Lewis Macpherson and Alexander Tilloch Galt, he established the firm of Gzowski and Company, and obtained the contract for building the Grand Trunk line from Toronto to Sarnia. Other contracts followed, and in 1857 Gzowski and his partners went into the iron and steel industry by establishing the Toronto Rolling Mills to make their own rails. Gzowski's masterpiece as an engineer and contractor was the international bridge at Niagara, built between 1871 and 1873.

Gzowski never forgot his military past and was closely involved in the Canadian militia, becoming lieutenant-colonel of the Toronto Volunteers in 1872, and in 1879 being appointed honorary A.D.C. to Queen Victoria with the rank of colonel. He saw no soldierly action after those distant days in Poland but loved to appear on public occasions in flamboyant uniforms, which with his flowing side-whiskers gave him an air of Central European splendour rarely seen in Victorian Canada. By the time of his death in 1898 Gzowski had added a knighthood to his hereditary Polish title of count and enjoyed his honours as much as the fortune he had made assisting Canada's expansion.

William Molson

Canada has never quite completed the process of transition from a colonial mercantile society to a fully industrial one. We are still too dependent on exporting resources and importing manufactured goods, and the multinational corporations now fill a similar role in regulating the two-way flow to that which traders and merchants did in the early nineteenth century. But parallel with that surviving colonial economic structure a native Canadian capitalism did develop. Its beginnings can be seen in the first decades after the conquest of New France, and no group was more deeply involved than the Molson clan–John Molson, who arrived from England in 1782 to establish his brewery at Montreal and who operated the first steamship on the St. Lawrence in 1809, and his sons John, Thomas, and William.

Of them all, the most far-sighted and perhaps the most important pioneer among Canadian industrialist-financiers was William Molson, born in 1793, who served as an ensign in the War of 1812 (from which the family profited greatly) and entered a series of shifting partnerships with his father and brothers, which led them to complete control of steamship traffic on the St. Lawrence, besides their brewery and foundry operations, and a considerable export-import business.

William Molson's important breakthrough came when he turned from brewing to more profitable distilling. This brought him–in what was known as "the battle of whisky against rum"–into conflict with the powerful mercantile interests that controlled the import of spirits from the West Indies, and it also brought him into conflict with the churches, which during this period of evangelical revival were conducting fervent temperance campaigns.

It may well have been to defend his interests as a distiller that William Molson entered politics. In 1835 he was involved in the Constitutional Association of Montreal, founded to counter the threat of rebellion by Papineau's Patriotes, and in 1840 he became a member of the municipal council of Montreal. But when he competed in 1844 for an assembly seat in the Tory interest he was defeated, largely through temperance opposition. He did not make a second attempt, but his political frustration was revealed in his active promotion of the famous 1849 manifesto in which a group of Montreal merchants demanded annexation to the United States.

By the 1840s Molson had realized that power in the developing capitalist world lay less in industry and commerce–the making and sale of goods–than in finance, the manipulation of the money that was the lifeblood of the industrial world. Already in 1837 the Molsons had attempted to set themselves up as a quasi bank by issuing their own bills, but they were forced to abandon this practice by the rivalry of the established banks. William Molson then decided to enter banking in a more regular way. In 1843 he became a director of the Bank of Montreal and later of the Mutual Insurance Company of Montreal, and in 1853 he took advantage of a change in the law to set up a private bank, Molsons Bank, which in 1855 became a charter bank, incorporated as a joint stock company under his own presidency. He retained this position until his death in 1875, and the bank, which carried on a successful business in the two Canadas, survived until its absorption by the Bank of Montreal in 1925.

Molson's interests ramified into varied fields, including mining and railways, soap making and real estate, as well as the brewery and distillery operations on which the family's fortune was founded. He owed his success and his wealth to the flexibility with which he adapted himself to the rapid changes in the Canadian economy during the nineteenth century.

But his interests did not lie solely in gathering money; like many of the nineteenth century financiers, he was also a judicious public giver, and the objects of his philanthropy included McGill University, the Montreal General Hospital, and the Hospice de Montréal.

John Alexander Macdonald

If our unheroic view of the Canadian past allows of culture heroes, one of them must undoubtedly be Sir John A. Macdonald, who has assumed in collective Canadian memory the mythic role of father of the nation. Yet the effects that Macdonald helped to precipitate were in fact the result of many minds working together to end at least two intolerable situations: the failure of the legislative union of Upper and Lower Canada, and the threat of American aggression during the period of the Civil War. That Macdonald has enjoyed so much of the credit for creating Canada is undoubtedly due less to his actual achievement than to his possession of that indefinable and unmeasurable quality known as charisma.

Macdonald's early career certainly did not seem to cast him in the role of nation maker. In 1815 – the year of Waterloo and Britain's emergence into ascendancy after the long Napoleonic wars – he was born in Glasgow of a Highland family which migrated to Canada in 1820 and settled near Kingston. Like many ambitious young men of his time, John Macdonald went into law and he quickly made a name as an eloquent defender in criminal cases. He entered politics on the municipal level, becoming a Kingston alderman in 1843. The next year he entered the Legislative Assembly of Canada as a Tory and in 1847 he became receiver general in the short-lived Draper cabinet. His mastery of intrigue and arrangement (which once led him to describe his profession jestingly as "cabinet-maker") was first shown to dramatic advantage in 1854 when he put together the centrist coalition government led by Allan MacNab out of which the Liberal–Conservative Party developed.

Macdonald was content to be attorney general for Canada West in MacNab's administration but in 1857 he became titular prime minister in the government that he and Cartier headed. The Macdonald–Cartier partnership lasted the rest of Cartier's life and depended so largely on the votes of French Canadians who distrusted Confederation that Macdonald long remained lukewarm on the issue with which his name was later to be indissolubly associated. In 1864, when the coalition government was created to bring

about Confederation as the only way out of the political stalemates that plagued the united provinces, Macdonald stood aside to allow the inoffensive Étienne-Paschal Taché to be brought out of retirement and act as figurehead premier. Yet once he did accept Confederation as inevitable, Macdonald put his manoeuvring talents to work and was more responsible than any other individual for steering the federalist idea through difficult conferences and also through the rapids of popular distrust in the Maritimes and Quebec. Undoubtedly it was Macdonald who gave Confederation the shape established by the British North America Act and endured by Canadians ever since, with too much power concentrated at the centre for a true federalism ever to emerge.

The achievement of Confederation did not end Macdonald's task. The union had to work, and for twenty out of the first twenty-four years of the dominion's life he presided over its destinies. It was no record of unbroken success. The completion of the CPR – needed for the effective settlement of the western prairies and the retention of British Columbia – was needlessly delayed by the Pacific Scandal, which surfaced when it was revealed that Macdonald and his fellow ministers had received immense sums in campaign funds from the railway promoters. The prairie rebellions of 1869 and 1885 were caused largely by Macdonald's inexcusable blindness to the wishes and needs of the Métis and the Indians. But the railway links were eventually made, and Canada – given a sense of unity by Macdonald's National Policy[4] – had changed by the time of his death in 1891 from a cluster of settlements along the St. Lawrence and the shores of the Great Lakes into a viable transcontinental nation.

Macdonald was one of Canada's few major statesmen. He was also a man of original, engaging character, with a mind well stocked by reading; a capacity for tenderness displayed in the care he lavished on his sick first wife and his retarded daughter; a ready verbal wit that made him the dread of ponderous Victorian orators; and an inclination to conviviality that at times of crisis would tip into alcoholic incapacity. Yet Macdonald was so politically conditioned that he could turn even his weaknesses to advantage, winning one gathering with the outrageous remark: "I know enough of the feeling of this meeting to know that you would rather have John A. drunk than George Brown sober." He died a few months after his victorious election of 1891, in which he had made his famous statement of imperial loyalty: "A British subject I was born – a British subject I will die." After his death, lacking a guiding hand, the Conservative party went into the long decline that paralleled the growing ascendancy of Laurier's Liberals.

George-Étienne Cartier

The rivalry between the federalist Trudeau and the separatist Lévesque, which has dominated Canadian politics in the 1970s, re-enacts a familiar situation, for the most fervent advocates of Confederation and its bitterest opponents have always been found in Quebec. Certainly, at the time of Confederation in 1867, no man did more to bring the Dominion of Canada into being than George-Étienne Cartier, scion of a family of seigneurs and merchants long established in New France and linked–according to tradition–to the founder of the colony, Jacques Cartier.

George-Étienne Cartier was born in 1814 on his father's estate at St. Antoine on the Richelieu River. At that time, when the War of 1812 was still in progress and both Upper and Lower Canadian militia were fighting beside British regulars against the Americans, attachment to the British crown ran high even in Quebec, and Cartier was called George in honour of the king most hated by Americans, George III; presumably nobody in St. Antoine knew that the unfortunate monarch had long been mad.

Such antecedents did not prevent George-Étienne Cartier, when he became a law student in 1831, from supporting Louis-Joseph Papineau and joining the Fils de la Liberté. In 1835 he was called to the bar but continued his connection with the Patriotes and in the Lower Canadian rebellion fought with courage against British regulars at the battle of Saint-Denis. He fled to the United States, and exile cooled his enthusiasms, for when he returned in 1838 it was to support the gradualist methods advocated by the Reformers under Louis-Hippolyte La Fontaine.

Cartier did not himself re-enter active politics until 1848, when he was elected to the Legislative Assembly. In the following year, 1849, he bitterly opposed the Montreal Annexation Manifesto, and throughout his career he stressed the perils of American domination. He developed an early interest in railways and in 1852 introduced into the assembly a bill creating the Grand Trunk Railway; next year he became the railway's legal adviser, and though he denied any connection between the two events, the suspicion of an inclination to profit by his political influence followed him for the rest of his life.

In 1855 he took up office as provincial secretary for Canada East in the MacNab government and the next year became attorney general in the Macdonald–Taché government. With La Fontaine's departure from the political scene he had become the virtual leader of the Mauves, the moderate reformers, and when Taché resigned in 1857, Cartier joined Macdonald at the head of a government that lasted until in 1862 it was defeated on a militia bill. He was one of the leaders of the opposition to John Sandfield Macdonald's centrist government, and with a thirteen-hour speech, beginning on 25 February 1864, he brought it down and started the series of compromises leading up to Confederation. Cartier was attorney general for Canada East in the Great Coalition of 1864 and entered enthusiastically into the Confederation campaign, posing the alternative to a Canadian union as absorption into the United States. Taking part in the Charlottetown and Quebec conferences, he was a member of the first official delegation to London in April 1865 and later attended the Westminster Conference that devised the British North America Act.

When the dominion came into being in 1867, Cartier became minister of militia, but he was almost Macdonald's equal, and when the prime minister was incapacitated Cartier would take his place. Many crucial tasks of ensuring the development of the dominion were entrusted to him; he conducted the negotiations for the surrender of Hudson's Bay Company rights in the North West and the negotiations leading to British Columbia's entry into Confederation.

His long-term interest in railways led Cartier to introduce in 1872 the bill authorizing the Canadian Pacific, and when the bill was passed he exultantly shouted, "All aboard for the West!" But the CPR was Cartier's political nemesis, for during the election campaign of 1872 he obtained funds from Sir Hugh Allan, whose syndicate expected to build the railway. When the Liberals exposed the deal, it was revealed that Cartier alone had received $85,000. The Pacific Scandal which followed broke the Macdonald government, but Cartier was already mortally ill of Bright's disease. He died in England, where he had gone in the hope of a cure, in May 1873. Long ago, as a student, he had composed a still remembered song, "O Canada, mon pays, mes amours," and despite his venial inclinations, Cartier was a true Canadian patriot at heart.

Joseph Howe

Hugh MacLennan invented the term "two solitudes" to describe the division between French- and English-speaking Canadians in our own day. Before Confederation there were as many solitudes as there were colonies in British North America, for in the days previous to effective railway communication they were divided by distance as well as administratively, and what went on in the Canadas created few ripples in such small, remote capitals as Halifax or St. John's or Victoria.

In many ways the political and cultural life of early nineteenth century Nova Scotia actually moved ahead of the Canadas. During the 1830s the province underwent a notable literary and intellectual renaissance, and it was in the Nova Scotia legislature, in 1848, that responsible government first became effective in British North America.

No figure more dramatically represents the local vigour of Nova Scotia in its classic age than Joseph Howe, as writer and as politician, and no man's career better shows the difficulty with which Nova Scotians accepted the limitations on autonomy that Confederation demanded.

Joseph Howe was born in Halifax in 1804. His father, the local postmaster and king's printer, was a Loyalist whose devotion to the British connection inspired his son. Joseph's formal education was scanty, but he was a natural autodidact, able to learn with great self-discipline, so that he quickly developed an eloquence in writing. He also learnt the printer's skills and combined his abilities to publish the *Acadian* in 1827 and in 1828 the *Novascotian*, which he quickly made the liveliest Maritime paper. In the *Novascotian* he set himself up as popular tribune, running a column called "Legislative Reviews" to criticize public men and uncover political abuses. In 1835 an attack on the exactions imposed by Halifax magistrates and police led to his prosecution for criminal libel. According to the law of the day, Howe was probably guilty, but he conducted his own defence so spiritedly that the jury acquitted him and the crowd carried him home in triumph. Howe had won a victory for freedom of the press but he had also shown himself a superb, convincing orator.

His election to the Nova Scotian assembly in 1836 as a Reformer was the consequence of his sensational trial. In 1840 he joined the Executive Council on condition that it become a genuine coalition of Tories and Reformers, but soon he began to suspect Lord Falkland, the governor, of intriguing with Conservatives, and in 1843 he resigned to carry on in his paper a series of scathing attacks on Falkland and to mount a campaign for responsible government, culminating in his celebrated *Letters to the Right Honourable Lord John Russell, on the Government of British America* (1846), which stated the case for reform more clearly and vigorously than it had ever been put before.

Howe's campaign concluded successfully in 1848 when the appointed government was defeated in the assembly and the new governor, Sir John Harvey, called on the Reform leader, James Boyle Uniacke, to form an administration, in which Howe became provincial secretary and virtual shaper of policies. In 1854 he left the provincial secretaryship to become chief commissioner of the Railway Board. In 1860 he became premier of Nova Scotia and conducted a surprisingly lacklustre administration, which was defeated in 1863.

Howe now moved out of politics, accepting appointment as imperial fishery commissioner under the 1854 Reciprocity Treaty, which meant that he took no part in the negotiations that led his province into the Dominion of Canada. But in 1866 he returned to lead the local opposition to the "botheration scheme" of Confederation. He argued that the terms did not offer enough guarantees in transportation and fiscal matters, and advocated instead an imperial federation linking the colonies to Britain. He took a protest delegation to London, and when that failed he led a campaign in Nova Scotia that defeated the confederationists in the 1867 elections. Early in 1868 he led an official Nova Scotian delegation to London, asking for a repeal of the British North America Act, but failed to evoke a response and accepted a compromise that gave Nova Scotia slightly better terms and himself a post in the dominion cabinet.

Howe's federal career was undistinguished. He was too closely tuned to Nova Scotian life to be happy elsewhere, and his health deteriorated. In 1873 he was appointed lieutenant-governor of Nova Scotia, and died within three weeks. His one great political triumph, the winning of responsible government, lay far in the past, and the vagaries of his later career obscured his other achievement – as one of Canada's finest writers of discursive prose.

Alexander Tilloch Galt

Alexander Tilloch Galt, the son of the Scottish novelist John Galt, was born in Chelsea, England, in 1817. His father came to Canada in 1825 on the land business of the Canada Company[5] and returned to Britain in 1829, leaving Alexander at school in Lower Canada until he joined his parents in England in 1830.

In 1835 Alexander Tilloch Galt returned to Canada as a clerk in the Sherbrooke offices of the British American Land Company, which his father had helped to found, becoming the company's chief commissioner in 1844. Land development, later accompanied by speculation in related fields like railways and mining, continued to interest Galt for the rest of his life, and his political concerns tended to be dominated by the thought of how best to further the opening of British North America and the exploitation of its vast resources.

Galt's first political act – the signing of the Montreal Annexation Manifesto of 1849 – revealed a certain despair at the fractional policies of colonial Canada. Although he was also elected to the Legislative Assembly of Canada in that year, he resigned in 1850 to devote himself to land and railway developments.

Galt returned to the assembly in 1853, working in alliance with the Lower Canadian Rouges, or Liberals. By now he no longer believed that annexation to the United States would solve Canadian problems. Instead, he showed himself in 1856 to be one of the pioneers of Canadian federalism by submitting – with A.A.Dorion – a resolution demanding the reconstruction of the existing Canadian union into a federation of Upper and Lower Canada. In 1858 he pushed this trend to its logical conclusion by proposing a federal union of all British North American colonies and making the adoption of this aim a condition for joining the Cartier–Macdonald government in that year as minister of finance. Macdonald agreed reluctantly. Cartier was more enthusiastic, and shortly afterwards Galt, Cartier, and John Ross went to England to try and convince the imperial government of the need for such a union.

The time was premature and the Colonial Office unreceptive, but Galt did not abandon his proposal. He went out of office with the Cartier–Macdonald combination in 1862 but returned as minister of finance in the coalition government established to achieve Confederation. He was present at the historic Confederation conferences in Charlottetown and Quebec, and took a leading part in the Westminster Conference of 1866 and the framing of the British North America Act, Canada's substitute for a constitution.

Having played so long and active a part in achieving Confederation, it was inevitable that Galt should become a member of the first federal cabinet, and he returned to the post of minister of finance. But he and John A. Macdonald were temperamentally antipathetic, and Galt resigned from the government in 1868 and retired from parliament in 1872, taking the opportunity to dissociate himself from all parties and to declare, again a pioneer, his belief in future Canadian independence. Later, in 1881, he advocated a federation comprising the whole British Empire.

During his last years Galt returned in nonpolitical ways to public service. He was a fisheries commissioner under the Treaty of Washington; he served from 1880 to 1883 as Canada's first high commissioner in London, and it was appropriate that he, whose vision always extended so far beyond his immediate horizons, should take Canada into the international community by negotiating the earliest trade agreements with France and Spain.

During his last decade Galt returned to the concerns of his earlier life and until his death in 1893 he spent most of his time on mining, railway, and irrigation schemes in the Canadian West.

Thomas D'Arcy McGee

D'Arcy McGee began as an Irish nationalist committed to violent revolution and ended as a Canadian patriot committed to constitutional change; the shift in his politics may well have cost him his life, for he died from an assassin's bullet in the first year of the confederation he was so active in promoting.

D'Arcy McGee was born in 1825 at Carlingford in Ireland, the son of a coast guard. In 1842 he sailed on a timber ship returning from Wexford to Quebec, travelling on to New England, where he joined the staff of a Catholic Irish newspaper, the *Boston Pilot*. His first year was spent collecting subscriptions and writing occasional pieces on Irish literature, but in 1844, at the age of nineteen, he was made editor of the *Pilot* and started a career in journalism that would last his life. At this time McGee was fervently anti-British, and advocated the American annexation of Canada.

In 1845 he returned to Ireland and became editor of the *Freeman's Journal*, but after he joined the nationalist Young Ireland movement his politics became too extreme for the *Journal*, and he joined the staff of the *Nation*, at the same time helping found the Irish Confederation, dedicated to ending the union of Ireland and Great Britain. In 1848 he returned to North America and started the New York *Nation* but fell out with the Fenians when his position shifted away from violent insurrectionism, and was forced to leave New York. In Boston he founded the *American Celt*, with which he moved back to New York in 1853.

McGee was not content with mere editing. From boyhood he was a prolific writer and started to publish poems in the Irish *Nation* during the 1840s. He wrote novels, articles on literature, and historical works, of which the best is the *Popular History of Ireland* (1863). Throughout his writing runs a pride in the Celtic past and a sense of Ireland's national destiny.

But if McGee's devotion to Ireland never diminished, his approval of American democracy did. In 1855 he began recommending Irish migrants to choose Canada over the United States, a preference he put into practice in 1857 by accepting the invitation of Montreal's Irish community and going there to publish the *New Era*. Almost immediately he began to write on Canadian affairs, attacking the powerful Orange Order and advocating better parliamentary representation for the Irish immigrants. His Irish background made him highly conscious of Canadian stirrings towards autonomy and soon he was dreaming of a "new nationality" inhabiting a "kingdom of the St. Lawrence" under a dynasty to be founded by one of Queen Victoria's younger sons. He urged a "federal compact" between British North American provinces and called for the absorption of Rupert's Land. He even foresaw the emergence of a distinctive Canadian literature and urged the public support for Canadian publishers that only came into being more than a century after his death.

McGee was first attracted towards the Reformers. Elected to the Legislative Assembly in 1857, he supported George Brown's brief government of 1858 and opposed the Cartier–Macdonald combination. In 1861 he withdrew support from George Brown because of the latter's opposition to separate Catholic schools, but in 1862 he joined John Sandfield Macdonald's government as president of the council, chairing an important conference on the Intercolonial Railway between the Canadas and the Maritimes. At this time he declared, "There is . . . far more liberty and toleration enjoyed by minorities in Canada than in the United States," and advocated a British American nationality and the retention of imperial links.

Shortly afterwards McGee moved over to the Conservatives. He allied himself to Cartier in Montreal and in the Great Coalition government of 1864 became minister of agriculture and immigration, and a delegate to the Charlottetown and Quebec conferences.

But to his fellow countrymen McGee remained an Irish as well as a Canadian politician, and he aroused hostility in 1864 by denouncing the Fenians for their plans to attack Canada. Next year, in Wexford, he made a speech renouncing his own nationalist past, and this lost him the support of the Montreal Irish. Macdonald and Cartier began to realize that he now represented a political liability. He was not invited to the crucial Confederation conference in Westminster (1866), nor was he included in the first dominion cabinet in 1867. He decided to leave politics and return to writing; instead he died on 7 April 1868, shot on the steps of his Ottawa lodgings. Patrick James Whelan was hanged for the murder, but Fenian complicity, though suspected, was never proved.

George Brown

In a country where political life has rarely led to violence, it is striking that two of the men who created Canadian confederation died by assassins' bullets. Twelve years after D'Arcy McGee's murder, the Liberal leader George Brown suffered the same fate.

The progress that led Brown to his dark tryst with destiny began in 1818, when he was born at Alloa on the Firth of Forth, son of an Edinburgh merchant – Peter Brown – who got into financial difficulties and in 1837 migrated to New York to run a dry goods store. George Brown worked at first in the family shop, but when his father turned to journalism in 1842 and founded the *British Chronicle*, George assisted him with the newspaper and the following year became its publisher.

Peter Brown was an ardent Liberal but also a devout Presbyterian, and in 1843, when the Free Kirk split from the Church of Scotland, he supported it and moved to Toronto to start a religious journal, the *Banner*, in the Free Kirk cause. But George Brown was more interested in political battles than in sectarian skirmishes, and in 1844 he founded a weekly paper, the *Globe*, dedicated to the cause of Reform. In 1853 it became a daily and in 1855 absorbed its rivals and became the official organ of the Reform party. The *Globe* developed into the most influential paper in British North America and remained the centre of Brown's life.

Brown became involved in political action somewhat indirectly in 1848 by accepting an appointment as secretary to the first of many commissions to investigate the Kingston penitentiary. The commission uncovered numerous abuses, and the scandal over its revelations made Brown a political figure. He fought a by-election in 1851 and was defeated by William Lyon Mackenzie, but in the 1852 elections he won a seat in the Legislative Assembly, where he began almost immediately his long campaign for representation by population, which he believed was necessary to prevent Upper Canadian interests being sacrificed to those of the French Canadians, who were falling behind in numbers but retained parity of representation. In 1859, foreseeing that the existing union of the two Canadas offered endless sec-

tional disputes with growing racial bitterness, he began in the *Globe* to talk of a federal union.

George Brown was neither an adept nor a happy politician; he preferred the independence and solitude of the journalist's role to the constant accommodations and compromises of politics, and so he tended to avoid rather than seek political office. The one government he led – in August 1858 – was the shortest in Canadian history, lasting two days. He chaired brilliantly the historic select committee of Parliament which in May-June 1864 studied the sectional problems of United Canada and on 14 June recommended in favour of a "federative system." But the only ministerial office he held for any length of time was the presidency of the council in the coalition government of June 1864. In this role he worked out the constitutional structure that the Canadians presented to the Charlottetown Conference on Confederation, and in the later Quebec Conference he established the pattern of central and provincial governments. In November 1864 he went to London for exploratory talks, which assured the Canadian and Maritime ministers that their proposals would get sympathetic hearing. He went again with Macdonald and Cartier in the summer of 1865 but was not present at the Westminster Conference of 1866, for he had already resigned from the cabinet. The ostensible issue was disagreement over the way a proposed reciprocity agreement with the Americans should be worked out, but Brown welcomed the excuse to escape from the intrigues of political office. The night of his resignation he wired his wife: "I am a free man once again."

Defeated in the parliamentary elections for the first dominion parliament in 1867, Brown took this as a signal to withdraw completely from the role of politician. This did not mean an end to political interest. He continued to manipulate the influence of the *Globe*, and on occasions like the Pacific Scandal of 1873 he was able to use it to steer events in a Liberal direction. His autocratic rule at the *Globe* led him into one of the more controversial incidents of his career, in 1872, when he had picketers arrested in the attempt to break a printers' strike. It led also to his death, for he was shot on 25 March 1880 by a worker discharged for drunkenness, and he died six weeks later from the effects of the wound.

Brown's was a difficult career, for he set out to be a man of political influence yet sought to keep his hands free of the intrigues inevitable in politics. This contradiction in motives explains why his great resources of intellect and personality were never fully used.

Samuel Leonard Tilley

Samuel Leonard Tilley, born in 1818 at Gagetown, was a New Brunswick apothecary who–at peril to his political career–became a Father of Confederation and gave the new Canada of 1867 a title and a motto.

Tilley entered politics in 1850 as a member of the Legislative Assembly of New Brunswick. In 1854 he became provincial secretary in a Liberal administration and introduced a highly unpopular Prohibition Act that caused the fall of his ministry in 1856. When the Liberals returned to power in 1857, Tilley resumed his post; in 1861 when the premier, Charles Fisher, resigned over a crown lands scandal, Tilley–who had avoided involvement–succeeded him.

This meant that Tilley was in control of New Brunswick's political destiny during the crucial years when Confederation moved from dream into reality. Involved from 1852 in the scheme for an Intercolonial Railway that would link the Maritimes with Lower Canada, by 1860 he had become the advocate of a union of the Maritime provinces under a single government, and he was also interested in the larger scheme of a federation that would include all British possessions in North America.

In 1864 the political leaders of the four Maritime colonies arranged a meeting in Charlottetown to discuss legislative union, but when the Canadian delegates arrived– after having requested an invitation–the dimensions of the issues changed and everyone agreed to continue discussions in Quebec later in the year.

At the Quebec Conference, the Newfoundland delegates rejected the idea of union and returned home to sing, "Come near at your peril, Canadian wolf!" The Prince Edward Island delegates held aloof, playing for time and better terms. But Tilley and Charles Tupper, who headed the Nova Scotian delegation, accepted Confederation and worked out with the Canadian delegates a scheme to be presented to the imperial government.

The politicians' enthusiasm was not shared by all their constituents, and when Tilley rashly called an election in 1865, his party was defeated and an anti-confederationist ministry took over in Fredericton. The whole plan of Confederation, as well as Tilley's career, was threatened, for

geographically New Brunswick was an essential link in the union. However, the lieutenant-governor, Sir Arthur Hamilton Gordon, under orders from Westminster to expedite Confederation, manoeuvred the new government into resignation, and in 1866 the Liberals returned to power. Tilley now assumed a necessarily low profile; the premier of the new confederationist government was Peter Mitchell, but Tilley had planned the election strategy and he worked out the mandate he and the other delegates took to the Westminster Conference in 1866.

Tilley's best known contribution to that conference is said to have come when the title of the new union was discussed. Macdonald would have made it a kingdom, but the British felt that would excite the American messianism which was resurgent at the end of the Civil War. Then Tilley, versed in scripture, made his apt quotation from the 72nd Psalm: "He shall have dominion also from sea to sea, and from the river unto the ends of the earth." Canada acquired a title–Dominion–and a motto, *A mari usque ad mare* ("from sea to sea"), which fitted the hope of bringing the North West and the Pacific Coast into their new Canada.

Like the other Fathers of Confederation, Tilley was rewarded with a post in Macdonald's first cabinet; he became minister of customs and later, on Galt's resignation, minister of finance, in which post he arranged–under the second Macdonald government–the financial aspects of the National Policy. He also served, before he died in 1896, two periods as lieutenant-governor of New Brunswick.

Tilley was a man of strict evangelical Christian principles, untouched by the shadows of corruption that darken the names of so many of his contemporaries, and one can only wonder at the strange bedfellows politics makes when one remembers that Tilley would not allow in his house, even when it was Government House, the liquor that was the lifeblood to Sir John A. Macdonald, his colleague and leader over so many years.

Charles Tupper

Many Canadians have found their way into politics through the law; comparatively few through the rival profession of medicine. An exception was Charles Tupper, born in 1821 at Amherst, Nova Scotia, son of a Baptist clergyman, Charles Tupper, and grandson of Eliakim Tupper who migrated to Nova Scotia from Connecticut in 1762.

Charles Tupper completed his studies at Edinburgh, then one of the world's best medical schools, and returned to practise in his home town, Amherst. He became an active local Conservative and challenged to such effect the hypnotic influence on Nova Scotians of Joseph Howe's oratory that in 1855 he was able to defeat him in Cumberland constituency. Tupper was a notable acquisition to the Conservative cause in Nova Scotia, and when the party took power in 1856 he became provincial secretary. By early 1864 he was leader of the party and premier of Nova Scotia.

Already, like Tilley in New Brunswick, Tupper had become convinced of the feasibility of legislative union in the Maritimes and also of a looser union of British North America, and he became premier in time to play an active part in organizing the Charlottetown Conference on Maritime unity, to which the Canadian delegates came. Here, and at the later Quebec Conference, Tupper established a close relationship with John A. Macdonald that would last until the latter's death and was perhaps fostered by the fact that Tupper's appetite for women was almost as strong as Macdonald's for alcohol. When Tupper returned from the Quebec Conference, which seemed to have assured the emergence of a Canadian federation, it was to find that Joseph Howe was arousing widespread feeling against the idea of Confederation. Only by very skilful political manoeuvres could Tupper ensure that Nova Scotia would be represented by a delegation–which he led–at the Westminster Conference.

When the time came, in 1867, to select the first dominion cabinet, Tupper was aware of the difficulties Macdonald faced in making a government that would be representative of the parties and factions that had supported the coalition cabinet of 1864, and one that would also be representative of all the provinces, all their peoples, and all their religions. He agreed to postpone receiving the reward of office and did not in fact enter the cabinet until Joseph Howe had been reconciled to Confederation and had received his ministry. Only then–in 1870–was Tupper's patience rewarded with the cabinet rank of president of the council.

When Macdonald and his government were defeated in 1873 over the Pacific Scandal, Tupper remained his strongest supporter in opposition, and on the Conservative return to power in 1878 it was he, as minister of public works (and later of railways and canals) who was responsible for ensuring the construction of the Canadian Pacific Railway. Before the first train ran from Montreal to Vancouver in 1885, Tupper had succeeded Galt in London as Canadian high commissioner, and there he remained from 1884 to 1896, with a single brief return to Ottawa politics. He watched from afar the steady decline of the Conservative party after Macdonald's death in 1891, and early in 1896 responded to appeals that he return to revivify the party. In January 1896, he entered Mackenzie Bowell's cabinet as secretary of state and in April took over as prime minister, too late to put enough life into the party to fight the summer elections, in which Laurier led the Liberals to federal victory.

Tupper's political career ended in 1900 when he was defeated in Cape Breton and went into retirement, which he lived out in Vancouver and later in England. He occupied his old age writing *Recollections of Sixty Years in Canada*, published in 1914, a year before his death as the last surviving original Father of Confederation.

Hugh Allan

Hugh Allan was a product of the shipbuilding culture that has existed along the Clyde in Scotland since the early eighteenth century. He was born at Saltcoats on the Ayrshire coast in 1810. His father, Captain Alexander Allan, was a shipowner who sailed his own boats and became involved in the transatlantic traffic in merchandise and emigrants. In 1822 Captain Allan started a regular service between Glasgow and Quebec with his sailing ship, *Jean*. The following year young Hugh Allan began work, at the age of thirteen, as office boy in a counting house at the port town of Greenock on the Firth of Clyde, and in 1826 he went to Montreal and joined the dry goods firm of William Kerr and Company, acting at the same time as agent for his father's modest shipping line.

Hugh Allan's interests lay far more in ships than in dry goods, and in 1831 he turned to shipbuilding, joining the firm of John Millar. He was made a junior partner in 1835, and when Millar, the head of the firm, died in 1839, Allan and the other surviving partner started a new firm which began to extend its scope to operating as well as building steamships.

This was the period when the whole character of sea transport was being changed by the development of steam propulsion and also by the substitution of steel for wood as the main material in boat construction. Allan and his partners (soon including his younger brother Andrew) moved ahead quickly in both these fields and in 1852 incorporated themselves as the Montreal Ocean Steamship Company. By 1854 they had already acquired iron-built screw steamers, and in 1856 they were able to institute a rapid fortnightly steamboat service from the St. Lawrence to Liverpool; in 1857 it became a weekly service, the earnings from carrying passengers and merchandise being supplemented by the contract, which Allan and his partners had received, for carrying Canadian mail to Europe.

A special stimulus was given by the outbreak of the Crimean War in 1853, when Allan was in a position to provide troop carriers for both Britain and France; later on Allan ships were used to transport British troops to South Africa. For long the Allan Royal Mail Line, as it became known, was the leading shipping line operating from Canadian base ports and owned in Canada; it was to transport hundreds of thousands of immigrants before finally being incorporated with its main rival, Canadian Pacific Steamships, in 1915.

Hugh Allan's interests quickly ramified. Like many early Canadian capitalists, he saw the advantage of having his own financial institutions, and founded the Merchant's Bank of Canada. He invested in cattle rearing, in mining, in various industries. And he developed the political links– mainly with the Conservatives and especially with George-Étienne Cartier–that were necessary for a firm depending so greatly on government contracts. When he was knighted in 1871, it seemed as though his name was as solid and secure as the great granite mansion called Ravenscrag that glowered like its owner over a Montreal still entirely dominated by English-speaking entrepreneurs.

It was his political connections and his desire to exploit them for increasing his profits that led Allan into discredit, if not into disaster. When the Canadian Pacific Railway was being planned immediately after Confederation, it was obvious that no single firm or individual capitalist could finance such a project, even with the subsidies in land and money that Macdonald's government was willing to provide, and various combinations of promoters came together, some of them obviously American dominated. Finally it was decided to award the concession to the Canadian group headed by Hugh Allan, but before the agreement could be ratified, the Liberals exposed the fact that, responding to Cartier's appeals, Allan had made large campaign donations to the Conservative leaders, including the prime minister, Sir John A. Macdonald. Under a storm of public protest, Macdonald resigned, and Alexander Mackenzie's Liberal government, which followed him in power, revoked the agreement. When the Canadian Pacific concession was finally awarded in 1878, it was to a syndicate in which Allan played no part. His public career had ended, though he continued to grow richer and his influence in financial circles was undiminished. He died in Edinburgh in 1882, a notable Canadian example of the great power that individual nineteenth century entrepreneurs wielded before the rise of corporate capitalism.

Alexander Mackenzie

It is hard to imagine that a man as dourly high-principled and personally charmless as Alexander Mackenzie entered politics for any other reason than a strong and puritanical sense of duty. Certainly, power when he gained it was no pleasure to him, and his success can be measured less in achievement then in endurance.

How far his original occupation conditioned Alexander Mackenzie it is now hard to estimate. Born in Scotland in 1822, he served his apprenticeship as a stonemason before he emigrated to Canada in 1842, and even then his life remained linked with stone, for he set up as a building contractor in Kingston and afterwards in Sarnia. His very face had the lines of a Gothic sculpture, and some of the rigidity of stone entered into his political principles, which enabled him to take up the leadership once only, and that for a brief but special period when corruption seemed to have captured the highest levels of the nation's life and a man of uncompromising sternness was needed.

An interest in journalism first drew Alexander Mackenzie away from stone and into politics. He became the friend of George Brown, editor of the *Globe*, and in 1852 started a local Reform paper, the *Lambton Shield*. His early interest in an active political career was so cool that he only sought election to the assembly of the united Canadas in 1861, in time to add his unvociferous support to the movement towards Confederation.

By the time the Dominion of Canada came into being in 1867, Mackenzie had acquired enough taste for political office to seek and win seats both in the federal House of Commons and in the Legislative Assembly of Ontario, and in 1871 he first acquired ministerial stature by becoming provincial treasurer for Ontario. In 1872 dual representation – the holding of seats in both federal and provincial parliamentary bodies – was disallowed, and Mackenzie chose Ottawa in preference to Toronto.

The choice led him to an encounter with destiny he can hardly have expected, when late in 1873 revelations were made of corrupt dealing between Macdonald and other Conservative ministers, and the promoters who hoped to build the Canadian Pacific Railway. If the Conservatives were embarrassed by accusations they could not effectively answer, the Liberals were embarrassed because they were not organized to seize the opportunity so unexpectedly presented. Mackenzie was a man entirely lacking in personal magnetism, but he had no immediate rival and the grimly moralistic tone he assumed in the debates on the Pacific Scandal led the Liberals to make him their leader. Thus, Mackenzie succeeded Macdonald, as the dominion's second prime minister, and the force of public disapproval directed against the Conservatives, rather than any positive programme the Liberals had to offer, provided him a comfortable majority in the 1874 elections.

Mackenzie ruled for almost five years, with little imagination or political courage. Because expenditure on the Canadian Pacific Railway was unpopular in Ontario and even more so in Quebec, Mackenzie – doubling as minister of public works – restricted his efforts to creating a patchy land and water route with only small stretches of railway. This led him into a bitter dispute with British Columbia, which came very near to secession by 1878, when Mackenzie decided to call an election. The lack of positive action by the Liberals, combined with a growing economic recession, enabled Macdonald and the Conservatives to stage a dramatic comeback, and the Liberals were defeated.

Mackenzie had to face the anger of his own supporters, led by Edward Blake, who somewhat unjustly blamed his inept administration for a defeat that was at least as much attributable to their own failure to insist on an imaginative alternative to Conservative programmes. In 1880 he resigned the leadership and Blake took over. Though Mackenzie retained his seat until his death in 1892, he now played the role of a minor politician.

Alexander Mackenzie was a man whose limitations suited him for a particular time in history and a very restricted role, which was little more than to hold Canada together while Macdonald and his dynamic following recovered from the wounds of the Pacific Scandal and prepared for a second and more positive term in office.

Donald Alexander Smith

Donald Alexander Smith is perhaps most remembered as Lord Strathcona, but his peerage came late in a life during which he played an extraordinary series of roles that profoundly affected the shape Canada assumed by the time he was metamorphosed, in 1897, into Baron Strathcona and Mount Royal.

Smith was born in the Scottish town of Forres in 1820, and like many unprosperous Scots he found his way into the service of the Hudson's Bay Company, which he joined in 1838. After a brief training at Lachine, he was sent to Labrador, and there he remained for almost thirty years, until 1868, rising in rank to chief trader in 1852 and chief factor in 1862. Such a remote area seems an unlikely place for financial talents to develop, but Smith served both his company and himself well. He built roads to make transport more economical; he diversified activities at the trading posts to give a wider range of salable products. He appointed himself a financial agent for the other fur traders, investing their salaries through his banking cousin George Stephen at three percent interest; he made good investments, paid the agreed interest, and invested the further profits in Hudson's Bay stock so that finally he became the leading shareholder in the company that employed him. Within the company hierarchy he advanced rapidly – to control of the Montreal department in 1869, and in 1870 to the post of chief commissioner and resident governor in Canada.

It was at this period that the company sold its rights in Rupert's Land[6] to the new Dominion of Canada, an act that sparked off the rebellion in 1869 of the Red River Métis under Louis Riel. When it was obvious that an impasse had been reached between Riel's provisional government and the dominion, Sir John A. Macdonald appointed Smith his special commissioner, and Smith managed to weaken local support for Riel among the non-Métis population so that the compromise resulting in the creation of Manitoba could be worked out.

After this exercise in practical diplomacy, Smith decided to turn to regular political activity, partly with an eye to protecting and furthering his business interests. He was elected in 1870 to the Legislative Assembly of Manitoba and at the same time to the House of Commons. When dual representation was abolished he decided to leave the assembly but continued in the House of Commons until 1880, and again from 1887 to 1896. He never entered the cabinet, largely because of the stand he took in 1873 as one of the dissident Conservatives who condemned Macdonald and his colleagues over the Pacific Scandal.

Smith's motives in taking this stand are distinctly suspect, for he himself was not fastidious in parliamentary practices. He was unseated from the House of Commons in 1880 for corrupt electioneering, and when, after the return of the Conservatives to power in 1878 the scheme for the Canadian Pacific Railway was revised, Smith – who had helped to destroy the chances of Sir Hugh Allan's consortium to build the railway in 1873 – emerged as a member of the new successful group.

Having in 1874 become land commissioner for the Hudson's Bay Company, administering the considerable real estate the company had acquired as part compensation for its Rupert's Land rights in 1869, Smith began to see the profitable possibilities of western railways, and he became involved with Stephen and other financiers in the purchase of the St. Paul, Minneapolis and Manitoba Railroad in 1879. Although not officially a member of the new CPR syndicate, for fear of offending Sir John A. Macdonald, he was the real power behind its organization, and it was with a fitting symbolism that in 1885 he drove the railway's last spike at Craigellachie in the Monashee Mountains. By this time Smith's versatile talents were already deployed elsewhere, and in 1887 he became president of the Bank of Montreal.

After Macdonald's death, Smith was ripe for political honour and in 1896 Sir Charles Tupper made him his own successor as Canadian high commissioner in London. Smith retained the post, at the same time ruling the London Committee of the Hudson's Bay Company with an iron hand, until his death in 1914. He received his peerage in 1897 and entered spiritedly into the glittering social life of Edwardian London, becoming conspicuously philanthropic and founding and funding a regiment of his own, Lord Strathcona's Horse, which he sent to the South African war under the command of Sam Steele. No man went farther from the chilly shores of Labrador than Donald Alexander Smith.

George Stephen

Unlike his cousin Donald Smith, who became Lord Strathcona, George Stephen was one of those men of immense wealth and power who move inconspicuously on matters that may affect the whole world. He was born in the small northern Scots community of Dufftown in 1829, received a sound Scottish grammar school education, and served his apprenticeship as a draper before he emigrated – in 1850 – to Montreal, then the Canadian commercial capital. There his relatives manufactured woollen textiles, and he entered their firm as an employee. By introducing more imaginative merchandising methods, he steadily increased profits and at the same time (by carefully investing his savings) managed to purchase a controlling interest in the firm.

Stephen was one of the astute businessmen of the time who realized that Confederation had greatly widened Canadian commercial horizons but that the best opportunities went to those who controlled finance and transport, rather than to those who controlled manufacturing. For this reason his speculative instincts turned towards banking and railways. In 1873 he was elected a director of the powerful Bank of Montreal; in 1876 he was made its president. In 1879 he became president of the St. Paul, Minneapolis and Manitoba Railroad Company, which he had bought with Donald Smith and two other financiers.

The gamble with the St. Paul railroad proved much more profitable than Stephen or his partners had hoped, largely because the acquisition was made when the development of the American prairies began to take on impetus. Even so, Stephen at first appeared hesitant when Smith came to him with the proposal that they should form another syndicate to build the Canadian Pacific Railway. However, when British capital was promised, and when the government – to whom the railway had become a political necessity – offered what seemed good terms in subsidies and land grants, Stephen finally agreed to head the consortium and secured the full support of the Bank of Montreal.

This was a gamble so great that it almost failed. The costs of pushing the CPR through the passes of the Rockies and over the granite and muskeg of the Shield were far higher than anyone had bargained for, and Stephen, in whose charge lay the financing of the whole scheme, had to exercise as much faith as ingenuity. He and Smith committed all their personal assets, and there came a time in 1884 when Stephen would say in desperation, "My friends and my enemies agree that this will be the ruin of us all." Finances ran out completely during the winter of 1884-85, and even Sir John A. Macdonald could not persuade Parliament to grant more subsidies.

Stephen and his associates were saved neither by their friends nor by their enemies but by the unknown Métis of the South Saskatchewan River, who in 1885 rose in rebellion under Louis Riel and Gabriel Dumont. A small army of eight thousand men was hastily assembled and had to be transported into the northern prairies. The CPR rose to the emergency by improvising links to cover the gaps where the line was not yet constructed, and a grateful Parliament voted the necessary subsidies to bring the work to a conclusion.

The tensions of the four years during which he was involved in the completion of the Canadian Pacific Railway convinced Stephen not to embark on further grandly speculative ventures but to retire with the ample means he had accumulated. Before even reaching the age of sixty, he abandoned his presidencies and directorates, and retired to England. There he bought himself a country house, lived in a quiet squirely way, nursed his investments, occupied himself discreetly with good causes, and quietly beat Donald Smith to the peerage by becoming Lord Mount Stephen in 1891.

William Van Horne

If any figure in Canadian history seemed a spiritual heir of the *condottiere* of the Italian renaissance, it was Sir William Van Horne, a ruthless industrial soldier of fortune and perhaps Canada's greatest and most perceptive patron of the arts.

William Cornelius Van Horne was born in 1843 to a family of Dutch descent living in Illinois. He was virtually a child of the railway generation, for at the age of fourteen he started work as a telegraph operator on the Illinois Central Railway, and from that time was deeply involved in the booming world of American railway construction and operation, rising up through the ranks until he became acting general manager of the Chicago, Milwaukee and St. Paul Railroad.

It was at this time that George Stephen, Donald Smith, and their associates were looking for a man who could be entrusted with the immensely difficult task of organizing the construction of the Canadian Pacific Railway, with the unparalleled problems of laying the railbed over the bogland and granite outcrops north of the Great Lakes and finding a way for it through the "sea of mountains" from the Rockies to the Pacific coast. Nobody in the existing Canadian railway systems seemed to have either the experience or the sheer force of will needed for such a task.

But Van Horne was such a man. His railway experience had been long and varied, and he had an immense appetite for life and its challenges. "I eat all I can, I drink all I can, I smoke all I can, and I don't give a damn for anything," he once declared, and it was all true. Van Horne met difficulties head on and usually defeated them by a combination of will and intelligence. His first difficulty after he became general manager of the Canadian Pacific in 1881 was one of acceptance, for American speculators had been trying for years to get control of the Canadian railway system, and there were many who regarded Van Horne as a Yankee "Trojan horse." In fact, he had as little sense of nationality as any soldier of fortune. He was quite happy to become a Canadian citizen, but all that really concerned him was the task ahead, a challenge greater than any railroad constructor before him had ever faced, and there was a great deal to the quizzical remark of one of his contemporaries, that "Van Horne is a citizen only of the Canadian Pacific."

Eventually, with assistance from George Stephen as financial wizard, from myriads of long-suffering workers (including thousands of Chinese), and from the North-West rebels of 1885, who scared Canadian politicians into granting adequate funding, Van Horne completed the railway in an extraordinary four years, and by so doing he kept British Columbia from leaving the dominion.

Van Horne maintained his links with the CPR almost to his death in 1915. He became vice-president of the company in 1884, president on George Stephen's retirement in 1888, and in 1899, on his own retirement from active work, president of the board of directors, which he remained until 1910.

Van Horne's appetites were not all physical. He had a high sense of beauty, both the beauty of nature and that of artifice, and among tycoon patrons of art he was remarkable for his adventurousness. He was the first Canadian to establish a collection of Post-Impressionist artists, he was one of the first to recognize the genius of Canadian avant garde painters like J.W.Morrice, and one of his earliest acts after completion of the Canadian Pacific Railway was to recruit artists and send them to record the beauties of the country which the railway had opened up. The result was a great broadening of the scope and quality of Canadian landscape painting as its exponents faced the challenge of rendering in paint the magnificence of the Rockies and the Selkirks.

Oliver Mowat

If the strong centralist government that Sir John A. Macdonald sought to impose on the new Dominion of Canada in 1867 did not result in the eventual erosion of provincial rights, it was largely due to the efforts of Oliver Mowat, who as premier of Ontario for twenty-four years–from 1872 to 1896–remained in office longer than any other first minister in a commonwealth parliament.

Mowat was born in Kingston in 1820; his family were Tories, and it seems natural that he should have studied law in the office of his Conservative fellow townsman, John A. Macdonald. But if Macdonald taught Mowat law, he did not strengthen his Toryism. A deep personal antagonism developed between the two men, and when Mowat did turn to politics, he repudiated the convictions of his family and his legal mentor, and became a strong Reformer.

Like Macdonald, Mowat began with municipal politics, becoming a Toronto alderman and helping found the city's park system. In 1857 he entered the Legislative Assembly of United Canada and quickly attained and lost office as provincial secretary in George Brown's two-day ministry in 1858. From 1863 to 1864 he served under John Sandfield Macdonald as postmaster general and continued in that role under the Great Coalition of the same year.

Mowat was not one of the delegates to the Charlottetown Conference on Confederation, but he did attend the subsequent conference in Quebec, where he showed his genuinely federalist tendencies by insisting, with Cartier's support, on the retention of substantial rights by the provinces.

Before Confederation came into being, Mowat temporarily withdrew from politics to take up a judgeship in the Upper Canada Court of Chancery, and he continued in this position after the old colony became the Province of Ontario. He was tempted back into politics when in 1872 Edward Blake decided to resign from the provincial premiership to devote himself to activities on the federal scene. Mowat retired from the bench, sought and won election to the assembly, and began his unparalleled period as premier and attorney general. In this position, during the vital early years of Confederation, Mowat carried on an obstinate battle against John A. Macdonald's attempts to turn Canada into a centralized legislative union rather than a true confederation. In this struggle, the knowledge of constitutional law and legal procedures that Mowat had gained on the judge's bench stood him in good stead. He followed the practice of re-enacting laws which Ottawa had disallowed and in the final resort appealing with a considerable degree of success to the Privy Council in Westminster, then the supreme court for Canada under the British North America Act. As was shown by repeated electoral success, Mowat had the support of most Ontarians in his struggles against Ottawa, as well as the admiration of many Canadians in other provinces. If genuinely federalist elements have survived in Canadian government, it has been largely thanks to Mowat's resolute defence of the rights of the provinces during the 1870s.

During his long period in office, Mowat also extended the provincial franchise, laid the foundations for orderly municipal government, and acquired the mineral-rich areas of the Shield when Ontario was extended northward to Hudson's Bay.

Mowat's reign as premier of Ontario came to an end not because of electoral defeat but because, when the Liberals returned to power in 1896, Laurier appointed him to the Senate and invited him to become federal minister of justice. Mowat was already seventy-six, and although he accepted the portfolio, he found the tasks it incurred too heavy and resigned to become lieutenant-governor of Ontario. He held that post until his death in 1903.

Others did more than Mowat to devise a federal system for Canada and to ensure that it came into being, but no man did more to defend the survival of the federal principle in the young dominion.

D'Alton McCarthy

If any man's career shows in dramatic form the influence that religious passions retained in late Victorian Canada, it is that of D'Alton McCarthy, the brilliant lawyer and political orator who was once regarded as Sir John A. Macdonald's likely successor but who never held a cabinet post.

D'Alton McCarthy was born near Dublin of Irish Protestant parents in 1836 and came to Canada with his family in 1847. In his early manhood McCarthy devoted himself to the law, being called to the bar in 1858. He had a high reputation as a barrister, specializing in the preparation of cases for submission to the Privy Council in London, but he also had a persuasive way with juries that led him often to be engaged for difficult cases before the Canadian courts; he became a queen's counsel in 1872.

Although always a Conservative in temperament and opinions, McCarthy did not become active politically until 1876, when he was elected to the dominion House of Commons. He remained a member of the House until his death in 1898; his personal popularity and the loyalty he inspired among Protestant Ontarians guaranteed him his seat even when his convictions led him to abandon regular party allegiances.

For more than a decade McCarthy worked in harmony with Macdonald and the Conservative party leadership; in 1884 he was offered the ministry of justice but rejected it because, for the time being at least, he preferred to organize support for the party outside the cabinet. His advice was sought by the Tory leaders and often accepted, and until the breaking point of 1889 nobody doubted that the highest posts in party and government were McCarthy's whenever he chose to claim them.

The breaking point came over the issue of the Jesuit Estates Act, which had been passed in Quebec by Honoré Mercier's nationalistically inclined government in 1888. The act proposed to give $400,000 to the Jesuits in compensation for lands which had been confiscated in Quebec when the order was temporarily suppressed by the pope in 1773. William Edward O'Brien, another Conservative M.P., introduced a motion for the disallowance of the Quebec act.

Macdonald's government, anxious to retain whatever precarious hold it might have over Quebec Catholic votes after Louis Riel's execution, decided to support the provincial government. Only eight Conservative and five Liberal members (known later in the Orange lodges of Ontario as "the noble thirteen") voted for disallowance. McCarthy was one of them, and he felt so strongly over the issue that he abandoned whatever future he had with the Conservative party to declare himself an independent.

McCarthy now began to tour the country, passionately denouncing what he regarded as the special privileges given to Catholics. He placed himself at the head of the newly founded Equal Rights Movement and stirred up Ontarians over such questions as denominational schools and the use of the French language. In 1890 he caused a bitter debate in the House of Commons by introducing a motion to end the use of French as an official language in the North-West Territories, and in the same year he made a fiery speech in Portage la Prairie, which is said to have led the Manitoba government to end denominational schools and the official use of the French language in their province. The dispute over the Manitoba Schools Act lingered in the courts, which in the end ruled that the federal government had the right of disallowance, and this was one of the factors that weakened the Conservative government after Macdonald's death and led to its final collapse in 1896.

By this time McCarthy's own ardour had been worn down by the rigours of public campaigning and the frustration of legal and political battles, and in 1897, when Laurier worked out a compromise that at least partially satisfied the Catholics, he did not protest. He died in 1898, a hero to thousands of Ontario Protestants, and yet in terms of achievement a man whose career had been wasted by fanaticism.

Edward Blake

Canada has had its fair proportion of political loners and eccentrics, but none perhaps of greater potentiality or finer intellect than Edward Blake, who was passionately concerned with political ideals but temperamentally unfitted for the manoeuvres of party politics, and who always evaded power when it lay most ready for him to grasp. Brilliant as an orator, erudite as a constitutional lawyer, moody of personality, and unpredictable as a leader, he seems in memory to fill more than any other man the role of Don Quixote in Canadian public life.

Blake was one of the many nineteenth century Canadian political leaders of Irish Protestant stock. His father, a distinguished lawyer who migrated in 1832, had served in Robert Baldwin's Reform administration and had also been chancellor for Upper Canada. Edward, who was born in 1833 and received a customary establishment education at Upper Canada College and the University of Toronto, followed his father into law and in his early thirties became one of the most successful barristers in the Canada of his time.

Blake developed early an interest in politics and leaned by family tradition and individual temperament to the Reform side, but at first he kept away from actual political activity, and it was only when Confederation seemed to offer a wide enough field for his activities that he allowed his name to stand in 1867 as a candidate for the new Ontario legislature and also for the House of Commons. He won both elections, and according to the easy rules of the young dominion he was allowed to keep the two seats.

At first Edward Blake concentrated on provincial politics, largely because the shadow of George Brown, formidable editor of the *Globe*, hung ominously over the federal Liberal party. He was a sharp and relentless critic of John Sandfield Macdonald's first government of Ontario, and in 1871, when Sandfield was defeated, he became premier of Ontario for a few months, the only occasion on which he actually held the highest office of any government. In 1872, when dual representation was abolished, he resigned his Ontario seat and turned his full attention to federal politics in time to play a decisive role in the Commons debates over the Pacific Scandal, which led to the downfall of Sir John A. Macdonald's first dominion government in 1873.

Blake had already been offered the leadership of the Liberal party and had capriciously declined it, so that Alexander Mackenzie became the new prime minister. Blake found it hard to forgive himself and impossible to forgive Mackenzie for the situation, and though he accepted a ministership without portfolio, he resigned within three months and in October 1874 shocked his party by announcing at a Liberal rally in Aurora, Ontario, that he was leaving the ranks to join Goldwin Smith in the Canada First[7] party, declaring his belief in the need for Canada's independence. Blake did not remain long with the doctrinaire nationalists of Canada First; in 1875 he was back in the Liberal fold and had accepted the post of minister of justice, in which role he founded the Supreme Court of Canada, though he was unable to get imperial consent to abolish appeals to the Privy Council in London as the ultimate arbiter of Canadian law.

When the Liberals were defeated in 1878 and the party blamed Mackenzie's ineptitude, it was Blake who in 1879 was chosen as leader. He proved uninterested in the responsibilities of guiding a party in opposition, and as he had made so many enemies–in British Columbia through his opposition to the CPR and in Quebec through his ambivalent attitude towards Louis Riel–the party was defeated in the 1882 elections. In 1887 Blake resigned the leadership, making way for Laurier, with whom he finally parted in 1891 over the issue of reciprocity, whose dangers as a way to American domination he saw quite clearly.

This was the end of Blake's public life in Canada, but almost immediately he responded to an appeal from the Irish nationalists, with whom he had been long in touch. From 1892 to 1907 he sat as a nationalist member in the British House of Commons, advocating Home Rule, achieving virtually nothing, retiring in 1907, and returning to Toronto, where he died in 1912. His political life in Ireland had been as lacking in consequence as his political life in Canada, and Blake can be seen in retrospect as a man of brilliant moments, of fine speeches, of decisive interventions in debates, but not as a man of sustained achievement. There were so many opportunities lost, and willingly lost, that it is hard to remember him except as the greatest might-have-been of Canadian history.

Wilfrid Laurier

"I am a Liberal," said Wilfrid Laurier in the famous speech he made in 1877 to protest the Catholic church's hostility to the Rouges, the Quebec Liberals. "I am one of those who think that everywhere there are abuses to be reformed, new horizons to be opened up, and new forces to be developed." On the whole he lived by such principles, though like all who profess them, he found they became compromised by the demands of power and the shifts of politics. So far as Canadian history is concerned, it is perhaps Laurier's nationalism rather than his Liberalism that is important. If Canada achieved unity from Macdonald's unlikely hands, it moved towards independence under Laurier.

The Lauriers–originally the Champlauriers–were old Quebec stock, tracing their ancestry to the companions of Maisonneuve who came to Montreal in 1642. Laurier's father was a prosperous farmer at St. Lin, Quebec, and also a surveyor. Wilfrid was born in 1841, and his parents' anglophilia was shown in his Christian name, taken from Scott's *Ivanhoe*, and also in his being sent to an English school in New Glasgow, René Lévesque's birthplace. Later Wilfrid went to the classical college at L'Assomption and eventually studied law at McGill, where he delivered the first valedictory ever presented in French. By this time–1864–he was already interested in politics, attracted by the Rouges, and he was a member of the Institut Canadien when that organization was placed under interdict by Bishop Bourget as heretical and subversive.

In 1866, suffering from a lung malady, Laurier left Montreal and moved to L'Avenir in the Eastern Townships, where he edited a Liberal newspaper, *Le Défricheur*. A few months later he moved to Arthabaskaville, where he settled down to practise law, and in 1871 became a member of the Legislative Assembly of Quebec. From this point on, while remaining a devout and practising Catholic, he opposed with growing success the practice among the clergy of directing the votes of their parishioners; the church, he believed, should stand outside politics.

In 1874 he was elected to the House of Commons. In April he made his maiden speech in English to protest the expulsion of Louis Riel from the House. He attracted the attention of the Liberal leaders, and for a brief period in 1877-78, until Mackenzie's government was defeated, he held the position of minister of inland revenue. Laurier had become the acknowledged leader of Quebec Liberal M.P.'s, but he did not acquire the general popularity he later enjoyed in Quebec until 1885, when he led the wave of French-Canadian protest against the execution of Louis Riel and in Montreal made another famous speech, declaring, "Had I been born on the banks of the Saskatchewan . . . I would myself have shouldered a musket to fight against the neglect of governments and the shameless greed of speculators."

When Edward Blake resigned from the Liberal leadership in 1887, it was Laurier who seemed the natural leader, and in 1896 he profited by the disintegration of the Conservative party after Macdonald's death to lead the Liberals to victory. As prime minister he established a strong cabinet that presided over the opening and populating of the West, authorized new railways that opened the northern prairies, and eventually created the provinces of Saskatchewan and Alberta. There were difficult problems in the West, reflected in the controversies over denominational schools in Manitoba and the rights of French speakers in the new provinces, and although Laurier made compromises which temporarily satisfied most parties, the issues left a residue of resentment.

Laurier combined a loyalty to the British connection with a desire to see Canada free of binding imperial ties. This led him into some apparent inconsistencies, for he supported Canada's participation in the South African war (which many French Canadians opposed) but at the same time he made the Canadian armed forces independent, laid plans for a Canadian navy, established Canada's right to negotiate commercial treaties, and frustrated at various imperial conferences Joseph Chamberlain's desire to turn the British Empire into a federation with an overriding imperial council to decide general questions concerning the commonwealth.

Perhaps Laurier's major inconsistency, one he shared with many Liberals since his time, was that he recognized the danger of political domination by Britain but was blind to that of economic domination by the United States. He accepted the programme of reciprocity–which involved wide-ranging commercial co-operation with American interests. On this issue his long period in office ended with defeat in the 1911 elections. Laurier never returned to office, and during World War I his Liberal party was almost destroyed over the issue of conscription. Many leading Liberals broke away to join Borden's coalition; in the 1917 elections Laurier was defeated everywhere but in Quebec, and he died in 1919 while attempting to reconstruct his shattered party.

Clifford Sifton

If Canada is now one of the world's few genuinely multicultural countries, the reason lies largely in the great migrations of eastern Europeans to the prairies between 1890 and 1914. More than any other man, Clifford Sifton – publicist and politician – was responsible for their coming. Sifton was one of the new energetic men who came into federal office in 1896, when Wilfrid Laurier brought an end to the decaying power of the Conservatives who had ruled almost continuously in Ottawa since Confederation.

Sifton was an Upper Canadian, born in London, Ontario, in 1861. His father, who began as a farmer, moved to the North West in 1875 on the wave of Upper Canadian immigration and became a contractor for telegraph and railway lines. He also dabbled in politics, was elected twice to the Legislative Assembly of Manitoba and in 1878 was voted speaker.

Clifford Sifton, who chose law as his profession, followed his father into provincial politics, entering the assembly as representative for North Brandon in 1888. In 1891 he was appointed attorney general and minister of education in Thomas Greenway's Liberal government. This meant that he represented the provincial government in the thorny Manitoba schools controversy with the federal authorities. Sifton was a devoted supporter of the idea of secular education, and if he was not actually responsible for the Manitoba law of 1890 revoking the right of French-speaking Catholics to establish their own schools with provincial support, he defended it in the law suits and negotiations with Ottawa ending in Laurier's 1897 compromise, which gave the Catholics limited rights.

By this time Sifton was himself a member of Laurier's cabinet. He had been elected to the House of Commons in 1896 and in the same year became minister of the interior, then one of the key Ottawa posts. The administration of the North-West Territories, including the prairie lands that later became Saskatchewan and Alberta, was Sifton's responsibility. He realized that the economic health and political security of Canada demanded that the vacant lands be settled quickly, and he began an intensive campaign to encourage Europeans with farming experience to immigrate. He tried first for British immigrants, but when they did not come quickly enough he turned to Scandinavians and to Slavic groups from the Russian and Austro-Hungarian empires. He brought in the first Mennonite colonies to settle in the Canadian prairie, and approved the acceptance of the Doukhobors in 1898-99.

The arrival of Slavic groups, and particularly the Ukrainians (or Galicians as they were often called), aroused great opposition among the many Canadians who wanted to make their country outside Quebec an Anglo-Celtic preserve. The Ukrainians – and also the Doukhobors – arrived wearing coats of sheepskin, with the fleece inside, and these garments became symbols in a bitter controversy, with Sifton maintaining that "men in sheepskin coats," because they came from Eurasian steppes similar to the prairies, were double the worth of an ordinary settler; while his critics declared that those who wore sheepskin were "the scum of Europe."

Sifton was acutely aware of the need to protect his local power base in the West, and for this purpose in 1898 he acquired the *Manitoba Free Press*, which not only supported his immigration policies but later, under John W. Dafoe's editorship, became one of the great organs of Canadian Liberal opinion.

Sifton was a maverick among the Liberals and refused to accept all the compromises by which Laurier sought to steer a course between Quebecois and English-speaking supporters, whose interests were often divergent. When Saskatchewan and Alberta were established in 1905, Sifton refused to accept the concessions to denominational schools, and resigned as minister of the interior. In 1911 he led a revolt of nineteen Liberal M.P.'s against Laurier's proposal to renew the reciprocity agreement with the United States, which Sifton suspected would lead to a surrender of Canadian resources. By this act he was largely responsible for the Liberal electoral defeat of 1911 and the return of the Conservatives to office under R.L.Borden.

For the rest of his life Sifton remained interested in politics, and his position as proprietor of the powerful *Manitoba Free Press* made him something of a Liberal grey eminence, influencing policies almost until his death in 1929 without returning to office or indeed to parliament. Earlier than most Canadians he understood the power of the mass media and used it. He was a man of strong, independent convictions, and was exceptional among politicians for his willingness, when the occasion arose, to place conviction before career.

Richard John Cartwright

Richard Cartwright was one of the best parliamentary debaters of his time and without exception the most offensive to his political enemies. Born in Kingston in 1835 of Loyalist stock, Cartwright was the son of an Anglican clergyman and received a good establishment education at Trinity College, Dublin, before returning home to take up commerce and become president of a small local bank. His political career started in pre-Confederation Canada, when he was elected to the Legislative Assembly as a Conservative in 1863. In 1867 he entered the federal House of Commons.

Never, even in youth, was Cartwright inclined to modesty, and in 1870, when his claims at the age of thirty-five to the Ministry of Finance were ignored in favour of those of the politically more experienced Francis Hincks, he developed a burning resentment towards Sir John A. Macdonald. This found ample fuel in the Pacific Scandal of 1873, when Cartwright, who already on occasion had voted with the opposition on such questions as the terms offered to British Columbia as an inducement to enter Confederation, finally left the Conservative party and received from Alexander Mackenzie the coveted post which the Tories had denied him.

Cartwright at last became minister of finance. Perhaps the most striking achievement at this time–one of which few Canadians are aware–was to establish the office of a politically independent auditor general to supervise government expenditure.

When the Liberals were defeated in 1878, Cartwright remained in their ranks and for the next eighteen years alternately amused and depressed the House of Commons with his speeches prophesying national disaster at the hands of the Conservatives. His opponents called him "Blue Ruin," his supporters "the Rupert of debate." He was a penetrating critic, but almost everything he said in opposition was marred by the bitter personal hatred he harboured for Macdonald, which led him in the end to oppose erecting a monument to his dead enemy unless it bore a plaque telling the story of the Pacific Scandal.

During the years of opposition Cartwright also built a more positive reputation as a very shrewd financial critic of the Tory administration. He supported Laurier's claims to leadership of the Liberal party and in fact became his main representative in English-speaking Canada, so that when the Liberals finally regained office in 1896 he was appointed minister of trade and commerce, a key post at a time when Canada was moving towards international recognition through the negotiation of trade agreements with countries in Europe and the Americas. When Laurier was absent, it was Cartwright who would act as prime minister. Cartwright's appointment to the Senate in 1904 did not diminish his authority in the councils of the Liberal party, and there seems little doubt that he disastrously encouraged Laurier in pursuing a reciprocity agreement with the United States, the issue that precipitated the Liberal defeat of 1911.

Cartwright did not long survive that defeat. He died in 1912, having found time to dictate his *Reminiscences*, in which he returned to his attacks on Macdonald with such vehemence that Sir Joseph Pope was stirred into replying with his *Sir John A. Macdonald Vindicated*.

By nature Cartwright was an intensely conservative man, and his long allegiance to the Liberal cause can be explained by a mixture of personal incompatibility with Macdonald and a genuine repugnance for the kind of political amoralism that the Pacific Scandal seemed to demonstrate.

Timothy Eaton

No man seemed a better example for the Victorian argument that sobriety and fair dealing are the best way to prosperity than Timothy Eaton, who parlayed rigorous principles into a business so successful that it initiated Canada's greatest commercial dynasty.

Timothy Eaton was a Protestant Irishman, born in 1834 at Ballymena in Ulster. His father, a farmer, had died before his birth, and Timothy was brought up according to the strictest Calvinist principles, so that to the end of his long life he condemned with equal rigour drinking and smoking, card playing and dancing. In 1854 Eaton migrated to Canada, where his two elder brothers, Robert and James, had already established a general store at St. Mary's, Upper Canada. Fourteen years afterwards, Timothy Eaton left the partnership to set up his own dry goods store in Toronto. A year later, having assessed the trading patterns of the city, he founded the firm of T. Eaton and Company, and began to do business on what he regarded as rational and moral principles.

In T. Eaton's stores everything was sold for cash and there was no bargaining, since all prices were fixed and based on cost plus a reasonable profit. Thus, the customer did not have to bear the cost of bad credit risks, and very soon he was further indemnified by Eaton's guarantee to return his money to a customer who was not satisfied with his purchase. Such methods, besides making Eaton and his heirs some of the richest men in North America, revolutionized the Canadian retail business and established standards of commerce which, if not foolproof, were certainly far better than the practices of earlier merchants who traded by haggling and refused to guarantee the goods they sold.

Timothy Eaton not only offered his customers a square deal within the profit system, and stood by the offer. He also realized that employees would work better if they in turn were treated fairly, and thus, though he was dictatorial and arbitrary in his decisions, he paid good wages by the standards of his day and he pioneered in early closing hours so that his workers would have more relaxation. In return, he demanded and received a degree of efficiency and loyalty that few other employers in his day could command.

By such methods Eaton built up a department store chain that was one of the biggest not only in Canada but in the whole of North America–an enterprise so securely founded that to this day it remains a family empire in the old style, which has not surrendered to the corporate capitalism of the later twentieth century; Timothy's great-grandsons still control it.

But Eaton was not content with the urban market which most merchants regarded as sufficient. He realized that the opening of the Canadian West provided a dispersed market which ordinary merchandising methods had barely touched. Accordingly he created a great mail order department, equipped to supply people in the most remote villages of the prairies and the western mountains with a choice of goods that no local storekeeper could possibly supply, and to inform such potential customers he began to publish in 1884 the famous Eaton's Catalogue. Appearing first as an unillustrated thirty-two-page brochure, it developed into a large, lavishly pictorial publication (nine hundred pages long before it ceased to be published in 1976) avidly read by its recipients and known as "the homesteaders' bible," or–among prairie Indians–as "the wish book." At its height the catalogue reached a circulation of two million, which is an index of the kind of empire Timothy Eaton created.

But it was an empire with self-imposed limitations. Eaton was consistent to the extent that if his principles forbade him to smoke or drink, he would encourage nobody else to indulge in these lapses from evangelical morality, and as a consequence his catalogue never advertised tobacco or liquor and his stores never sold them. Timothy Eaton died in 1907, dourly convinced that he was the one camel who might pass through the eye of the biblical needle.

Margaret Murray

Margaret Murray, who founded one of the classic Canadian social organizations, was born in Scotland, the daughter of a wealthy Paisley textile manufacturer, William Polson. In 1865 she married the philosopher, John Clark Murray, also a native of Paisley, who held the post of professor of mental and moral philosophy at Queen's University. Murray attained some fame in his time as the author of a number of now outdated texts on psychology and ethics, and in 1872 he was appointed to the chair of philosophy at McGill University, where he remained for the rest of his academic career. From this time onwards the Murrays lived in Montreal, where Murray himself died in 1917 and Margaret in 1927.

Like so many academic wives, Margaret Murray took to social welfare work, partly from boredom, partly from a genuine desire to be of service. At first it was the YWCA that attracted her attention, but during the Boer War she became involved in an association to tend the graves of soldiers killed in South Africa, and at this time she became acutely aware of the considerable opposition to Canadian participation in the Boer War, which she interpreted as a sign of the disintegration of imperial loyalties.

Undoubtedly Margaret Murray was influenced by the strong current of Imperial Federalist thought in Canada, and she conceived the idea of forming a patriotic organization of women who would uphold British ideals and traditions, and preserve the unity of the Empire. Encouraged by the governor general's wife, Lady Aberdeen, with whom she discussed her idea, she launched her campaign with a series of telegrams to the mayors of provincial capitals, suggesting that they call on women with public interests to form an association which at first she called Daughters of the Empire. It is clear she had in mind a Canadian counterpart to the Daughters of the American Revolution, founded in 1890, and the Daughters of the Confederacy, founded in 1894.

The early response was negligible. Receiving little support in her own town of Montreal, Margaret Murray was prepared to abandon her efforts when the news arrived that a group had formed itself in Fredericton, New Brunswick, where the United Empire Loyalists were strong. Encouraged

by this first success, Margaret Murray went back to work with such energy that by the end of 1900 the movement had spread over the country and the Imperial Order of Daughters of the Empire (IODE) came into existence. The motto of the organization, "One Flag, One Throne, One Country," links it to the Imperial Federation movement, which had countered talk of Canadian independence by advocating a reconstruction of the British Empire into a federation that would give Canadians and other citizens of colonial territories a share in imperial decisions so that the Empire could operate internationally, with the strength and unity of a single country.

Margaret Murray became director as well as founder of the IODE and guided its activities until after the war of 1914-18. Wars and similar imperial crises stimulated the activities of the IODE. Its first project was to supply comforts for Canadian soldiers in South Africa, and during World War I it raised five million dollars for wider purposes. In periods of peace the order was little distinguishable from other service clubs (with which it competed in such fields as providing scholarships) except in ideological terms; under Margaret Murray's direction, and ever since, it supported both a strong and centralized Canadian state and also close ties in a commonwealth based on British traditions.

John Wilson Bengough

The pen may not be mightier than the sword, but the pencil of a witty cartoonist can be a formidable weapon in political battles, and Canada has had a notable contingent of artists whose caricatures have contributed a salutary element of irreverence to our national life.

Undoubtedly the first of the great Canadian cartoonists, certainly in time and perhaps also in merit, was John Wilson Bengough who started in life as a printer and whose versatile artistic talents–for Bengough was a satirical poet as well as a cartoonist–were linked all his life with the newspaper world, particularly in his native Toronto, where he was born in 1851.

Bengough was essentially a post-Confederation man, developing his talents in the period of strong political personalities and gamey politics that lasted from 1867 until Laurier's accession to power in 1896. To draw out the bizarre aspects of this vigorous and often corrupt scene Bengough decided to create his own paper, and in doing so he created the tradition of the political cartoon as a feature of Canadian journalism.

His paper was called *Grip* after the speaking raven in Dickens's *Barnaby Rudge;* it was a twelve-page weekly, consisting mainly of cartoons and satirical verse. Fortune smiled on its appearance in 1873, for that was the year of the Pacific Scandal, which Bengough exploited in a series of devastating drawings. Bengough's hatred of corruption led him to ally himself loosely with the Liberal interest at the time, and the fact that Sir John A. Macdonald and his associates ruled for most of the life of *Grip*, which Bengough left in 1892 and which died two years later, assured an abundance of personalities and issues ripe for mockery. With a less colourful and ambiguous man than Macdonald at the head of the nation, Bengough would have found it much more difficult to build up, as he did, *Grip*'s circulation and his own repute as a cartoonist, which he enhanced by a whole series of subsidiary activities.

These included reprinted volumes of his cartoons, like his two-volume *A Caricature History of Canadian Politics*, which appeared in 1886, and humorous lecture tours across Canada. These tours, which began in 1874, were popular and entertaining, for Bengough would not only tell satirical tales of what was happening in the public life of Ottawa, Toronto, and Montreal, but he would also bring his easel onto the stage, and while he talked he would draw cartoons to illustrate the events he discussed or make lightning caricatures of local personalities in the towns he visited.

Bengough's nimble and sharp-toned mind produced a great amount of good satirical verse, only a proportion of which was published in volumes like *Motley* (1895) and *In Many Keys* (1902). He was too individual in his viewpoint to remain an orthodox Liberal and so he became a dedicated advocate of Henry George's scheme for a single tax based on land values and a confirmed free trader, producing polemical pamphlets to support his views, like *The Up-to-date Primer: A first book of Lessons for Little Political Economists* (1896). He supported his ardent advocacy of prohibition with an eccentric little book called *The Gin Mill Primer* (1898).

When the energy began to run out of *Grip*, Bengough abandoned his creation and went on in 1892 to become cartoonist for the Montreal *Star*, and afterwards for the Toronto *Globe*. But he never seemed so happy or so effective in the setting of a large newspaper as with *Grip*, the magazine he created and dominated, the magazine that in so many ways *was* J.W.Bengough. He lived on into the era between the two world wars, dying in 1923, but he had long ceased to be a figure of public significance; his real age was the yeasty formative years of Canadian national politics between Confederation and the century's end.

Alexander Graham Bell

There have been many Canadian inventors, and most of them have gained less than the fame they deserved. This was certainly not the case with Alexander Graham Bell, whose name survives in the Bell Telephone Company which he created and which plays so large a part in the lives of Canadians–a people more addicted to telephone conversation, according to statisticians, than any other nationality.

Alexander Bell, as he was born in 1847 (the Graham was added only eleven years later), was the son of a Scottish expert in speech correction, Alexander Melville Bell. The elder Bell was author of a classic manual, *The Standard Elocutionist*, which passed through two hundred editions, but he was also an early expert on speech correction, inventing a system called Visible Speech by which the congenitally deaf could be taught to speak.

Alexander Graham Bell was mainly taught at home by his father, though he studied for periods at both Edinburgh and London universities. After a brief spell as a teacher he became his father's assistant in speech training. The fear of tuberculosis, which had killed Alexander's two brothers, led the family to move to Canada, and in 1870 they settled in Brantford, Ontario. Three years later Alexander became professor of vocal physiology at Boston University, and it was here, working with a repair mechanic called Thomas Watson, that he put into practice in 1876 the idea for a telephone which had come to him at Brantford in 1874. The invention was described, when Bell patented it in the United States, as "The method of, and apparatus for, transmitting vocal or other sounds telegraphically . . . by causing electrical undulations, similar in form to the vibrations of the air accompanying the said vocal or other sounds." Bell recorded that the first long-distance speech by telephone took place in Canada–from Brantford to Paris, Ontario, a distance of eight miles. There followed years of litigation in the American courts over rival claims to the invention of the telephone, but in the end Bell was vindicated.

Alexander Graham Bell went on to many other inventions, some of which contributed greatly to the technology of modern times. One was the photophone, by which Bell contrived to transmit sound on a beam of light. Another was the graphophone, a rival system of sound recording to Edison's phonograph.

In 1885 Bell acquired on Cape Breton Island a property which he called Beinn Bhreagh, and from this time onwards he spent all his summers in Canada, where he died in 1922. At Beinn Bhreagh, where he owned a large stretch of deserted land, he carried out his experiments, founding the Aerial Experiment Association in collaboration with young Canadian scientists. He designed a working model of a man-carrying tetrahedral kite and worked at solutions to the problems of solar distillation and sonar detection. Perhaps his most spectacular late achievement was the invention of the hydrofoil, of which before his death he produced a number of experimental models; in 1918 one of them–which weighed five tons–attained a speed of seventy miles an hour.

Bell was, in fact, something of a Leonardo da Vinci of modern times. His surviving notebooks reveal that for every invention he carried through to fulfilment or even to the experimental stage, hundreds of ideas remained as jottings. In this way Bell anticipated, at least in conception, many inventions that have only been carried to fruition in the later twentieth century. In many fields of applied science he was a great seminal intelligence.

Yet to the end Bell remained devoted to the original concern that had led him on his long path of invention, the alleviation of the condition of congenitally deaf people by enabling them to communicate with others by means of speech, and among his more humanly satisfying achievements was the beginning of the long education of Helen Keller.

Louis-Joseph Papineau

Louis-Joseph Papineau was a conservative with the temperament of a revolutionary. He believed essentially in an oligarchical republic, ruled by country gentlemen; he differed from Canadian democrats of his time in his rejection of the idea of responsible government, just as he differed from Canadian Conservatives in his eventual rejection of the British connection and the monarchical system. He is often presented as the precursor of Quebec independence, but even on this issue he wavered; there were times when he would have accepted the immersion of Lower Canada in the United States. In action as well as theory his record is equivocal; he did not even stay to risk his life in the Rebellion of 1837 that was fought in his name.

Papineau was born in Montreal in 1786. His father, the notary Joseph Papineau, was a seigneur and a Liberal monarchist who had been active in the defence of Canada against the Americans in 1776. Louis-Joseph, educated at the College of Montreal and the Quebec Seminary, at first followed his father's example; he served as a militia officer in the War of 1812 and he was present at that fine day in our history when General Brock and Tecumseh captured Detroit.

Before this, and even before he was called to the bar in 1810, Papineau had been elected in 1809 to the Legislative Assembly, and he continued to serve intermittently in various parliamentary bodies until 1854. He joined the moderately liberal Parti Canadien and in 1815 was chosen speaker of the assembly, a post he held for most of the next twenty-two years. His brilliance was evident, and in 1820 the governor-in-chief, Lord Dalhousie, persuaded him to join the Executive Council of Lower Canada. Friction with Dalhousie was the beginning of Papineau's shift into disaffection. He felt that the governor was disregarding his advice and he resigned from the council. In 1822 the British government proposed a union of Upper and Lower Canada, and Papineau went to London to oppose the bill. It did not pass. Nevertheless, from this point Papineau became an increasingly firm opponent of British rule in the Canadas.

In 1826 the Parti Canadien, of which he was by now virtual leader, became the Patriote party, moving steadily in the direction of radical activism, and Papineau himself fell under the influence of American political thought, particularly the variations of Jeffersonian–Jacksonian democracy which favoured his own conservative social and economic views; at heart he remained a seigneur to the end of his life and ruled as an authoritarian squire over the ancestral estate, which in honour of Jefferson he named Montebello.

Papineau interpreted his office as speaker of the assembly as a mandate to be spokesman for Quebecois discontent. He quarrelled with successive governors, each of whom he regarded as a symbol of British injustice, and in 1834 he was responsible for the celebrated Ninety-two Resolutions, a statement of grievances so extreme that it alienated moderate Liberals as well as Conservatives in Lower Canada and drove the Patriotes into the isolation where they became as much a conspiratorial movement as a political party. As so often happens in such situations, the lead fell into the hands of men who advocated violent insurrection, to which Papineau was opposed. As late as the assembly of the Patriotes at St. Charles on 23 October 1837, Papineau was still advocating peaceful means, but a crisis was precipitated when the government began to arrest Patriote activists. Papineau went to St. Denis, where he accepted the rank of commander of the rebels, and then slipped over the border to the United States while his followers fought their way into tragedy.

Papineau never again became an effective political leader. In exile he avoided the activists and took no part in the later rebellion of 1838. He went to Paris and lived there, poor and lonely, until an amnesty allowed him to return to Canada in 1845. He was immediately elected to the assembly of the united Canadas but followed an erratic course. He opposed the Reformers led by La Fontaine and even supported the manifesto of the Montreal merchants, who in 1849 demanded the American annexation of Canada. Some of the young men who formed the Parti Rouge in the 1840s gained inspiration from him, but his influence on the whole was slight, and in 1854 he resigned from parliamentary life to devote his remaining years, until his death in 1871, to the role of lord of Montebello, a Jefferson without slaves.

Rodolphe Laflamme

Toussaint Antoine Rodolphe Laflamme was a Montrealer by birth and at heart, born in 1827, son of one of the city's merchants. He was a devoted Quebec patriot, and like many of those who passionately defended the province's rights, he took up the profession of law, after studying at the College of St. Sulpice and later at McGill; he was called to the bar in 1849.

The effect of the priestly education at St. Sulpice was to turn Laflamme into a lifelong anticlerical; at the age of seventeen, in 1844, he was one of those who founded the liberally-oriented Institut Canadien. In 1847 he became the institute's president, and he was associated with Antoine-Aimé Dorion in the formation of the radical-liberal Parti Rouge.

Laflamme was actively opposed to the ultramontanist conservatism of the mid-nineteenth century Catholic hierarchy in Montreal and accepted excommunication rather than submission when a papal ban was imposed on the Institut Canadien in 1869.

One of the results of the ban was the famous Guibord case, in which Laflamme played an active role. Not long after the papal ban had been imposed, Joseph Guibord, a member of the Institut and printer of its *Annuaire*, died and was refused burial in his own plot by the parish priest of Notre Dame because he had not submitted to the church. Bishop Bourget supported the priest's refusal, and Guibord was temporarily interred in the Protestant cemetery, while Laflamme took up the case in the courts on the widow's behalf. He fought it through stage after stage until finally in 1874 the Judicial Committee of the Privy Council ordered that Guibord be buried in the plot which he had owned. The burial took place under heavy military escort on 16 November 1875, and Guibord's grave was closed with reinforced concrete to prevent its desecration. Bourget gained a kind of pyrrhic victory by immediately deconsecrating the spot where Guibord lay.

Laflamme's radicalism, like that of Papineau (whom he greatly admired) was riddled with inconsistencies, and when the feudal seigneurs of Quebec fought through the courts up to the Privy Council, seeking compensation for the privileges they had lost under legislation passed in 1858, he acted as their counsel.

Perhaps the other most interesting fact about Laflamme's career as a lawyer is that Louis Riel was one of the young men who worked in his office – for a few months after he left the College of Montreal in March 1865. There are no records to suggest how far Laflamme influenced Riel's later actions. Certainly, although Riel always remained a deeply religious man, there were times when he became strongly anticlerical, and his concern over the autonomy of the people of the Red River, which led him to lead the provisional government there in 1869-70, may have been influenced by Laflamme's passionate defence of Quebec autonomy when Riel was working for him. Laflamme was a strong opponent of Confederation as it worked out in 1867, since he believed it could only harm the interests of French-speaking people in Quebec and elsewhere.

Despite his political activities, Laflamme seems to have had an initial mistrust of ordinary political methods, for he did not seek any office until his middle forties, preferring to act through journalism and through the Institut Canadien. It may indeed have been the Institut's decline after the Guibord affair that led him to seek election to the House of Commons in 1872. He supported Alexander Mackenzie's Liberal government in 1873, and in 1876 became minister of inland revenue, moving in 1877 to the ministry of justice. He was defeated in 1878, when Sir John A. Macdonald returned with a landslide majority, and retired from public life. His youthful ardour spent, he lived on, in the growing loneliness of an ageing bachelor, until his death in 1893.

Antoine-Aimé Dorion

The Dorions were one of the great political clans of Quebec during the years of the union of Lower and Upper Canada. Antoine-Aimé was born in 1818 at Ste. Anne de la Pérade in Champlain county, and his brother, Jean-Baptiste-Eric (generally known as Eric Dorion) was eight years younger. Both brothers became deeply engaged as young men in the Institut Canadien and in the more radical wing of Canadian liberalism. Antoine-Aimé, who followed the familiar Lower Canadian legal route into politics, was called to the bar in 1842, and when Louis-Joseph Papineau returned from his French exile in 1845, he was the leading member of a group of young men who gathered around the old leader to discuss political ideas. It was out of this group that the Parti Démocratique, otherwise known as the Parti Rouge, emerged in 1848. Antoine-Aimé was its acknowledged leader, and Eric, whose extreme radicalism earned him the title of "l'enfant terrible" among Lower Canadian politicians, became its publicist, founding and editing the party mouthpiece, *L'Avenir*.

From this point the brothers tended to go their own somewhat different ways. Although Eric served in the Legislative Assembly of United Canada for two terms, he was less interested in parliamentary activity than in political journalism and in direct forms of social action, like the founding of colonies in the unsettled regions of Lower Canada. He himself was the leader of one such colony in Lower Canada, which he called L'Avenir after the paper he had founded, and here he started a second paper, *Le Défricheur*, which Wilfrid Laurier subsequently edited.

Eric Dorion died young in 1866; Antoine-Aimé lived on to become something of an elder statesman. He was elected to the assembly of the united Canadas in 1854 and with one small break remained a member until Confederation, when he entered the House of Commons. As leader of the Rouges, he was the natural ally of the Grits of Upper Canada, and when George Brown formed his ill-fated four-day government in 1858, Dorion was leader of the Lower Canadian section and minister of crown lands. Later, in 1862, John Sandfield Macdonald established a hardly less precarious Reform government, and Dorion became provincial secretary for Canada East. In 1863 he moved up to equality with Sandfield as attorney general for Canada East, holding the position until the government fell in 1864.

The collapse of the Macdonald–Dorion administration was the beginning of the events that led up to Confederation. Dorion had long been an advocate of the replacement of the legislative union of the two Canadas by a federal union of the two provinces, which he believed would remove many of the divisive factors by giving local control over local affairs and yet would present a federally united Canada to pressure from either Britain or the United States. Confederation as it emerged after the Charlottetown and Quebec conferences of 1864 was another matter, since it would mean three English-speaking provinces against one French-speaking, and Dorion was acutely aware of the perils of such an arrangement. Accordingly, he campaigned strongly within Quebec against Cartier, the main French-Canadian advocate of Confederation, but he was unsuccessful.

Once Confederation came about, Dorion was too astute a politician to continue a hopeless opposition, and like his former associate, John Sandfield Macdonald, he accepted with the best possible grace. He was elected to the House of Commons in 1867 and was immediately accepted as leader of the French-Canadian members in opposition. When the Liberals came into power under Mackenzie in 1873, Dorion was chosen as minister of justice, but like many other members of that administration he felt uneasy under the uninspired leadership of the grim-faced, Baptist stonemason, and in 1874 he accepted with gratitude the offer–which he may well have arranged as minister of justice–of the post of chief justice of Quebec, a refuge for a passé politician where he quietly rusticated until his death in 1891.

Canada before and just after Confederation was too small a stage for all the brilliant men who crowded it, and Dorion was one of the many whose talents were never given full expression.

THE FACT OF QUEBEC

Ignace Bourget

The nineteenth century Catholic hierarchy in Quebec was not as homogeneous as it sometimes appears in retrospect. One wing was inclined to be sympathetic to Liberal causes and to seek a certain independence of outlook, rather in the manner of the great Gallican prelates of France in the seventeenth and eighteenth centuries. The other wing–the ultramontanists–was inclined to stress the supremacy of the papacy and its views in church affairs, and to follow a conservative course in political and social matters. The personification of the liberally-minded Gallicans in Quebec was Archbishop Taschereau of Quebec; the personification of the ultramontanists was Bishop Bourget of Montreal. Both of them saw the role of the church as central to the community of French Canada; it was the interpretation of the role in which they differed.

Ignace Bourget was born at Point Levis in Lower Canada in 1799. He was educated at Nicolet College and in the Quebec Seminary, and ordained in 1822. In 1836 he was appointed vicar general of Montreal, and coadjutor bishop in 1837, the year of the uprising in Lower Canada, when Bourget sympathized with the rebels though his conduct was shaped to give the impression of loyalty to the existing authority. Throughout his life he was to be deeply concerned with maintaining the symbiosis between the French-Canadian culture, with its distinctive language, and the Catholic faith. He feared the influence of English Protestantism more than he supported the idea of French independence.

In 1840 Bourget succeeded to the see of Montreal, and with full control of the diocese he was able to reveal the extent of his ultramontanist beliefs. According to such beliefs, the pope's authority should govern all aspects of the life of good Catholics, including their political actions and their opinions in every field. One of Bourget's first acts as bishop of Montreal was to invite the Jesuits in 1842 to return to Canada, from which they had been absent for more than sixty years, and the Jesuits in turn encouraged him in policies that inevitably brought him into conflict with the modern trends emerging in Quebec as well as in other parts of Canada during the mid-nineteenth century.

Bourget's famous conflict with the Institut Canadien,

which began as early as 1858, when he warned Catholics against supporting it, and reached a climax in 1869 with the papal ban and the Guibord affair, is discussed elsewhere in these pages. It was only one aspect of his attempts to interfere deeply in the social and political affairs of Quebec. He encouraged his priests to preach against the Parti Rouge and to threaten parishioners who voted for the Liberals, and he openly supported the so-called Castors (or Beavers), the wing of the Quebec Conservatives who issued a Catholic programme and supported his ultramontanist views. Only in 1877 when the papacy finally decided that Bourget was exceeding its wishes, did he grudgingly call off his attempt to shape the political behaviour of Quebec Catholics. From this point the fortunes of liberalism began to improve in the province.

At the same time, Bourget was energetic in many practical ways, and while he is said to have delivered almost a thousand directives of various kinds to his flock during his thirty-six authoritarian years as bishop of Montreal, he was also responsible for the foundation of charitable institutions and colleges, as well as ecclesiastical foundations. It was nevertheless as much because of his controversial role in political affairs as because of age that he was finally removed from the see of Montreal in 1876 and elevated to the essentially honorary position of archbishop of Marianopolis *in partibus*, in which role he died near Montreal in 1885.

Elzéar Alexandre Taschereau

There is a certain irony to the fact that the first Canadian to wear the cardinal's hat should have been the liberal-minded Archbishop Taschereau rather than Bishop Bourget with his fanatical loyalty to the papacy. Yet there were ways in which Elzéar Alexandre Taschereau was the man more fitted for that princely role. He was, if not an aristocrat, at least a descendant of the gentry of New France; his grandfather, his father, and his brothers held high judicial posts; his maternal grandfather had been for many years speaker of the assembly of Lower Canada, and he himself was a scholar of ability and discrimination.

Elzéar Taschereau was born at Ste. Marie de la Beauce in 1820 and began to attend the Quebec Seminary at the age of eight, but it was not until he made a trip to Rome at the age of seventeen with one of his tutors that he finally accepted his vocation and went on to seek ordination.

For many years his role was that of teacher, and he never served as an ordinary parish priest. Soon after his ordination in 1842 he was appointed professor of philosophy at the Quebec Seminary, where he was afterwards director and then superior, in which role he became in 1860 rector of Laval University, founded in 1852 as a daughter institution of the Quebec Seminary. There is no doubt that over the years Taschereau's interest and protection helped Laval to maintain the tradition it quickly developed of resistance to the intellectual conservatism represented by the ultramontanist doctrines supported by Bishop Bourget in Montreal and Bishop Laflèche at Trois Rivières.

Taschereau was always willing to leave the study and the lecture hall when human suffering was involved, and in 1847 he nearly died from a fever caught when caring for Irish immigrants among whom an epidemic had broken out in the quarantine station of Goose Island. He became very popular among the Irish Catholics, and this may have been one of the reasons why he was appointed vicar general of Quebec in 1862 and simultaneously bishop and archbishop in 1871.

In this role Taschereau threw his considerable influence on the side of a liberal interpretation of church doctrine, and in the great hidden struggle within the hierarchy in Quebec at this time, his influence was almost always on the side of moderation. It is true that under great pressure he signed a joint pastoral letter which Bourget and Laflèche had concocted in 1875, declaring that no one could be a Liberal and remain a Catholic, but in 1876 he reversed his position, issuing a *mandement* which declared that the church's position must be one of neutrality between conservatism and liberalism. It was, significantly, in Taschereau's diocese that Laurier made his classic speech differentiating the "political" liberalism of Canada and of the British tradition in general from the doctrinaire and anticlerical liberalism of continental Europe.

Undoubtedly Taschereau's attitude during this period did a great deal to heal the scars caused in Quebec society by the dispute between the Rouges and the more conservative representatives of the church, and to ensure the continued role of Catholicism in the province's cultural life, including the dominant role it played in Quebec education until very recent decades.

To the social and educational role of the church Taschereau also contributed in more concrete ways, founding and reforming colleges, and establishing a hospital in Quebec, besides encouraging traditional forms of devotion by reconstructing the ancient pilgrimage shrine of Ste. Anne de Beaupré near Quebec. Cardinal Taschereau resigned his diocese in 1894 and died in 1898, a man of lifelong devotion and modesty, yet one of the respected figures–among non-Catholics as well as Catholics–in the Canada of his times.

Honoré Mercier

The career of Honoré Mercier in Quebec, like that of Oliver Mowat in Ontario, reminds one that there are more kinds of federalism than that which became enshrined in Canada through the British North America Act. Classic federalism – the federalism of the great French political thinker, Pierre-Joseph Proudhon – is based on building upward from the regions, not on attempting the more precarious feat of building downward from the centre. This was nearer the view of men like Dorion, Mowat, Laflamme, and Mercier, who opposed Confederation in the form it took in 1867, or if they did not directly oppose it, accepted it with caution. The national crisis of the 1970s suggests that their caution may have been justified and that more thought might have been given a century ago to the particular mix of central government and federal autonomy appropriate to the Canadian situation.

Honoré Mercier, whose life was short and whose career was to be abbreviated by scandal, was born in 1840 at St. Athanase, the son of a Quebec farmer. He was educated at the Jesuits' college in Montreal and remained under the influence of the order for the rest of his life. His interest in politics began early; at the age of twenty-two he was already editing *Le Courrier de St. Hyacinthe* in the interest of the Parti Bleu, the Quebec Conservatives, and though he changed parties over the issue of Confederation, he remained a man of conservative approach, deeply attached to tradition.

In 1866, having been called to the bar, Mercier abandoned journalism and at the same time severed his links with George-Étienne Cartier and the Bleus, since he believed there were not enough guarantees in the confederation plans to protect French-Canadian rights. At the same time, like most nationalists of his era, Mercier recognized that he had to operate within the given situation of Canada as he found it, and at no point did he seriously advocate independence for Quebec. But he did gather from among disgruntled Conservatives and right-wing Liberals enough sympathizers to form in 1871 the Parti National, remote ancestor of the present-day Parti Québécois. By avoiding anticlericalism and other radical extremities he hoped that he would be able to enlist the support of the Catholic church in the struggle for Quebec's greater autonomy.

Mercier's political career began very haltingly. He sat in the federal House of Commons from 1872 to 1874 and then turned to his law practice until in 1879 he was elected to the Quebec provincial assembly. By now the Parti National had dwindled, but Mercier was able to inject many of its attitudes into the provincial Liberal party, to which he now belonged. He became solicitor general in the administration run by Joly de Lotbinière, but the government lasted only a few months, and Mercier went into opposition for the next six years, in 1883 succeeding Joly as leader of the Liberal party. It was by playing on Quebecois indignation over the execution of Louis Riel in 1885 that Mercier was able to muster enough strength to defeat the Conservatives and take over the administration of the province in 1886.

Mercier was a bold leader in office and some of his initiatives were good, particularly the conference of provincial premiers which he called in 1887 and at which he and Oliver Mowat of Ontario were responsible for strong resolutions on the rights of the province, which – though Sir John A. Macdonald pretended to ignore them – helped in the 1880s to halt the trend towards a more highly centralized kind of government in Canada.

At the same time, Mercier became involved in a number of highly controversial situations through his anxiety to enlist the Catholic clergy (who had traditionally supported the British element) on the nationalist side. He appointed a priest, Antoine Labelle, as deputy minister of colonization, and in 1888 angered the Orange Order and Protestants throughout Canada by compensating the Jesuits for property lost when the order was banned by the pope in the eighteenth century.

Mercier had so much support in Quebec that he might have weathered these crises if he had not been discredited by disclosures, before a senate committee, of corruption in connection with railway contracts in Quebec. The lieutenant-governor of Quebec abruptly dismissed Mercier's government, and he lost heavily in the election that followed. He retired from politics, dying three years afterwards.

Mercier was a strange combination of idealism and veniality, but such men were not uncommon in his time and exist among us today. Perhaps his great misfortune was that – unlike Macdonald – he did not survive long enough to outlive the one great scandal of his career.

Joseph-Israel Tarte

Joseph-Israel Tarte was – in Carlyle's phrase – the "sea-green Incorruptible" of Quebec politics, for he was not only a man of highly publicized personal probity but declared himself "an uncompromising enemy of robbery and corruption" wherever he smelled it out, and he put his principles into such effective action that he ended the careers of at least two distinguished French-Canadian political leaders, Sir Hector Langevin and Honoré Mercier. When he himself was eventually expelled from office, it was from an excess rather than a lack of honesty.

Tarte was the son of a farmer, born at Lanoraie, Lower Canada, in 1848. He was educated at L'Assomption College, and in 1871 became a notary public. Soon afterwards he took to journalism and began to edit *L'Evènement* in Quebec as an organ of the Castors, the right-wing Catholic Conservatives. He continued to edit *L'Evènement* until 1891, while he found his way first into provincial and then into federal politics.

Tarte sat as a Conservative in the Quebec assembly from 1877 to 1881, and in 1885 he became deeply involved in the agitation against the execution of Louis Riel. This led him into an alliance with Honoré Mercier and the Parti National in Quebec, and also into a lasting hostility towards Sir Hector Langevin, who had succeeded George-Étienne Cartier as leader of the Quebec federal Conservatives and had refused to break party ranks by denouncing Riel's execution.

In 1891 Tarte was elected as an independent to the House of Commons. The election was contested and the seat eventually given to Tarte's opponent, but not before he had been able to bring charges in the House against Sir Hector Langevin, then minister of public works, and Thomas McGreevy, a railway contractor who was also a member of parliament. There was no doubt that corruption existed in the Department of Public Works, and when Sir John Macdonald refused to move against one of his chief lieutenants, Tarte persisted until a senate committee was set up and showed that McGreevy had indeed been involved deeply in corruption and that Langevin had been culpably unobservant. McGreevy was expelled from the House of Commons and Langevin resigned, his career ended. But Tarte found himself in the position of the sorcerer's apprentice, for once the senate committee had started sweeping, it did not stop. Tarte's friend Honoré Mercier was also found to be tainted by the same pattern of railway corruption; Mercier's government fell and the Parti National faded away.

Tarte meanwhile joined the Liberal party and became Laurier's confidant and chief lieutenant. Perhaps more than any other party worker, Tarte was responsible for orchestrating the massive and permanent shift of Quebecois political allegiances at this time from the Conservatives to the Liberals.

After Laurier's triumph in the elections of 1896, Tarte was rewarded with the office from which he had been instrumental in expelling Langevin, the Ministry of Public Works. There is no doubt that Tarte proved very effective in cleaning up a department that had become notorious during the years of Conservative government for patronage and sheer graft, and he also guided Laurier to an acceptable compromise in the Manitoba schools dispute. But in 1902 he broke party ranks, regardless of the consequences, to make a public plea for higher protective tariffs, and Laurier dismissed him from the cabinet.

Tarte, who in 1897 had acquired another newspaper, *La Patrie*, returned to journalism and also to his old Conservative allegiance, recognizing the party reforms Robert Borden had achieved and supporting the Conservative policy on tariffs against the reciprocity with the United States that the Liberals advocated. Tarte died in Montreal in 1907, and his departure was viewed with mixed feelings by those who granted his honesty but resented the strain of acerbic self-righteousness that was exhibited, *inter alia*, in Tarte's fanatically intolerant prohibitionism.

Henri Bourassa

Henri Bourassa was one of those quixotic and intensely appealing figures in Canadian history, who by their very failure to meet our conventional criteria of success or consistency, seem to project something real and deep in our collective nature. Today Bourassa is claimed as an ancestor by the Quebec separatists, yet he was never in their narrow way a francophone nationalist. He always saw clearly how history had brought French and English Canadians together, separate from the Americans and politically adult enough to shake free from British imperialism. There was never any time that he felt either of the two Canadian nations could exist alone; the price of their survival, he always argued, was a mutual recognition of their separate and complete identities.

Henri Bourassa was the son of the painter and architect, Napoléon Bourassa; more relevant to the traditions he absorbed is the fact that his mother was Azélie Papineau, youngest daughter of the Patriote leader Louis-Joseph Papineau. Much of Henri's childhood, after his birth in 1868 in Montreal, was spent on his grandfather's estate of Montebello, which as a young man he helped to administer and colonize. His education was irregular, yet–though he never graduated in a formal sense–it was good enough to make him in later years a brilliant journalist and a maverick politician whose voice never went unheard.

As a young man, he attracted the attention of Wilfrid Laurier, and he was among the Liberal members elected to the Canadian House of Commons in 1896, the year of Laurier's great victory. He was regarded as one of the most promising young Liberals, destined for a cabinet post, perhaps for the party leadership, but very soon–in 1899–he quarrelled with Laurier over Canada's participation in the South African war, which seemed to him an acceptance of imperial domination, and he remained the rest of his life a political *franc-tireur*, outside the major parties.

In 1903 Bourassa helped Olivar Asselin to found the Ligue Nationaliste; in 1907, despairing of achieving anything through federal politics, he resigned from the House of Commons and entered the Quebec provincial assembly; in 1910 he founded *Le Devoir*, which became and remained one of the best Canadian newspapers, always anti-imperialist, always loyal to the French language and tradition in Canada, but never willing to accept without criticism that counsel of despair called separatism.

With their opposition to Laurier's compromises over the question of Canadian participation in British naval expansion, Bourassa and *Le Devoir* contributed to the defeat of the Liberals in 1911. Later, during World War I, Laurier and Bourassa came closer together, though the latter never returned to the Liberal party. He opposed the idea of Canada's automatic entry into the war because she was part of the Empire; he opposed conscription. Although by now he held no political post, his influence in Quebec was considerable and it helped to solidify French-Canadian resistance to unquestioning participation in the war.

Bourassa returned to open politics as a member of the House of Commons from 1925 to 1935. During the 1930s he withdrew from the French-Canadian nationalists, since he did not agree with the inclination to alienate English Canadians who in their own way he recognized to be also nationalist and anti-imperialist. However, when World War II revived the old spectre of imperial conflict and conscription, Bourassa and his immediate followers closed ranks with the nationalists against Mackenzie King and the advocates of compulsory service, and in 1943 he supported the creation of the Bloc Populaire[8] in Quebec as an expression of his people's opposition to Canada's automatic acceptance of Britain's wars. Then he retired into the seclusion from which he did not emerge until his death in 1952.

Bourassa, as André Laurendeau once said, "asserted in clear terms that we must be Canadians before being either Frenchmen or Englishmen." Implied in such an assertion was the argument that we can remain Canadians only if we recognize and make room for each other's special traditions and aspirations.

Camillien Houde

One of the most enigmatic and yet in his own bizarre way one of the most appealing figures of recent Canadian history was Camillien Houde, the gigantic and colourful mayor of Montreal, most spectacular of municipal politicians and also a true– and irrepressibly comic–Canadian rebel.

Houde can best be seen as a personality of the Chaplin era, a raffish figure who appeared from nowhere to entrance the public imagination. He was born in Montreal in 1889, and his early career, before he first appeared in 1923 as a successful Conservative candidate in the Quebec provincial elections, was seedily unimpressive. He had been a bank clerk and an insurance agent, and by 1928, when he was first elected mayor of Montreal, had gone on to manage a biscuit factory and a candy factory, both of which failed. He was literally on the edge of bankruptcy when he became mayor of Montreal, standing on a reform platform as the people's candidate, but supported financially and in print by the *Montreal Star*.

Houde had both wit and a striking appearance–an elephantine body clad in old and baggy suits, and a nose so immense that he was once able to play Cyrano de Bergerac in an amateur performance without needing an artificial nasal appendage. He had also a genuine feeling for the Montreal poor as well as a healthy historical instinct that made him one of the first Canadians to warn against American cultural colonization, which he did early in the 1930s.

Houde was defeated in the 1932 mayoral election but returned in 1934 to run a reform programme, spending heavily on relief and public works, and soaking the rich with a municipal income tax. He resigned in 1936 during a dispute with Maurice Duplessis, then premier of Quebec, but returned in 1938 for his most spectacular term in office. Already he had run for the House of Commons as an independent on an anti-armament platform, declaring that "if the administration continues its programme of armaments, it will drive Quebec to complete independence." He did not gain his federal seat, but in 1939–at the same time as he entertained King George VI and the queen lavishly–he continued to warn Mackenzie King against trying to impose conscription. He advocated defensive precautions, perhaps

even an alliance with the United States, but he opposed the sending of Canadians to fight foreign wars.

The decisive confrontation with the federal government came on 2 August 1940 when Houde made a speech attacking the National Registration Act, which he warned– truthfully enough–was a harbinger of conscription, and urging Montrealers to resist registration. Three days later, in a move of extraordinary obtuseness, Mackenzie King had Houde arrested and interned, at Petawawa and later at Fredericton. Houde immediately became a hero in Quebec, and the government's attempts to brand him as a fascist were unavailing and certainly unjust. Although Houde shared the vague sympathy for Mussolini and Franco that was then general among French Canadians, he was so temperamentally uncommitted that when he met the Quebecois fascist leader, Adrien Arcand,[9] in internment he snubbed and avoided him.

At last, after massive protests, Houde was released on 16 April 1944, and he returned to a hero's welcome in Montreal, where he was immediately re-elected mayor, a position he held, virtually unopposed, until his retirement in 1954. In 1945 he moved towards Quebec nationalism and became one of the early leaders of the Bloc Populaire. In 1949 he was elected to the House of Commons; he allowed the parliamentary officials to carry out the comedy of converting two seats into one so that he would have a whole desk to accommodate his vast bulk–and then showed his contempt for high politics by never appearing. He died in September 1958, and 150,000 Montrealers attended the funeral when he was buried at the Côte des Neiges Cemetery in a tomb already built to his order and modelled on Napoleon's tomb at the Invalides in Paris.

"As long as we keep a good balance between prayer and sinning," Houde once said, "I know my city is not going to sink into wickedness." It might serve as an epitaph for the man as well as for the now vanished Montreal that he once governed.

Lionel-Adolphe Groulx

In France there were many who from various points of view sought to revive social messianism in the Catholic church. Sometimes they were radicals like Charles Péguy or liberals like François Mauriac, passionate devotees of a concept of love in action that made them willing at times to defy the church itself to save the church's soul. At other times they were conservatives like Charles Maurras, the founder of L'Action Française, who linked religion and patriotism, and saw their country as a kind of materialized Jeanne d'Arc, especially favoured of God.

In French Canada the Catholic radicals have always been few. The left–in the nineteenth century–was the domain of the Rouges; and the fanatical ultramontanist illiberalism of church leaders like Bishop Bourget and Bishop Laflèche ensured that Rouge protests against social injustices and inequalities would take a secular form, unblessed by the church. There is no one in the French-Canadian Catholic tradition who might be regarded as the equivalent of Péguy in France or even of Graham Greene in England. The hierarchy of the church in Quebec discouraged any true manifestation of radical Christianity, and so when the Quiet Revolution came and Quebec moved away from the world of the seigneur and the habitant, it also moved away from the church.

Yet among the Catholic intellectuals of Quebec there were some who in their own conservative way anticipated and even provided a theoretical foundation for Quebec's movement towards collective self-realization, and among them the most important was undoubtedly Lionel-Adolphe Groulx, whose life spanned several phases of his province's intellectual life and whose writings inspired men in many ways far removed from his religiously-oriented nationalism.

Lionel-Adolphe Groulx–Abbé Groulx as he became generally known–was born of a habitant family at Cheneux near Montreal in 1878. He attended the seminary in Montreal and was ordained priest in 1903.

Groulx never became a parish priest; he taught for two spells at the seminary in Valleyfield, he studied in Rome, Fribourg, and Paris, and in 1915 he became professor of Canadian history at the University of Montreal.

Yet, though he was an internationally celebrated scholar, founder of the Institut d'Histoire de l'Amérique Française in 1946, and first editor of the *Revue d'Histoire de l'Amérique Française* in 1947, Groulx never ceased to be in attitude completely a priest and in feeling completely a peasant, so that his historical teachings and writings were directed towards rediscovering a Catholic folk tradition in Quebec that might be strong enough to resist the influence of English cultural domination, which he perpetually feared. His earliest books, like *Chez nos Ancêtres*, were written in praise of the customs and virtues of the Laurentian habitants.

Early on, Groulx realized the importance of an emblematic hero to a national movement. His sympathies were drawn towards the Catholic nationalism of Charles Maurras and L'Action Française in France itself, and envying them the great symbolic resource they had in Jeanne d'Arc, he set out to make a Quebecois hero out of Dollard des Ormeaux–the hero of the battle of the Long Sault against the Iroquois in 1660–defending his evocation of Dollard as an exemplification of the Quebecois spirit in books like *Si Dollard Revient* (1919) and *Dollard: Est-il un Mythe?* (1960).

Groulx's own political pilgrimage extended along the verges of the ultraright. Not content with supporting Charles Maurras in the 1920s, in the following decade he at times praised figures like Mussolini, Salazar, and Dollfuss. But in spite of this ultraconservative orientation, Groulx's major historical works proved an inspiration to Quebec nationalists of all complexions, whether conservative or socialist, separatist or merely autonomist. An ably argued vision of a French Canada in constant struggle to survive a relentless English urge to domination emerges from his massive *Histoire du Canada Français depuis la Découverte*, which appeared in several volumes between 1950 and 1952. The whole intellectual basis of Quebec nationalism is enshrined in that book; in the decade that followed Groulx's death in 1967 it has only needed the political talents of men like René Lévesque to give it practical manifestation. If any one man was the spiritual father of Quebec separatism, it was Lionel-Adolphe Groulx.

Louis-Honoré Fréchette

Louis-Honoré Fréchette was the best known French-Canadian poet of the nineteenth century, and because he was honoured once by the vastly prestigious French Academy he was better known abroad than any other Canadian writer of his time.

Fréchette's achievements went deeper than honours. In his *La Légende d'un Peuple*, which appeared in 1887, he apprehended more fully than any earlier Canadian writer the myths implicit in the Canadian past. And this was appropriate, for Fréchette came of an old Quebec family; his ancestor, François Frichet, came to New France in 1677, and he himself was a seventh generation Canadian.

Born in 1839, Fréchette grew up in the uneasy atmosphere of Canada after the Durham Report and the artificial union of Lower and Upper Canada in 1841. But his initial rebelliousness, which led him to be expelled in turn from two different classical colleges, seems to have been personal rather than political. It was only in 1860, when he became a law student at the newly founded Laval University in Quebec City, that Fréchette's youthful rebelliousness assumed a social character. He became a devoted supporter of the Rouges, or Liberals, with their somewhat anticlerical orientation, and edited two ephemeral radical sheets, *Le Journal de Québec* and *Le Journal de Lévis*, as well as publishing his first collection of rather fragile poetry, *Mes Loisirs*, in 1863. Fréchette was called to the bar in 1862, but the priests scared customers away from his practice in Lévis, and late in 1865 he departed to Chicago, where besides editing two successive and equally unsuccessful papers for French-Canadian emigrés, he worked in the land office of the Illinois Central Railway.

When Fréchette came back to Canada in 1871, it was to find the atmosphere greatly changed by Confederation, and the Rouges of Quebec in considerably better political shape. After running for Parliament in 1871 and failing, he was successful in the election of 1874, which brought Alexander Mackenzie to power, and he sat in the House of Commons until 1878 when the Conservatives returned, and Fréchette, defeated, dropped out of active politics.

In the meantime, he had published two more books of verse, which drew the attention of critics in France as well as readers in Canada, and his political rejection was tempered by the fact that in 1881 his fourth book, *Les Fleurs Boréales*, was awarded a prize by the French Academy. The award he won, the Prix Montoyon, was not one of the highest, the criterion being "virtue" rather than literary quality, but few people in Canada were aware of this, and the mere name of the French Academy was enough to sustain Fréchette's reputation for the rest of his life. His material survival was assured when in 1889 he was appointed to the clerkship of the Legislative Council of Quebec, a virtual sinecure which he held until his death.

By this time Fréchette had already published *La Légende d'un Peuple*, since acknowledged as his masterpiece and as perhaps the only Canadian historical poem to rival the great quasi epics of E.J.Pratt. Not always accurately, but always impressively, Fréchette celebrates not only the heroes and heroic events of the Canadian past but also the landscapes in which the events were enacted. There were other books of verse; there were also plays which rivals had little difficulty in exposing as plagiarisms; there were autobiographical essays and one curious work, *Christmas in French Canada* (1899), which Fréchette wrote in English and later himself translated into French. But these were works of little significance, and during the later years until his death in 1908 Fréchette was mainly content to sustain his image as the French-Canadian laureate and as the benign public figure known to generations of Quebec children (owing to his habit of carrying candy for spontaneous distribution) as "le grandpapa chocolat."

Philippe-Joseph Aubert de Gaspé

To those who imagine the springs of creation run dry at the end of youth, the career of Philippe-Joseph Aubert de Gaspé, who began writing in his seventies and then produced one of the classics of Quebecois and Canadian literature, is a reproach and–one hopes–an inspiration.

Aubert de Gaspé was born at the manor house of St. Jean Port Joli in 1786 of a family that had been noble in the days of the *ancien régime* and was still seigniorial under British rule. His father, Pierre-Ignace, was a member of the Legislative Council of Lower Canada, which meant that he was one of the "Château Clique" of wealthy landowners who co-operated with the British governors. His ancestor, Charles Aubert de la Chesnaye, had come to Canada from Amiens in 1655 as a fur trader and had been chief agent for the Compagnie des Indes Occidentales; in 1693 he was granted a patent of nobility by Louis XIV, and his descendants retained the rank until the British conquest of Quebec.

Aubert de Gaspé was educated at the Quebec Seminary and then studied law under the Loyalist, Jonathan Sewell, who became chief justice of Lower Canada and president of the Executive Council. In 1813 Aubert de Gaspé was called to the bar of Lower Canada, and in 1816 he was appointed sheriff of Quebec. He held the post for six years, until 1822, when he had to relinquish the office because the mercantile transactions which he had carried on parallel to his public duties had proved disastrous. In 1834 he was declared bankrupt, and he was confined to a debtor's prison from 1838 until 1841, when he finally straightened out his affairs and fled to the seclusion of the family seat at St. Jean Port Joli. There he lived in retreat the rest of his life and contented himself with managing the estate, which had been miraculously saved from the downfall of his fortunes.

Aubert de Gaspé began to spend his rustic leisure studying local history and folklore, and particularly searching through family records, in which he found accounts of the burning of the previous manor house by the British troops during the Seven Years War. He also read François-Xavier Garneau's classic *Histoire du Canada*, whose first edition had appeared in 1845, inspired originally by a desire to disprove Lord Durham's remark in his famous report that the French Canadians were a people "without a history and without a literature." Garneau proved that the French Canadians had a history, and Aubert de Gaspé was one of those who were awakened by reading him, and he began to see a meaning in the past his own house and family represented.

Since Garneau had effectively written the history of the French-Canadian past, Aubert de Gaspé proceeded to fill in the other half of the equation by contributing to its literature, and late in the 1850s, when he was already more than seventy, he sat down to write a massive historical romance, much influenced by Walter Scott, which he entitled *Les Anciens Canadiens*.

Les Anciens Canadiens is at first sight a fairly conventional story of historical adventure, of which hundreds were written in both French and English during the nineteenth century. The setting is the house at St. Jean Port Joli, the hero is a French-Canadian ancestor, and the other leading figure–his beloved enemy as it were–is a boyhood friend, Scottish son of a Jacobite, brought up in France and educated in Quebec, who has returned to Scotland and become an officer in the British army invading Quebec. The theme of the love-hate between the two cultures has echoed through Canadian fiction in both our languages ever since, but Aubert de Gaspé embellished it with all the lore of rural customs and folk tales that he had gathered during his long retirement, to such an extent that material he could not use in the narrative was crammed into footnotes. It is the sense of reading a chronicle of the long past of Quebec as well as the history of a special house that gives *Les Anciens Canadiens* its compelling interest and explains why it stands as such a significant book in the history of Quebec literature.

Les Anciens Canadiens appeared in 1863, when Aubert de Gaspé was seventy-six, and was immediately translated into English. Having started to write, he had little desire to stop, and three years later, in 1866, he published his *Mémoires*, which is a mine of information about late eighteenth century Quebec. He died in 1871, and in 1893 his son, also a novelist, published a posthumous collection of Aubert de Gaspé's unpublished sketches, full of the zest for curious knowledge, entitled *Divers*.

Émile Nelligan

Perhaps no Canadian writer has come closer to the romantic image of the accursed poet (*le poète maudit*) than Émile Nelligan, whose creative life was so brilliant and so tragically short. Nelligan was one of the undoubted geniuses of our literature, and the modern tradition in French-Canadian poetry began with him, but he was also the Canadian equivalent of Thomas Chatterton and Arthur Rimbaud, and by the age of twenty his work was at an end.

Nelligan was born in Montreal in 1879, son of an Irish doctor and a French-Canadian mother. His background was essentially Quebecois. He was educated at the Collège Sainte-Marie in Montreal, but apart from literature he took no interest in his studies, and he left the college without completing his course.

One at least of the reasons for his lack of interest in other studies was that he had encountered and become deeply absorbed in the poetry of Charles Baudelaire and Paul Verlaine; in the work of these great French symbolists he found the stimulus from which his own poetry emerged.

Nelligan had already been writing poetry for some time when he came into contact with two young law students, Jean Charbonneau and Paul de Martigny, devotees of modernist poetry, who established the *École Littéraire de Montréal,* a group of young writers–critics and journalists as well as poets–who held regular meetings at the Château de Ramézay in Montreal and who created an atmosphere of mutual excitement out of which emerged a kind of poetry quite different from anything that had been written in Quebec before, cosmopolitan in the sense that the poets were much aware of what was going on in Paris at this period, but also experimental in form and theme.

The group included many poets who have since become celebrated as ancestors of modern writing in Quebec, including Charles Gill, Albert Lozeau, Charles Dantin, and Gonsalve Désaulniers, but the most brilliant of all was Nelligan, who was hailed with enthusiasm by his fellow poets and in turn gained from his contact with them. The reading of his great poem, "La Romance du Vin," at a gathering in the Château de Ramézay is regarded as one of the seminal events in Quebec literary history.

Nelligan's poetry showed an amazing technical virtuosity for a poet so young. Many of the individual poems are of a haunting beauty in tone and image alike, but most of them also show the evidence of a tormented mind, and in the case of Nelligan this was not a matter of mere romantic agony. He had strong depressive tendencies, and in 1899, before he was twenty, his mind broke down completely and he wrote no more. He lived on, in mental institutions, until his early sixties, dying finally in 1941 after four decades of silence in which the light never seemed to shine again in his mind. He was not even able to appreciate the publication of the first book of his poems in 1903.

Nelligan's career was tragically brief but also magnificently intense, and the poems he wrote during the five years before his mental collapse have now become classics of French writing, as honoured in Paris as in Quebec. Even today it is moving to read such pieces as "Le Vaisseau d'Or," whose last lines seem to prophesy Nelligan's own sad fate:

> Qu'est devenu mon coeur, navire déserté?
> Hélas! il a sombré dans l'abîme du Rêve!
>
> (What has become of my heart, abandoned ship?
> Alas, it has foundered in the abyss of dreams!)

À mon ami Albert Lozeau, ce
portrait du grand Nelligan.
Tous trois, nous avons adoré
la Poésie; nous l'avons
adorée, puisqu'elle
est divine. Est-ce
pour cela que
nos trois nous
se rencontrent
ici, ou bien
est-ce
parce que le
malheur
nous a
frappés
tous trois ?
Charles Gill

Louis Riel

The metamorphosis of Louis Riel in the eyes of English Canadians from one of the villains of our past into one of its hero-martyrs – a fit subject for operas and postage stamps – is one of the extraordinary phenomena of our recent history. It reflects not only a changing attitude to the native peoples of our country but also a shift in our perception of French-English relationships that may yet help Canada survive as an unbroken land.

In the past, the image of Riel and his execution in 1885 was a divisive element among Canadians; it created a rift between Quebec and the rest of Canada that was deepened by the conscription crises of two world wars, and by virtually destroying the former influence of the Conservative party in Quebec it brought about a preponderance of Liberal government in Canada over the past eighty years.

Yet Riel's tragedy was acted out on very small stages, and only a few thousand people were involved in each of the major acts – the Red River rising of 1869-70 and the North-West Rebellion of 1885. Riel himself, the son of a Métis miller on the Red River, was born at St. Boniface in 1844. As a boy he attracted the attention of Bishop Taché, who sent him to the College of Montreal to study for the priesthood. By 1865 Riel realized that he had no vocation and left the college. He spent a year finding he was no better suited for a career in law than for the church, and in 1868, after a couple of years as a store clerk in American cities, he was back on the Red River.

It was a critical time. There was already talk of the territory being sold by the Hudson's Bay Company to the new Dominion of Canada, and even before the transfer took place Canadians were building a road to the Red River and beginning to survey the settlement. The Métis, who had no legal title to their lands, became alarmed. It was Riel who led them in the first passive resistance of standing on the surveyors' chains and stopping them working. But more drastic action was needed if the people of Red River were to have a real say in their future, and in 1869 the Comité National des Métis was formed. Its mandate halted the entry of Canadian representatives seeking to reach Fort Garry through American territory, and after the Métis mili-

tia had seized the fort a provisional government was formed with Riel at its head, which eventually gained the support of most of the people of Red River, with the exception of the extreme Canadianist faction led by Dr. Schultz.

The only violence during the rising was caused by this faction, which twice attempted armed rebellion against the provisional government. Only one person was killed by the Métis, but this single killing – the execution after court martial of the Orangeman, Thomas Scott – was the error that clouded the whole of Riel's future.

Eventually, after complex negotiations involving Bishop Taché and the future Lord Strathcona, the rising came to an end with the creation of the Province of Manitoba, but the dominion government's promise to amnesty Riel was not kept, owing to the bitter resentment Scott's execution had caused in Ontario. Riel was forced to flee to the United States, but he retained the loyalty of his people on the Red River, who twice elected him to the House of Commons, in 1873 and 1874. He was not allowed to take his seat. Finally, in 1875, he was banished from Canada for five years.

At this time Riel showed symptoms of mental disturbance and for a period lived secretly in institutions in Quebec. Then he moved to the United States and finally on to Montana, where he became a teacher in a Métis settlement and an American citizen. He seemed to have slipped out of history. But his people remembered him, and in 1884, when the Métis of the South Saskatchewan could not obtain satisfaction on their land claims, Gabriel Dumont invited him to come to Canada and lead the protest.

Riel returned and started a peaceful agitation that won wide support. But the petition he and others devised had no effect on the federal government, which was procrastinating as it had done years before on the Red River, and in March 1885 the Métis rose in rebellion. By May they were defeated, largely because the vacillating Riel had prevented Dumont from carrying out effective guerrilla action. Riel himself surrendered. He was tried in Regina, found guilty of treason, and executed on 16 November at the orders of the Conservative government, who very unwisely placed political tactics above humanity and in the process permanently alienated Riel's fellow francophones in Quebec.

Alexandre-Antonin Taché

In the tangled historical web of the Red River rising of 1869-70, one of the men who stands out for good sense, humanity, and honesty is Alexandre-Antonin Taché, bishop of St. Boniface.

Bishop Taché was not himself a Métis. He had been born at Rivière du Loup in 1823, a member of an old New France family. His uncle, Sir Étienne-Paschal Taché, three times headed governments of Canada in association with Sir John A. Macdonald; his elder brother, Joseph-Charles Taché, was a well-known nineteenth century Quebecois journalist.

Alexandre-Antonin was educated at the College of St. Hyacinthe and at the Seminary of Montreal. There he decided to dedicate himself to missionary work among the peoples of Rupert's Land, and particularly the Métis, and in 1844 he became a novice in the Oblate order. In 1845 he was sent to Red River, where he was ordained by Bishop Provencher, founder of the mission at St. Boniface.

Taché remained on the Red River for the rest of his life –another forty-nine years. At the age of twenty-eight he became coadjutor bishop, and when Provencher died in 1853 he took his place as bishop of St. Boniface; in 1871 he became archbishop and metropolitan of St. Boniface.

Taché reached the Red River at a time of great changes. The Hudson's Bay Company maintained a rather loose rule over the Red River country, but the Métis, who had formerly lived as nomad hunters or voyageurs, were beginning to settle in villages mingled with those of Scots immigrants and English half-breeds along the banks of the river. The spread of American power in the Midwest did a great deal to alter the situation in the Red River settlements, and Métis hunters wishing to trade with American fur buyers virtually forced the company to accept free trade across the border.

Americans began to look at Rupert's Land as a possible target for annexation; Upper Canadians also, from the late 1850s, showed a growing interest in this great reservoir of land and resources, and as Confederation drew near, the talk of eventually including the North West in the new Canada became more pointed. Canadians settled in Fort Garry

as traders and professional men, and began to talk arrogantly of union. By the time the Hudson's Bay Company finally sold its rights to Canada in 1869, the inhabitants of the Red River area, who had never been consulted, were thoroughly alarmed, since to them the Canadians were threatening strangers, and although it was the Métis who took armed action to prevent Canadian representatives entering the settlements, all sections of society shared their anxiety, including Bishop Taché, who had followed events with growing anxiety.

Taché was in touch with members of the Canadian government during the negotiations with the Hudson's Bay Company, urging them to make some clear statement of intent before taking over the territory and especially to reach a settlement with the Métis regarding land claims. His representations were ignored until the rebellion took place, when he was in Rome. Then he was regarded as a possible saviour, and he returned in response to a cable from Sir Hector Langevin.

Taché was sympathetic to the Métis and recognized the justice of their grievances; after discussions in Ottawa, he consented to go to Fort Garry and attempt to make peace. When Taché arrived, he promised the Métis on behalf of the government an amnesty for acts committed under the provisional government, and it was largely on this understanding that agreement was reached for the acceptance of Canadian rule and the establishment of the Province of Manitoba.

In the event, the government did not grant a full amnesty. Sir John A. Macdonald claimed that Taché had exceeded his instructions. Taché disagreed, and in fact he was probably the victim of a political shift due to the dominion government's fear of incurring Ontario hostility by amnestying Riel. Although Taché felt personally humiliated by this incident, he did not condone Riel's later resort to violent rebellion in 1885. He did, however, carry on a long and bitter campaign of his own in Manitoba for the retention of separate Catholic schools, but he died in 1894, three years before Laurier's government worked out a compromise which the Catholics accepted. Taché was a man with a fervent sense of justice, particularly justice to minorities, and his life was shaped and saddened by it.

THE OPENING OF THE WEST

Adams George Archibald

One of the most difficult tasks of early Confederation was entrusted to Adams George Archibald when he was appointed first lieutenant-governor of Manitoba in 1870, but he controlled a tense situation with tact and firmness, and if the peace he established in the North West was broken by rebellion in 1885, other men, mainly in Ottawa, were to blame.

Archibald began as a colonial politician in the Maritimes, whose early career in no way anticipated his later role in western Canada. He was born in Truro, Nova Scotia, and educated at the famous Pictou Academy. He studied law and was called to the Prince Edward Island bar (1838) a year before he was called to that of Nova Scotia. In his late thirties he turned to politics and in 1851 was elected to the Nova Scotia assembly, of which he remained a member until in 1867 he entered the dominion House of Commons.

Archibald was a Liberal and served as solicitor general for Nova Scotia in 1856 and attorney general in 1860. Unlike Joseph Howe, he was a staunch advocate of Confederation, attending the Charlottetown and Quebec conferences of 1864, and representing Nova Scotia at the Westminster Conference of 1866-67, which formulated the British North America Act. As a reward for his loyalty to Confederation in a province notoriously lukewarm to union with Canada, Archibald was given cabinet rank as secretary of state in Macdonald's first dominion government in 1867.

When difficulties arose on the Red River in 1869 and the Province of Manitoba was finally created as a result of the agreement reached between the dominion authorities and Riel's provisional administration, the government in Ottawa was faced with the problem of choosing a lieutenant-governor who would wield authority until a regular provincial administration had been established and yet who would not be compromised in any way by the passions that the events at Red River had aroused in Upper and Lower Canada. An Ontarian would offend the Métis and a Quebecois would offend the noisy Canadian element in the new province. A Maritimer was the only possible choice. Archibald was offered the post and accepted.

Already Colonel Wolseley's expedition, a mixed force of British regulars and Canadian volunteers (including many Ontarians bitterly hostile to Riel) had started to cross the Canadian Shield on its way to Red River, and Archibald hastened through American territory in the endeavour to take over the government from Riel in a regular manner before the troops arrived. Wolseley got there on 23 August, Riel having prudently ridden away when he saw the troops approaching Fort Garry; Archibald did not appear until 2 September, by which time the Ontarians had already started to molest the Métis.

Archibald's sympathies – if he had any bias – were with the Métis, and he gradually established order in Manitoba, setting up an executive council there, supervising the elections for the first assembly in November 1870, and creating the infrastructure of a government for the North-West Territories, of which he was also lieutenant-governor. He concluded treaties with the local Cree and Ojibwa Indians, and he won the hearts of the Métis by accepting their support when the threat of Fenian invasion arose in 1871, and by appearing at a rally of Métis volunteers headed by Riel (nominally in exile) and shaking Riel's hand without asking his name. If other Canadian leaders had behaved with as much tact and understanding in the North West during the years after Archibald's term of office, the whole history of white-Métis relations might have been something other than the sorry affair it was to become.

But Archibald left the West in 1873 to become a judge in Nova Scotia, and when Joseph Howe died later that year he took over the lieutenant-governorship of Nova Scotia, which he held until 1883. In 1888 Archibald returned to the House of Commons, but his heart was no longer in politics and he retired in 1891, dying in the following year.

6209

THE OPENING OF THE WEST

John Norquay

Although it was the uprising of the French-speaking Métis under Louis Riel that brought about the creation of the Province of Manitoba, most of the political rewards of that achievement went to men of other groups, one of whom was the English half-breed leader, John Norquay.

John Norquay was born in 1841 in the Red River Protestant settlement of St. Andrews, a few miles from Fort Garry. Orphaned as a child and brought up–though not adopted–by Mrs. James Spence, he grew up in a society of Scottish farmers and Métis buffalo hunters, dominated by the Hudson's Bay Company, which was concerned to maintain as long as possible the traditional fur trade that had given it possession of the vast area draining into Hudson's Bay, then known as Rupert's Land.

John Norquay was a sharp, intelligent boy who attracted the attention of the Anglican bishop of Rupert's Land, David Anderson, and was educated in the Anglican school, St. John's Academy, in Winnipeg. There he learnt Latin and Greek to supplement the English, French, Cree, and Ojibwa which he had acquired naturally in the intensely multilingual Red River Settlement. At the age of seventeen he began teaching in the parish school of St. James, but the schoolroom seemed too constricting an environment for this man who was vast in both energy and size (he eventually turned the scales at three hundred pounds) and in 1866 he began farming at High Bluff (or Council Bluff) west of Fort Garry on the Assiniboine.

During the Red River rising, Norquay appeared as a leader of the English half-breeds, critical of Riel's tactics but sharing his alarm at the prospect of Canada taking over the North West without making terms with its people. He was elected to the council of the provisional government, and there he acted as spokesman for the English half-breeds, offering support for Riel's aims of provincial status and responsible government on condition that the opponents Riel had imprisoned were released.

Norquay's role in 1869-70 led him naturally into the politics of the new province. In 1871 he was elected to represent High Bluff in the Manitoba assembly and he retained his seat until his death eighteen years later. Carrying over from the days of the rising a distrust of the dominion government, Norquay was at first disinclined to give himself any political label, since he believed the provincial government should present a united front to defend Manitoba's interests. But eventually, when a local Liberal party began to coalesce under the leadership of Thomas Greenway, he declared himself Conservative.

Norquay was minister of public works in the first provincial government. In 1875 he became provincial secretary, moving back the next year to public works. In 1878 he became premier of Manitoba and attempted to unite the ethnic groups within the province by including French leaders like Joseph Royal and Métis leaders like Charles Nolin in his cabinet.

Norquay's administration was distinguished by a fervent pursuit of provincial interests; he was one of the closest allies of Oliver Mowat, premier of Ontario, in his defence of the rights of the provinces under Confederation. Under his premiership Manitoba gained new and enlarged boundaries. By representing his province as the "Cinderella of Confederation," Norquay gained substantial increases in the annual federal grant. And he was one of the first advocates of the Hudson Bay Railway, completed long after his death.

It was over railways that Norquay waged his most bitter battles with Ottawa and eventually came to grief. Under his premiership the Manitoba assembly passed legislation allowing for the provincial chartering of railways running south to link up with the American railway system. Ottawa disallowed the legislation on the grounds that it conflicted with the monopoly granted the CPR under its charter. Norquay decided to defy this decision by building the Red River Railway with provincial funds, and he proposed to continue even when the provincial act was again disallowed. He was outmanoeuvred by Sir John A. Macdonald, who verbally promised land for the Hudson Bay Railway; when Norquay issued $300,000 in Manitoba bonds, Macdonald reneged on the promise, claiming he had never made it. Norquay was left in the position of having issued bonds without the collateral the land had seemed to provide; although even his enemies made no reflections on his personal integrity, he resigned, politically destroyed because he was too loyal to the Manitobans who had elected him. He died two years later, in 1889.

James Morrow Walsh

James Morrow Walsh of the North-West Mounted Police was one of those flamboyant and complex men who seem destined to become myths and find their way into literature, as Walsh eventually did, becoming the central figure in a well-known Canadian play of the 1970s, Sharon Pollock's *Walsh.*

Walsh was born in Prescott, Upper Canada, in 1843, and early on he developed a taste for military activity of a kind not easy to satisfy in Canada after the War of 1812. He joined the militia and saw service during the Fenian raids of 1866, but not until the North-West Mounted Police was organized in 1873 did he find a career that seemed likely to fulfil his double hunger for adventure and display. Walsh was one of the first recruits to the Mounted Police, and on the strength of his militia experience and his age (for men of thirty were among the elders in that young man's enterprise) he was appointed inspector, with the courtesy title of major.

Walsh rode out on the great march of 1874, which took the Mounted Police into the prairies, and in 1875 he led his troop into the sensitive area of the Cypress Hills, a favourite haunt of Métis hunters and a place where Plains Indians from both American and Canadian territories had traditionally wintered together. American wolf-hunters and liquor traders had also used the region, and here a party of them had massacred a group of Assiniboines early in the 1870s, an incident that was among the causes of the foundation of the Mounted Police.

By the time Walsh arrived in the region, the American traders had decamped. The Mounted Police built a stockaded barracks, which Walsh characteristically named after himself, and soon Fort Walsh became a centre of attention, since the Sioux who had destroyed General Custer and his force at the battle of Little Big Horn in 1876 began to drift over the border to evade American revenge, their leading chief, Sitting Bull, arriving in 1877.

Walsh became responsible for carrying out the Canadian policy of containing the influx of Indians without allowing them to take up permanent residence in Canada. He had an advantage in the red coats of the Mounted Police, which the Indians equated with the red coats of earlier British soldiers and the tradition that the British had always been fairer in their treatment of native peoples than the American "long knives." He rode fearlessly into the Sioux camps with small escorts and calmly informed the armed braves of the "Queen's laws" which they were expected to observe. It was a role Walsh enjoyed, for it allowed him to dress up elaborately in sombreros and frilled buckskin jackets when he went for his interviews with Sitting Bull; he also played it well, and a real friendship sprang up between the romantically-minded police officer and the war chief who had started out in life as a tribal shaman.

A critical point came in 1880, when the buffalo were almost exterminated in the prairies and the Sioux began to starve. The Ottawa government, already alarmed at the condition of Canadian Indians, refused to feed the Sioux, who consequently were faced with the alternative of famine or returning over the border. Sitting Bull asked Walsh, who was going to eastern Canada, to plead with the American president on behalf of the Sioux, and Walsh agreed–only to find that his superiors regarded what he proposed to do as an unwarranted interference in international relations. He was kept in eastern Canada until Sitting Bull had gone back to surrender in 1881, and he returned to find himself under a cloud of disapproval which he dispelled by resigning from the force in 1883 and setting up the Dominion Coke, Coal, and Transportation Company in Manitoba.

Fourteen years later Walsh was called out of oblivion at the time of the Klondike gold rush, when men capable of dealing with delicate and potentially violent situations were needed urgently. He was appointed a superintendent in the Mounted Police and also commissioner of the newly created Yukon Territory. He helped to bring order into the chaos of the gold rush, but once again he retired under a cloud, giving up his appointment in 1898 to the tune of accusations of corruption; later it was proved that the errors in recording gold claims which caused the accusation had been due to plain inefficiency, but the aura of wrongdoing hung over Walsh's name until his death at Brockville in 1905, and few people remembered his extraordinary feat of keeping the peace on the border, among thousands of starving and warlike Indians, with a scanty force buttressed by bluff. More than any other man, Walsh in the 1870s prevented Indian warfare in its most violent form from spreading into the Canadian prairies.

Samuel Benfield Steele

Samuel Benfield Steele, better known as Sam Steele (and to his subordinates as Smoothbore), was perhaps the most flamboyant of all the bounding extroverts who found their way into the North-West Mounted Police when it was founded in 1873. Steele, born in 1849 at Purbrook, near Orillia in Upper Canada, came of fighting stock. His father had been a captain in the British Royal Navy, and early on Sam Steele followed the family tradition by enlisting in the Simcoe militia during the Fenian raids of 1866. He qualified for an ensign's commission but did not take it up, and in 1870 when Wolseley led his expedition to the Red River, Steele was in the ranks as a mere private. He returned to Ontario with the idea of a military career still in his mind and in 1871 was the first man to enlist in the first Canadian regular unit, "A" Battery of the Royal Canadian Artillery. But the kind of garrison duty he might expect in the artillery did not compare with the appeal of the North West, and when the Mounted Police was created in 1873 Steele was the third man to enlist, receiving the rank of troop sergeant-major. He took part in the first great western march of the NWMP in 1874 and on that expedition travelled 1,255 miles on horseback.

Steele was not involved in the more sensational early assignments of the NWMP, such as the supervision of Sitting Bull's Indian bands when they came over the border or the early encounters with Gabriel Dumont's Métis militia at the beginning of the North-West Rebellion of 1885. He was engaged during that period mainly in policing the area through which the Canadian Pacific Railway was being built, enforcing prohibition and generally keeping order, as when–on one occasion in April 1885 when the railway organizers had been unable to send cash for wages–he had to quell a riot of three hundred armed men with seven constables. That year Steele was appointed superintendent, and when the North-West Rebellion broke out he organized a mounted force called Sam Steele's Scouts and commanded the cavalry that went in pursuit of Big Bear. In 1887 he was sent into the Kootenay area of British Columbia, where American miners were moving in and clashing with the Indians, and there he founded Fort Steele, now a historic park. In 1898, when the Klondike gold rush took place, Steele was crisis controller once again, sent to police the passes from the Alaska seacoast into Canadian territory. He was put in charge of the Mounted Police in the Yukon and British Columbia, as well as being appointed to the North-West Council. No sooner, however, had the Klondike simmered down than the South African war broke out. Steele went out in 1899 to lead Strathcona's Horse, and he stayed to command, from 1901, the Transvaal section of the South African Mounted Constabulary. He resigned from that post in 1906 and returned to Canada, where he joined the permanent army, commanding in turn the Calgary and Winnipeg military districts and rising to the rank of major-general. In 1914 he became inspector-general. He raised and trained the Second Canadian Division in 1915 and accompanied it to England, though not to the front. He stayed as commander of the Shorncliffe Camp until his retirement from the army in 1918. He had already published his reminiscences, *Forty Years in Canada,* in 1915, and perhaps that was a good thing, for a man who all his life had been so active did not take well to retirement and Sam Steele died in 1919, a few days older than seventy.

With Sam Steele, an age passed away; the Canadian West could never again be the land for the adventurer and the adventurous that it had been when he first saw it in 1870, and other kinds of men would control and shape the vast region he had helped to make secure for Canada.

Albert Lacombe

Albert Lacombe, whom the Blackfoot called Good Heart, was probably the best known, and certainly the best loved by the native peoples, of all the Catholic priests who went as missionaries to the West. He was born in 1827, son of a habitant farmer at Saint Sulpice in Quebec; a trace of Indian blood ran in his veins, for his great-grandmother had been kidnapped as a girl by the Ojibwa, and his grandfather was born of her union with one of the men of the tribe.

The Lacombes were prosperous enough as farmers to dedicate one of their sons to the priesthood, and Albert was chosen. He attended L'Assomption College, and in 1849 he was ordained and went out to the North West, then the domain of the Hudson's Bay Company, where the Métis rode as horselords of the prairies. Lacombe first served at Pembina, and here his association with the Métis began. In 1850 he went out as chaplain on the greatest of their buffalo hunts, and he was also present at the hunt of 1851 when a company of Métis hunters fought and won the famous battle of Grand Coteau against the Sioux Indians. The next year he went to Fort Edmonton, and over the following winter he learnt Cree so well that two decades later, in 1874, he was able to publish a Cree grammar and a Cree-French dictionary which are still of value.

The missions in this region were operated by the Oblate order, in which Lacombe was professed in 1854. In 1853 he had taken over from its founder, Father Thibault, the mission at Lac Ste. Anne, where he stayed until 1861 when he organized the Métis settlement of St. Albert. From this centre he was able to work among both the Cree and their traditional enemies, the Blackfoot, and much of his time was spent trying to reconcile the two peoples; there were occasions when he was actually caught in the fighting, and though he was often unable to stop bloodshed, there is no doubt that his influence contributed in the end to terminating the state of endemic warfare that existed in the western prairies and the foothills of the Rockies.

In 1874 Lacombe was called back to Winnipeg, where he combined priestly duties with the task of assisting French-speaking settlers from Quebec and New England to set up prairie colonies. In 1880 he was sent back into the plains as Catholic chaplain to the construction camps on the Canadian Pacific Railway, and during the two years he retained this position his reputation among the Indians served to calm a number of tense situations when the Blackfoot became angry over the invasion of their lands. Later, during the 1885 rebellion, it was largely Lacombe's influence over Crowfoot, high chief of the Blackfoot, that prevented this formidable tribe from joining Gabriel Dumont's forces; in this way Lacombe affected the course of the rebellion, for better or perhaps for worse.

By this time he had left his work with the CPR construction crews and had established a mission at Fort Macleod in what later became southern Alberta. He spent a great deal of time organizing Indian residential schools, and when he was released from active service in 1897, he was still involved in many special duties, as well as writing his *Memoirs of the Half-Breeds of Manitoba and the Territories of the Canadian North West.* In 1909, already more than eighty years old, he began his last work, the establishment of the Lacombe Home for the Poor, near Calgary, and there he lived the remainder of his life and died in 1916. He was buried in the settlement of St. Albert, which he had founded more than fifty years before, among the Métis to whom – with his own mixture of ancestries and traditions – he felt closest of all the peoples of Canada.

Edgar Dewdney

Edgar Dewdney represents a type relatively common in the early days of Canada's Confederation: the man of action whom politics emasculates into the ineffectual sycophant.

Dewdney was a west-countryman, born in Devon in 1835. He reached British Columbia in 1859 with some knowledge of surveying and engineering, and was immediately accepted by Governor James Douglas as one of the group of energetic young Britishers with whose help he hoped to solve the problems of a newly born mining country and turn it into a colony capable of resisting American encroachment. Dewdney helped lay out the site of New Westminster, the recently chosen capital of British Columbia. Then in 1860 he and Walter Moberley, later active in the construction of the Canadian Pacific Railway, built the Dewdney Trail through the Coast Range from Fort Hope to the Similkameen; it was eventually extended via the Okanagan Valley to Rock Creek and made by the Royal Engineers into a wagon road, fragments of which can still be seen running beside the modern highway through Manning Park.

For a number of years Dewdney continued his surveying in British Columbia, at the same time dabbling in real estate and drifting into politics – not difficult in a colony with a permanent population of about ten thousand whites. Dewdney's interests aligned him with the colonial establishment, and he detested the radical democrat Amor De Cosmos, who stood at the head of the movement to take British Columbia into Canada. However, by the time Dewdney was elected to the Legislative Council of British Columbia in 1869, entry into Confederation was a foregone conclusion, and all that remained was for him, like the rest of the province's official clique, to make the best possible terms for himself.

Dewdney did this by attaching his fortunes to those of Sir John A. Macdonald. Elected to the House of Commons in 1872, he sat as a Conservative, and through the Pacific Scandal he remained faithful to Macdonald. When Macdonald returned to power in 1878, he rewarded Dewdney by appointing him, in 1879, Indian commissioner responsible for overseeing the implementation of the treaties with the native peoples of the plains. In 1881 he was appointed – as well – lieutenant-governor of the North-West Territories.

It was perhaps the most difficult time of all for anyone to hold the almost dictatorial powers of a governor in the North-West Territories. The whole economic foundation of the old prairie way of life – the way of the Indians and the Métis – was shattered by the extermination of the buffalo. The Indians were starving; the Métis recognized that they must shift to an agrarian economy but had no assurance that they owned the land they occupied; white settlers were surging into the prairies in the wake of the railway, and some kind of clash between them and the old inhabitants seemed inevitable. The best of administrators would have found his task difficult; it was doubly difficult for Dewdney, who was too weak to present an alternative to Macdonald's vacillating policies and who allowed his personal interest in land speculation to cloud his judgment, so that he put himself in a very equivocal position in 1882 when it was found that he had acquired large parcels of land in Regina just before it was officially designated the new capital of the North-West Territories.

Thus, it was Canada's misfortune that Dewdney was still lieutenant-governor when the North-West Rebellion erupted in 1885. Other men warned Macdonald of the perils of the situation and were ignored, but Dewdney – who could have forced serious attention to the Métis grievances by strong representations to Ottawa – let matters slide and became one of the men responsible for the tragedy of Batoche.

Macdonald, however, repaid party loyalty. Dewdney's failures in 1885 were quickly forgotten, and in 1888 he was made minister of the interior; in 1892 he became lieutenant-governor of British Columbia. In both posts he performed with a lack of distinction that made it hard to recognize the young man of initiative who had created the basic road system of British Columbia in the 1860s. After nineteen years of retirement, Dewdney died in Victoria in 1916.

Gabriel Dumont

The names of Louis Riel and Gabriel Dumont have been habitually associated as leaders of the North-West Rebellion of 1885, but Dumont was a man of power and influence in the prairies long before he rode down into Montana in 1884 to fetch Riel to Batoche, and in many ways he was far more representative than Riel of the Métis people.

The Dumont family had been leaders among the Métis of the western prairies for two generations before the North-West Rebellion. The first of them was a French-Canadian voyageur, Jean-Baptiste Dumont, who arrived in the 1790s to work at the Hudson's Bay Company post of Fort Edmonton and there married a Sarcee Indian woman. All his sons were great hunters. One of them, Isidore, operated from Fort Pitt until the 1830s, when he migrated to the Red River, where his son Gabriel was born in 1837. By 1840 even the Red River seemed too settled for Isidore, who was a natural nomad, and he returned to the Saskatchewan, where he made Fort Pitt once again the centre of a wandering life of hunting and trading in which young Gabriel gained a first-class prairie education. He never learnt to read or write, but he could speak six Indian languages as well as French, he was a superb rider and marksman, an excellent tracker, and a huntsman so accomplished that he could call the buffalo, an art most of the Indians themselves had lost by this time.

Dumont combined such arts with a flair for diplomacy and leadership. He was present as a boy at the decisive battle of Grand Coteau in 1851 when the Métis defeated the Sioux, but he realized that Indians and Métis had common interests against the strangers who would eventually come into the West, and he and his father arranged treaties between the Métis and the Sioux, and later between Métis and Blackfoot. In 1869, when the Red River rising broke out, Gabriel Dumont had already been for several years chief of the Métis hunters of the South Saskatchewan, leading them out each year in quasi-military formation on the great buffalo hunt. He offered to bring Riel five hundred horsemen if he wished to resist the advance to Red River of the forces under Colonel Wolseley in 1870. Riel refused, and Dumont went back to the West to consolidate his links with the Indians and to organize the Métis along the Saskatchewan River into settled communities, since he foresaw the day when the buffalo would diminish and the native peoples would have to turn to farming.

In 1873 the Métis gathered at St. Laurent on the South Saskatchewan to set up a local government. They voted a series of laws and elected a council, with Dumont as their president. For two years Dumont ruled his people, introducing sensible regulations for land rights, timber rights, and buffalo conservation, until in 1875 the Mounted Police arrived and Métis local government was dissolved. But Dumont remained a leader of the Métis. He built a store and established a ferry at a spot which is still called Gabriel's Crossing. By the early 1880s he was aware that the influx of settlers into the Saskatchewan country would create a situation similar to that on the Red River in 1869. The Métis had no titles to their land, and they petitioned the government in vain to look into their grievances and to guarantee them the holdings they had long occupied. The governments of Alexander Mackenzie and Sir John A. Macdonald alike turned deaf ears. Finally, Gabriel Dumont rode down to St. Peter's mission in Montana to fetch Louis Riel in the hope that he could help them. Assisted by equally aggrieved English half-breeds and white settlers, Riel and Dumont framed a joint petition, in its turn ignored. Finally, in 1885, the Métis declared a provisional government, with Dumont as its military leader or "adjutant general."

The rebellion began in earnest when Dumont and his men surrounded and defeated a force of Mounted Police at Duck Lake. The survivors retreated to Prince Albert, and for a period, while the dominion government organized its forces, the Saskatchewan region was in Dumont's control. He organized his Métis force of three hundred men and planned a guerrilla war that might have held off the government forces long enough to force a compromise. But Riel refused consent until the last minute, when Dumont ambushed General Middleton's small army at Fish Creek. It was already too late. The beaten Canadians reorganized and advanced on Batoche, and although Dumont's men resisted for four days, defeat was inevitable. Riel surrendered; Dumont fled south to Montana, tried unsuccessfully to rescue Riel, and then joined the Buffalo Bill show. He finally returned to Batoche in 1893 and lived on quietly until his death from a heart attack at the end of a hunting trip in 1906. His name has been obscured by that of Riel, the martyr, yet he was one of the great Canadian rebels, a brave and chivalrous man whom even his enemies remembered with respect.

Crowfoot

While chiefs of the Cree Indians like Poundmaker and Big Bear rebelled violently against the misery of their people and were physically defeated, Crowfoot chose the path of conciliation and lived to endure the moral discomfiture of learning how fragile were the promises of Canadian governments.

Crowfoot was born about 1830 in a Blood Indian encampment. The Bloods were members of the great Blackfoot Confederacy, and when Crowfoot's father was killed his mother married a Blackfoot, and Crowfoot was brought up in that tribe. He grew up to be a famous warrior in the recurrent conflicts between the Blackfoot and the Cree. He fought in nineteen of the skirmishes that passed for battles in Indian warfare, was wounded six times, and killed several of his adversaries. Eventually, in 1865, he became a minor chief, and in 1885 he was elected one of the two leading chiefs of the Blackfoot.

By this time Crowfoot recognized that the world of the prairies was changing and that the Blackfoot must adapt themselves to it. Attacks on white men brought inevitable reprisals and should therefore be avoided. At the same time, intertribal wars merely made the Indians more vulnerable to alien pressures, and Crowfoot sought to end them and also to end the horse stealing that so often led to them.

He fell under the influence of Father Lacombe, the Oblate missionary whom he once rescued from a Cree attack, and when the North-West Mounted Police arrived among the Blackfoot in 1874 under James F. Macleod, Crowfoot ensured that his tribesmen kept the peace. Having learnt that the Mounted Police made the eradication of illicit whisky trading their first aim, Crowfoot welcomed their presence, and when he signed Treaty No. 7 at Blackfoot Crossing in 1877 on behalf of his people, he made his famous statement: "If the police had not come into this country, where would we be now? Bad men and whisky were killing us so fast that very few of us would have been alive today. The Mounted Police have protected us as the feathers of the bird protect it from the frosts of winter."

Crowfoot was to modify his good opinion of the white men in a very few years, when the buffalo were extermi-nated and the government failed to give the Indians the relief promised under the treaties. Crowfoot did his best to persuade his people to take up farming as a substitute for hunting, but such profound changes in ways of life are not made quickly, and the Blackfoot, like the other Indian peoples and the Métis, suffered greatly during the early 1880s.

Nevertheless, Crowfoot continued to believe that rebellion would merely worsen the condition of his people. When the construction crews of the Canadian Pacific Railway reached the territory of the Blackfoot Confederacy in 1884, he co-operated with Father Lacombe in restraining his young men from attacks. During the rebellion of 1885 he received appeals from Gabriel Dumont and his friend Poundmaker to join them; again he refused to become involved in a warfare that would inevitably lead in the long if not the short run to defeat.

After the rebellion Crowfoot was feted in eastern Canada by Sir John A. Macdonald and other leaders whose task of suppressing the rebellion he had helped to make easy, but his last years were shadowed by personal illness and the distress of his people. He died in 1890 at Blackfoot Crossing, where he had signed the treaty in 1877, and as he looked out over the Bow River he made a dying speech couched in the poetic phrases loved by traditional Indians: "A little while and I will be gone from among you, whither I cannot tell. From nowhere we came, into nowhere we go. What is life? It is as the flash of a firefly in the night. It is as the breath of a buffalo in the winter time. It is as the little shadow that runs across the grass and loses itself in the sunset."

Poundmaker

Poundmaker was the last Canadian Indian chief to defeat the white men in battle, yet it was only under great provocation that he was led into riding on his last warpath, for by nature he was a man of peace.

He was born in 1826 in the valley of the North Saskatchewan near the place where the white settlement of Battleford arose some fifty years later. His name–which in Cree was Pito-kanow-apiwin–was a reminiscence of the days when the buffalo were so numerous that they could be driven into great enclosures, or pounds, where they were slaughtered, a wasteful method that was only possible when the herds were large. By the time Poundmaker was a young man it was already obsolete.

Poundmaker's early life was lived in relative obscurity, for he had no fame as a great warrior and did not emerge into prominence until the days when the Indians had to find a way to live with the new conditions on the prairies, which included the arrival of considerable numbers of white men intent on acquiring land, and the extermination of the buffalo.

One of the results of these new circumstances was a tendency for the Indians to forget their old tribal hatreds and make peace, in view of the presence of a potential common enemy far stronger than any individual tribe. In 1872 the Cree and the Blackfoot finally settled their differences, and one of the tokens of the treaty was the adoption of Poundmaker as his son by the famous Blackfoot chief, Crowfoot.

Poundmaker was still a relatively minor chief when in 1876 he signed Treaty No. 6 between the Cree and the Canadian government. Like Big Bear he was uneasy about the provisions of the treaty, and he refused to settle down immediately on a reservation, wandering on the prairie as a moving focus of discontent for at least another three years, until, in 1879, realizing that the buffalo had almost vanished from the plains, he finally settled down on the Battle River.

There followed a period when Poundmaker attempted to live according to the treaty and become a model farmer. Leadership of the reservation at Battle River gave him an independent status he had not enjoyed before, and his behaviour so pleased the authorities that in 1881 he was chosen as official guide to the governor general, the Marquis of Lorne, on his viceregal journey from Battleford to Calgary, a task which Poundmaker carried out with a panache in keeping with his aristocratic good looks.

But the interlude of contentment did not last long. Poundmaker's people were not happy farmers, and the retrenchment of grants to the Indians by the dominion government in the early 1880s caused growing distress, so that Poundmaker began to lead an agitation demanding more considerate treatment. Like all the discontented groups in the North West–Indians or Métis, English halfbreeds or white settlers–Poundmaker and his followers were ignored by Sir John A. Macdonald, who was attempting to administer Indian affairs as well as carry on his multiple concerns as prime minister; and in March 1885, when the Métis rose in rebellion at Batoche and Duck Lake, Poundmaker and his warriors descended on Battleford, demanding food, and besieged the settlers and the Mounted Police in Fort Battleford.

This seems to have been the spontaneous action of people made desperate by hunger, for Poundmaker at first rejected Gabriel Dumont's attempts to persuade him to join the rebellion and only moved when there were no more supplies on his reservation. His later actions were those of a man who did not desire war. He retreated when Colonel Otter reached Battleford in April and only fought back at Cut Knife Hill when Otter's forces mounted an early morning surprise attack. He defeated Otter but did not pursue him, and in the end, on 26 May, he surrendered voluntarily to General Middleton. "Had I wanted war," he told his judge, "I would not be here but on the prairie. You did not catch me, I gave myself up. You have me because I wanted peace. I cannot help myself, but I am still a man."

Despite his plea, he was sentenced to three years in prison. Soon it was evident that he was dying of tuberculosis, and although he was released after six months through the pleas of Crowfoot, his adoptive father, he died a few weeks later, in July 1886, on Crowfoot's reservation at Blackfoot Crossing.

Big Bear

Big Bear was the great irreconcilable among the prairie Indians. He realized more clearly than any other of the chiefs of the plains that the Indians were doomed to subservience by the advent of the white men in the prairies, and his realization led him into resistance and tragedy.

Big Bear was born round about 1825 in the region of Fort Carlton, of mixed Cree and Ojibwa parentage. He grew up in the traditional life of the old prairies, with its great buffalo hunts, its feast-and-famine economy, and its endemic tribal warfare; it was a time when the white men were present only as fur traders who deliberately avoided interfering with the Indian ways. By middle age Big Bear saw the first threats to that way of life, as other kinds of white men began to arrive, intent on taking over the land.

Big Bear was not one of the great chiefs of the Cree; he led a small band of about a hundred people who traded furs to Fort Carlton and Fort Pitt during the 1860s. When the North West was brought into Canada and the Red River rising ended with the creation of Manitoba as the first prairie province, the threat to the traditional life of the plains became more manifest, especially after the North-West Mounted Police was established and the dominion government began to make treaties with the Indian peoples, aimed at locating them on reservations and leaving the rest of the land free for white settlers.

Big Bear was one of the few Indian leaders who understood how much the Indians were sacrificing for the derisory benefits which the treaties offered; he also blamed the white men – with a good deal of justification – for the disastrous diminution of the buffalo, which was removing the whole basis of the Indian way of life. When most of the Cree chiefs accepted the Canadian terms and signed Treaty No. 6 at Fort Carlton in 1876, Big Bear refused, though at the time he declared a desire to avoid interracial warfare: "It was not given to us by the Great Spirit that the red man and white man should shed each other's blood."

Having rejected the treaty, Big Bear also refused to settle on a reservation, and attracting other dissident Indians to his cause, he went with his followers to the gathering for treaty payments at Sounding Lake in 1877 and there again demanded better terms. He was refused, and went south to establish himself in the Cypress Hills, where for a time it was feared he would form an alliance with Sitting Bull and the Sioux. Big Bear's situation was made more difficult by the final destruction of the buffalo herds, and he had to accept rations to save his people from starving. But he still refused to settle on a reservation, and he moved back to the Fort Pitt area, where he now had a following of between three and four hundred people. As the situation of the Indians worsened throughout the prairies, many of them began to think that Big Bear had been right in resisting the treaties, and in 1884 he called a grand council which some two thousand Indians attended; there he urged united action to win better terms from the government.

Up to this time Big Bear was using essentially political means, and there is no evidence that he ever believed violence would achieve his aims. Nevertheless, when the government threatened to cut off rations unless he and his followers finally settled down, Big Bear began to gather ammunition and to listen to the overtures of Gabriel Dumont, the Métis leader, who was already preparing for the North-West Rebellion.

Big Bear was hastened into a tragic pattern of violence and flight when his authority failed to restrain his young braves, who on 2 April 1885 killed nine white people at Frog Lake and then, taking others with them as prisoners, went on to besiege Fort Pitt (commanded by a son of the novelist Charles Dickens) and to burn it after the Mounted Police retired.

Instead of joining the Métis at Batoche, Big Bear's followers entrenched themselves at Frenchman's Butte and fought General Strange's Alberta Field Force to a draw. Then, however, they scattered, and Big Bear led Sam Steele's scouts on a long chase through the northern forests until he surrendered on 2 July. He was tried for treason and sentenced to two years' imprisonment. Prison broke his spirit and his health, and he emerged to die – at last an inhabitant of a reservation – early in 1888.

William Dillon Otter

No man's career more eloquently demonstrates the rule that generals are produced by survival rather than military success than that of Sir William Dillon Otter. He was the first Canadian to become a general; he never won a battle.

Otter was born in 1843 near Clinton in Upper Canada. His parents were well-to-do, and he had an upper class education at the Toronto Model School and Upper Canada College. In 1861 he joined the volunteer militia, in 1864 was promoted to lieutenant, and in 1865 became adjutant of the Queen's Own Rifles, with which rank he took part in the Battle of Ridgeway against the invading Fenians in 1866. Eventually, in 1874, he became lieutenant-colonel of the Queen's Own and during this period acquired an interest in military organization which he developed in his only book, a manual on military logistics entitled *The Guide* that was popular in Canada and ran into a number of editions.

Largely as a result of this book, Otter became a career soldier, joining the permanent militia in 1883 as commandant of the School of Infantry in Toronto, where he organized "C" Company of the Royal Canadian Regiment. Between the Fenian raid and 1885 he saw no action other than being called out on a couple of occasions to overawe rioters in Toronto and Belleville.

When the North-West Rebellion erupted in 1885, Otter was naturally involved. The expeditionary force into the Saskatchewan country was commanded by General Frederick Middleton, who himself led the column that advanced on the Métis headquarters at Batoche. Otter was given command of the column sent to relieve the policemen and settlers besieged at Fort Battleford by Poundmaker and his Cree warriors.

Marching quickly northward, Otter arrived at Battleford late in April and raised the siege without difficulty, the Indians retreating into the country outside the town. Concerned that Poundmaker might join forces with the other rebel Indian chief, Big Bear, Otter advanced with his little army of five hundred men to attack the Cree camp on Cut Knife Hill. The Indians were surprised by the early morning attack on 2 May but quickly took up excellent firing positions, and Otter was forced to retreat for fear of being surrounded; indeed, his column was only saved from heavy losses because Poundmaker held his warriors back from pursuit. Otter drew back to Battleford, where he remained for the rest of the rebellion; it was to Middleton that Poundmaker eventually surrendered after the Métis had been defeated at Batoche.

Time erases the memory of failure, and in 1899 when the first Canadian contingent was sent to fight in the Boer War, Otter was placed in command. History repeating itself, he won his decoration in that war for being wounded while conducting a retreat from an impossible position at Bloemfontein.

Remaining in the army, he continued to rise through his abilities as a desk officer. In 1908 he became first chief of the Canadian general staff and a brigadier-general. In 1910 he became inspector-general and ranked as major-general. In 1913 he was knighted, and in 1914, aged seventy-one, he stayed on in the service to become director of Canadian internment camps. He died in Toronto in 1929.

Sandford Fleming

When the Montreal mob burned the Canadian parliament buildings in their rage over the Rebellion Losses Bill in 1849, a young Scot named Sandford Fleming rushed into the flaming building to rescue the portrait of Queen Victoria. The loyalty and the daring were characteristics that marked Fleming throughout his audacious career; he remained until his death a devoted imperialist, and as a surveyor and engineer he carried out some of the most arduous feats in the history of Canadian transport. It was his long exploratory journeys through the prairies and mountains that eventually provided the keys to unlock the treasures of the Canadian West.

Sandford Fleming, born in 1827 at Kirkcaldy, Scotland, received some training in surveying and engineering when he reached Canada in 1845 and entered the service of the Simcoe and Huron–later the Northern–Railway. Eventually, in 1857, he became chief engineer of the Northern, but his thoughts were already expanding beyond the horizons of Upper Canada, and in 1858 he published a pamphlet, *A Railway to the Pacific through British Territory*, which introduced to the public a project he had close to his heart and in whose realization he would eventually play a great role.

But before he could turn his attention to the Far West, which did not yet interest many Canadians, there were other important tasks for Fleming to undertake. In 1863 he was appointed simultaneously (though not jointly) by the Canadian, New Brunswick, and Nova Scotia governments to carry out the survey for the Intercolonial Railway; later he became chief engineer for the construction of the line, at the same time supervising railway construction in Newfoundland. But the Intercolonial was not finally completed until 1874, and by then Fleming was already engaged in what he regarded as his main life's task, the construction of a railway to the West.

By 1871 he was appointed chief government engineer for the planning of a railway to the Pacific. The following year he made a journey by horse and foot across the prairies and through the mountains, suggesting the Yellowhead Pass route, which is now used by the Canadian National Railway; the Canadian Pacific itself actually used a more southerly route, and here again it was Fleming and his assistants who in 1882 showed the feasibility of a way through the Kicking Horse and Rogers passes. By this time Fleming had already retired–in 1880–from regular government service, but he maintained his interest in the West, where he had considerable investments, and he was a director of both the Canadian Pacific Railway and the Hudson's Bay Company.

Fleming was a man of wide interests, original vision, and varied accomplishments. In 1849 he took part in founding the Royal Canadian Institute, and in 1882 he became a charter fellow of the Royal Society of Canada, of which he was elected president in 1888, while from 1880 to his death in 1915 he was chancellor of Queen's University. In 1851 he designed the first Canadian postage stamp, the Threepenny Beaver, and he devised the present international system of standard time, by which the world is divided into twenty-four equal time zones; Fleming proposed the idea in 1879, and it was adopted at a Washington conference in 1884. He was also a strong advocate of the development of imperial cable communications, which he saw both as a practical necessity and also as a symbol of the political links, which like so many of his contemporaries he believed would be best achieved through a system of imperial federation.

Piapot

Close to the 50th parallel, on the highway between Swift Current and Medicine Hat, and somewhat to the northeast of the Cypress Hills, lies a prairie hamlet where the grain elevators bear in their bold lettering the name of Piapot. This was the result of an ironic gesture on the part of the railway engineer who named the halt, for it was here that the Cree chief Piapot showed most actively his opposition to the penetration of the Canadian Pacific into the prairies, which he regarded as his inalienable homeland.

While chiefs like Poundmaker and Big Bear are remembered for the part they played in the North-West Rebellion by actually fighting the encroachment of the white men, and other chiefs like Crowfoot for the unwilling realism with which they tried to adapt themselves to an invasion that seemed inevitable, Piapot is remembered most of all for his faithful adherence to the beliefs and ceremonies of the prairie peoples.

Piapot was a Plains Cree, born somewhere around 1816 and originally given the name of Kisikawawasen, which meant Flash in the Sky. When he was a small boy, smallpox devastated the camp to which he belonged, and only he and his grandmother survived. They kept alive on the prairie until they were discovered and captured by a band of Sioux, who adopted the boy and trained him in the ways of prairie hunting and warfare. A few years later, when Kisikawawasen was fourteen, the Sioux camp was raided by a band of Cree and he and his grandmother were reunited with their people.

From this time he was regarded as a man related to both tribes of traditional enemies. The name under which he eventually became a chief, by virtue of his warlike exploits against the Blackfoot and other prairie peoples, was Piapot, or Hole in the Sioux, and the band that eventually accepted his leadership was called the Nehiyawapot—the Cree-Sioux.

Piapot owed his ascendancy over his followers and his repute throughout the southern Canadian prairies to something more than his abilities as a warrior and his charisma as a leader. He was also—like Sitting Bull—a great medicine man. His visions were regarded as potently prophetic, and he was reputed to have great powers as a rainmaker.

Piapot's band hunted mainly in the region of the Qu'Appelle Valley, and in 1855, when the Hudson's Bay Company post was established, they traded there and developed such a good relationship with the company that in 1869, when it was feared the local Métis–fired by the Red River rising–might attack Fort Qu'Appelle, Piapot and his warriors arrived to protect the traders there.

But the fact that Piapot accepted the trading relationship between the Indians and the Hudson's Bay Company did not mean that he viewed with any joy the spread of Canadian government and white settlement in the prairies, and in 1874, when the newly established administration in the North-West Territories negotiated Treaty No. 4 with the Cree, Assiniboine, and Saulteau Indians, Paipot chose to be absent hunting in the Cypress Hills.

More than a year later, on 9 September 1875, he was persuaded to sign an adherence to the treaty, though he refused to settle on a reservation while there were still buffalo left to hunt. His attitude, in fact, was ambivalent, since he opposed the settlement of the prairies yet welcomed the North-West Mounted Police for what they had done to rid the region of whisky traders and American desperadoes. He established friendly relations with J.M. Walsh after the latter built Fort Walsh in 1875, and remained in the Cypress Hills until the early 1880s.

By this time the Canadian government–with the problem of Sitting Bull on its hands–was becoming anxious about the concentration of Canadian and American Indians in the Cypress Hills area and tried to persuade Piapot to move back to the Qu'Appelle Valley. He resisted and in 1882 and 1883 attempted to halt survey and construction work on the Canadian Pacific Railway. In the latter year the police persuaded him to settle on a reservation southeast of Indian Head, but after a winter of famine and sickness he and his band moved to the Qu'Appelle valley where Piapot remained the rest of his life.

When the North-West Rebellion began in 1885, it was feared that Piapot, with whom Gabriel Dumont was in touch, would join the insurrection, but he remained neutral. Later he became a focus of resistance to attempts at assimilation when he defied the government by promoting the forbidden rain dances. Because of this he was officially deposed as chief in 1899, but his band refused to elect a successor, and Piapot, who remained true to the beliefs of his fathers, continued as *de facto* chief and as a revered figure among the Indians of the Canadian prairies until his death in 1908.

Nicholas Flood Davin

Nicholas Flood Davin was one of those brilliant, erratic men who seemed irresistibly drawn to the western prairies during the years after Confederation. He was born in 1843 at Kilfinane in Limerick County, the son of an Irish doctor, and began by training for the law, being called to the bar at the Middle Temple in London in 1868. Newspaper work seemed more immediately profitable and exciting than a briefless practice, and after editing the short-lived *Monthly Journal* in London, Davin went off to the Franco-Prussian War as correspondent for the London *Standard.* He succeeded in the unusual feat of covering both sides in the conflict, but he was wounded at Montmédy and returned to London, whence in 1872 he travelled to Toronto.

In these early Canadian years in Ontario, Davin, always a man of varied parts, combined journalism and the law. He wrote dispatches for the *Pall Mall Gazette* on the prospects of American annexation, and then he worked for the *Globe,* but he was temperamentally and politically out of sympathy with the Grit editor, George Brown, and shifted to the *Mail.* In 1874 he was called to the Ontario bar and carried on an intermittent legal practice, his best known brief being an eloquent but unsuccessful defence of George Bennett, the killer of his old enemy George Brown, in 1880.

Meanwhile Davin had turned to authorship and politics. He published his first book, *British Versus American Civilization,* in 1873, followed it up with a political skit, *The Fair Grit,* in 1876, and with a popular history, *The Irishman in Canada,* in 1877. In 1878 he competed unsuccessfully as a Conservative candidate in the federal elections.

Early in the 1880s Davin heard of the fortunes being made in the new towns of the North West, and in 1882 he arrived in Pile of Bones, only that year transformed into Regina, intending to indulge in land speculation. Instead, he settled down to newspaper publication and poetry, founding the *Leader* in 1883 and the next year publishing *Eos: A Prairie Drama, and Other Poems,* which attempted to adapt the story of Canada's West to the form of a classical myth. *Eos* first appeared in Ottawa; a revised version published in Regina in 1889 was the first book of verse to be published in the North-West Territories.

Davin found the raw, frank society of the North West suited to his journalistic style, and he turned the *Leader* into a lively, hard-hitting newspaper. He attacked the Mounted Police and the Liberals, who he believed were betraying the interests of the West, and when Riel was awaiting execution he disguised himself as a priest so that he could enter the prison for an interview.

The *Leader* gave him a way into politics, and from 1887 to 1900 he represented the people of what later became Saskatchewan in the House of Commons. He was deeply aware of the divisions that began to plague Canada after Riel's execution, and he tried in vain to check the bitterness that arose between Ontario and Quebec, intensified as it was by the Orange-oriented propaganda of his fellow Irishman, D'Alton McCarthy. But despite his abilities, he was regarded by the Conservative leaders as too erratic to be entrusted with ministerial office.

Because of his political involvements, Davin sold his interest in the *Leader,* which in 1895 fell into the hands of the Conservative, Walter Scott (later the first premier of Saskatchewan), who completely changed its policy. Davin then started a newspaper, the *West,* in the Liberal interest, but it never achieved the popularity or influence the *Leader* had enjoyed in early years. In 1900 Davin was defeated by Scott, his arch-rival, in the federal election. Already drinking heavily, he became acutely depressed, and on 18 October 1901 he shot himself in Winnipeg after addressing an unresponsive political gathering.

Davin was a man of great brilliance and sensitivity, drawn irresistibly to the flamboyant and ruthless life of the West, yet in the end incapable of finding a place within it. But perhaps there was an essential flaw in his nature that would have defeated him in any situation. He did many things well but lacked a persistent drive, and so he seemed to succeed in nothing. Undoubtedly that was the judgement by which in the end he condemned himself to death.

Robert Chambers Edwards

Bob Edwards was one of those maverick figures whom it is difficult to place in history and whose talents were so wayward that they are hard to classify. Yet he is part of the Canadian western myth, and a collection of his humorous columns (Hugh A. Dempsey's *The Best of Bob Edwards*) was a publishing success in 1975, more than fifty years after Edwards died; a posthumous triumph that could happen to very few Canadian journalists.

Bob Edwards was born in Edinburgh in 1864 and received the excellent education which in the nineteenth century was provided by Scottish universities; he attended both St. Andrews and Glasgow. In 1895 he migrated to Canada, at the beginning of Clifford Sifton's great drive to fill the prairies with immigrants from all parts of Europe. He went far west, but not beyond the Rockies, and settled down to newspaper publication on a modest scale. From 1898 to 1902 he launched a series of weekly small-town newspapers, none of which was particularly successful. Then, in 1902, he had the idea that what the West needed was a satirical paper to attack the corruption which was coming in on the wave of western settlement and the speculation it involved. In the little foothills town of High River he began to publish what he called a "semi-occasional" paper called the *Eye-Opener*, which justified its name by exposing every abuse that found its way into Bob Edwards's whisky-illuminated vision.

The paper was so successful that in 1903 Edwards moved it to Calgary; it became the *Calgary Eye-Opener* and reached a circulation of thirty thousand. Since the population of Calgary was considerably less than thirty thousand at the time, this meant that the journal was mailed all over Canada, often without the co-operation of the Canadian Pacific Railway, which was so annoyed by the *Eye-Opener*'s repeated attacks that it frequently refused to freight the paper. The CPR was not the only target that Bob Edwards attacked; he went for the land sharks, for the liquor interests (in spite of his own interest in the bar of the nearest hotel), and he was particularly forceful in his warnings of the encroachment of bureaucracy as government became stabilized and moved toward the ossification it has reached since Edwards died.

The *Eye-Opener* was not all attack. Some of the humour was gentle, like that surrounding Edwards's famous character, the remittance man Bertie Buzzard-Cholmondeley, late of Skookingham Hall; and something of the shy idealist who was the other side of the satirist emerged at times, as in the *Eye-Opener*'s favourite and oft-repeated personal prayer: "Lord, let me keep a straight way in the path of honour and a straight face in the presence of solemn asses. Let me neither truckle to the high nor bulldoze the low; let me frolic with Jack and the Joker and win the game. Lead me into truth and beauty and tell me her name; keep me sane but not too sane. Let me condemn no man for his grammar or woman for her morals, neither being responsible for either. Preserve my sense of humour and proportion; let me be healthy while I live but not live too long. Which is about enough for today, O Lord!"

Almost entirely a one-man operation, with Edwards as publisher, editor, and principal writer, the *Eye-Opener* continued for nineteen years, the remainder of Edwards's life. Nobody dared to continue it. A copy of the last issue was buried with him when he died in 1922, together with a silver flask of whisky.

Canadians have prided themselves on their humorists, perhaps because humour is so rare a thing among us; Bob Edwards was one of the best of that rare breed.

Almighty Voice

There were probably more white than Indian outlaws in the Canadian West, but the Indian fugitives from an imposed authority have a peculiar appeal, partly because they represented the tragic clash of different cultures and partly because, while the white "bad men" were outcasts from their own people, the Indians usually demonstrated in various ways their solidarity with rebels of their own race and remembered them afterwards as heroes. To this day, in the parkland around the junction of the North and South Saskatchewan rivers, the tragic story of Almighty Voice is almost as strong a legend among the native peoples–Métis as well as Indians–as that of Gabriel Dumont.

Almighty Voice was a Swampy Cree from One Arrow's reservation north of Batoche. He was born about 1874, and when he was a boy he saw the braves of his band ride down to play their part with Dumont and Riel in the Métis rebellion of 1885. He was known in Cree as Kakee-manitou-wayo and to the Indian agent as Jean Baptiste. Until October 1895 he was regarded as a peaceful young man, who caused no trouble, and was known as a good hunter and marksman.

In October 1895, however, he was arrested with another Indian–Young Dust–and charged with killing a cow. It is still unclear whose cow it actually was, but it seems certain that Sergeant Colebrook of the North-West Mounted Police, who carried out the arrest, went beyond his duty by threatening Almighty Voice, perhaps in ill-considered jest, with a heavier punishment than the crime, such as it was, merited.

That night Almighty Voice slipped away from the lock-up at Duck Lake and fled northeastward, crossing the South Saskatchewan and heading for the Touchwood Hills. It was several days before Colebrook, with a Métis tracker, came on the fugitive and his young wife. Almighty Voice shot at Colebrook and killed him. Then he fled into the wilderness of coulees and poplar bluffs, where a volunteer posse failed to find him, and vanished for a year and a half.

There is no doubt that friends and relatives knew of Almighty Voice's whereabouts, for he could not have kept alive without ammunition and other supplies, but in spite of the posting of a reward of $500, a small fortune in that time of Indian destitution, nobody provided a clue to his whereabouts until late May 1897, when a cow was killed on the farm of a Batoche Métis named Napoleon Venne, who sometimes scouted for the Mounted Police.

Venne suspected the presence of the Indian fugitive, and he and Corporal Bowbridge in their search for clues flushed out Almighty Voice and another young Indian. Venne was shot and wounded, and he and Bowbridge decamped to return next day with a posse of Mounted Police and volunteers who set out for the Minichinas Hills, towards which Almighty Voice had fled. They trapped Almighty Voice and two companions in a grove of trees isolated by prairie. They were able to surround the bluff, but in an attempt to rush the fugitives, two policemen and a volunteer were killed and two other policemen wounded. An old brass seven-pound cannon brought from Prince Albert started to blast the wood but proved ineffective.

On the second day a large party of Mounted Police arrived from Regina with a modern nine-pound gun. Meanwhile, the three Indians kept up their defiance; they lived on crows they had killed and on the sap from peeled maple trees and kept up a sporadic fire with their dwindling ammunition, which was enough to keep the besiegers out of the trees. There was never any thought of surrender, and Almighty Voice called out defiantly his intention of fighting to a finish.

Eventually, on the morning of 31 May, as the Indians from the neighbouring reservations watched silently from the hills that overlooked the bluff, the nine-pound cannon went into action, pounding the wood for four hours with canister and shrapnel. The second assault was then made. There was no opposition. Almighty Voice and his companions were dead, and the Indians who had witnessed their killing treasured the memory of the rebel who became transformed into a figure of heroic myth during the long years of neglect and acquiescence that followed.

John Ware

The black population of Canada has been built up by many small accretions. Long before the recent influx of immigrants from the West Indies, there had been small groups in Ontario and the Maritimes who were the descendants of slaves escaping by way of the famous underground railway and by other means in the decades before the Civil War. Another group migrated from California to less prejudiced Victoria at the time of the Fraser Valley gold rush of 1858, and many of these later settled on Salt Spring Island, where until very recently a distinctive black community survived. But there were few blacks who took part in the ranching life that developed in the eastern foothills of the Rockies during the decades following on Confederation, and of this few the best known was the cowboy and cattle rancher, John Ware.

John Ware was born in 1843, a slave in South Carolina. After liberation at the end of the Civil War, he drifted as a young man southward into Texas, where he found employment on ranches and learnt the skills of the cowboy. Ware was a tall, massive man of great strength, and he had an understanding of and with horses that made him a first-rate breaker. After a while in Texas, Ware moved northward with the drift of ranching into the newly opened rangelands of Wyoming and Montana. By 1882 he was in Idaho, and shortly afterwards he moved north over the border into Canada on a cattle drive and became a range rider on the Bar U ranch near Macleod.

Ware suffered a great deal of the kind of discrimination blacks endured even in Canada during the late nineteenth century, but his size and strength saved him from physical attacks, and his good humour and evident skill as a cowboy earned him the affection and respect even of those who still referred to him as "Nigger John." His imperturbable competence allowed him to turn even the tensest situation to his own advantage. There were many times when malicious or merely impish employers tried him out with an untamed mustang, and Ware calmly rode the horse to a standstill and turned the disdain of his fellow cowboys into admiration. "If there is a man in the roundup who keeps up the spirit of the boys more than another and provides amusement to break the monotony," wrote an anonymous hand in the Macleod

Gazette during 1885, "this man is John Ware. John is not only one of the best natured and most obliging fellows in the country but he is one of the shrewdest cow men."

Ware moved on from ranch to ranch in the Alberta country, until by 1891 he had finally saved enough money to establish his own outfit on the north fork of Sheep Creek in the foothills southwest of Calgary. There he prospered as a cattleman and was able to hire land for grazing beyond his own property, until by 1900 the homesteaders crowded in and John Ware found the space he needed was no longer in existence. He sold out, but his mark remains on the land he originally settled; there is a stream named Ware Creek near the site of John's old ranch, and a peak in the hills called Ware in his honour.

From the well-watered slopes around Sheep Creek, John Ware moved north to dry prairie land on the Red Deer River, and here his fortunes changed abruptly for the worse. The house he built when he settled on the ranch was washed away in 1902 in a great flood. Resourceful as always, Ware lassoed enough lumber floating downstream from a demolished mill to build himself a new home. But that did not mend his luck. The grass was poor; his cattle were afflicted by mange; his family found the isolation of their new situation hard to endure. Finally, as he was riding over the ranch in 1905, Ware's horse stepped in a badger hole; he was thrown and died of a broken back. In the ranching country of the Far West the name of this admirable man has survived; John Ware is as much a part of the mythology of the Canadian West as Gabriel Dumont or Almighty Voice.

George Mercer Dawson

In the records of far western Canada during the decades after Confederation it is hard to escape the traces of a restless little hunch-backed geologist named George Mercer Dawson. He is the Dawson after whom Dawson City on the Yukon was named in 1897; he is the Dawson who took the invaluable photographs which tell us what the long-vanished groves of totem poles looked like in the Haida villages of the 1870s. A geologist by profession, he bestrode the natural sciences, and in spirit at least was one of Canada's first true anthropologists.

Dawson was born at Pictou, Nova Scotia, in 1849. His father, Sir John William Dawson, was a naturalist of the pre-Darwinian school, who collaborated with Sir Charles Lyell and published a formidable series of books in the realm of popular science. George Mercer Dawson grew up a sickly boy, deformed by a childhood illness that stunted his growth and left him with a hump on his back. No one looked less like the stuff great travellers are made of, but few people can have had a father so daunting in his achievements as Sir John William Dawson, and George Mercer quickly left home to develop a life of his own, as active and in its own way even more productive than his father's.

He studied at McGill and went on to the Royal School of Mines in London. His first major assignment came in 1873 when he was appointed geologist and botanist for the North American Boundary Commission, which was surveying the international frontier line along the 49th parallel. The section with which he was involved lay in the prairies, and it enabled him to record, in the report he published at the end of his two years of service, a good deal of still valuable information about the prairies and their natural life in the days before the buffalo were destroyed, before the railways and the settlers came.

Dawson's period with the boundary commission displayed his passion for knowledge in every area of the natural sciences; it also whetted his appetite for travel and adventure, and when he was appointed to the Geological Survey of Canada in 1875 he availed himself to the full of the opportunities the service brought him. He became assistant director of the survey in 1883 and director in 1895, but

neither of these high-sounding positions kept this active little perpetual bachelor from spending as much of his short life as he could wandering the western wildernesses of the new Canada. No travel was too tiring or hazardous for him, and he seemed to challenge his crews by the very frailty of his appearance so that they would do more under him than under the other surveyors of the mountains and islands of the West. "He climbed, walked, and rode on horseback over more of Canada than any other member of the Survey at that time," said one of his colleagues, "yet to look at him, one would not think him capable of a day's physical labour."

It was Dawson who did the first intensive geological surveys of areas vital to Canadian development, like the Peace River and the Yukon, and it was he who first drew attention to the vast coal fields in the Crow's Nest Pass area of the Rockies. He investigated the Missouri Coteau and demonstrated its glacial origins, and he explored the interior plateaus of British Columbia. In 1892 he spent a year on the remote Bering Sea as member of a mixed commission investigating the pelagic sealing industry and co-authored the report on it with Sir George Baden-Powell.

Dawson's survey of the Queen Charlotte Islands, the first of its kind, was important because it led him into the study of Indian customs and languages, and he was one of the earliest scientists to describe the native cultures of the British Columbian coast with perception and sympathetic insight. His writings on this subject are vivid and valuable but unfortunately are mostly hidden away in the proceedings of the Royal Society of Canada and in the reports of the Geological Survey. It was perhaps the example of his ever-publishing father that made George Mercer Dawson so modest about seeking the wide public his discoveries and discussions merited. Yet after his early death in 1901, he became recognized as one of the greatest of those essential men in the early days of Confederation, the geographers and geologists who described and defined our vast land.

Charles Edward Saunders

When Canada acquired the vast stretches of the western plains from the Hudson's Bay Company in 1869, the government was faced not only with such immediate problems as the resistance of the people of Red River but also (once that had been overcome through the creation of the Province of Manitoba) with the double questions of how to populate this vast area and how to use effectively the combination of a virgin soil of great fertility and a climate with long hard winters and short hot summers, in which the annual average of frost-free nights decreased sharply as one travelled north.

Clifford Sifton solved the first part of the problem, largely by bringing in immigrants from eastern Europe who were accustomed to similar climatic conditions to those of the prairies. Sifton's migration was in full swing by the later 1890s, but as the lands along the CPR and south to the American border were taken up, it became evident that more hardy strains of wheat would have to be found if the northerly prairies were ever to be turned into productive farms.

The man who finally solved the problem was Charles Edward Saunders, born during the year of Confederation, 1867, at London, Ontario. The achievements he made can best be seen in the context of a family partnership, for the long process of discovering hardy and disease-resistant grains for the northern plains began with Charles Edward's father, William Saunders, a Devon man who came to Canada with his parents as a boy of twelve in 1848. Saunders, an energetic and rather overbearing man, became a manufacturing chemist and set up his own private experimental farm in 1868. When the federal Ministry of Agriculture established an Experimental Farms Branch in 1886, William Saunders was the obvious man to direct it, and he remained in charge until he retired in 1911, developing a number of new strains of fruit and grain adapted to various Canadian environments.

Charles Saunders, his son, was a sensitive young man, deeply interested in the arts, a good amateur musician and an occasional writer, who in later years published a volume of poetry and prose in French—*Essais et Vers* (1928). If his father had not been so insistent on the family mission of making Canada fruitful, Charles might very well have become a professional musician. As it was, he studied chemistry and botany at the University of Toronto, and later at Johns Hopkins where he took his doctorate in 1891. For a while he taught chemistry and geology in Kentucky, but he also developed his interest in music, dabbling in criticism and teaching a little at girls' colleges. But William Saunders was an insistent man, and in 1903 the post of dominion cerealist was created virtually for Charles Saunders to occupy.

Saunders moved back to Ottawa and set to work on the urgent task of finding an effective strain of wheat before too many precarious winters had passed in the northern prairies. Very soon he isolated a hardy and rust-free grain called Markham, which he renamed Marquis. It fitted the two prime requirements: it ripened quickly enough to survive most prairie seasons and it produced a good quality bread flour. By 1909 enough seed grain had been grown to distribute to the prairie farmers, and by 1920 fifteen million acres were sown with Marquis.

Saunders went on to develop refinements on the Marquis strain, adapted to variant conditions on the prairies, and of these Ruby, Garnet, and Reward were the best known. By then their creator was glad to make his health an excuse to give up his researches, and in 1922 he retired to Paris and lived there for many years before returning to Toronto, where he died in 1937. Yet his true monument is not to be found in the ephemeral poems he composed in France or in the music he loved most to make, but in the millions of northern prairie acres where each year the wheat ripens and grows golden in the brief blazing summer.

James Douglas

If one had to pick a single man to credit with the fact that Canada eventually stretched, as its motto proclaims, from sea to sea, the choice would have to fall on James Douglas, who in the 1840s and 1850s resisted American pressure on the Pacific Coast and so preserved the Colony of British Columbia to become the westernmost Canadian province.

James Douglas, the "Scotch West Indian" as he was called in the fur trade, was born in 1803 at Demerara, British Guiana, son of John Douglas, a Glasgow sugar merchant, and a creole woman remembered as Miss Ritchie. John Douglas brought his son to Scotland; James was educated at Lanark, where the training in French was good, an asset when at the age of sixteen he entered the service of the North West Company and sailed for Montreal.

For a few months James Douglas was stationed at Fort William, the company's Lakehead headquarters. He went on to Île à la Crosse, to be immersed in the last months of violence between the North-westers and the Hudson's Bay men; at the age of eighteen he fought a duel, with no fatalities. When the rival companies were united in 1821, Douglas stayed on as a clerk. In 1825 he was transferred to Fort St. James in New Caledonia (as northern British Columbia was then called) and in 1828 he married Amelia Connolly, the Métis daughter of Chief Factor William Connolly. He also became involved in violent disputes with the local Carrier Indians and in 1830 he prudently went south to Fort Vancouver, on the north bank of the Columbia River, where he became the accountant; in 1834 he was appointed chief trader and in 1839 chief factor.

These were difficult times for the Hudson's Bay Company on the Pacific Coast. An agreement between Britain and the United States in 1818 had thrown the region between California and Alaska open to trading by subjects of both countries, but by 1840 large numbers of American settlers were crossing the mountains over the Oregon Trail and their supporters were demanding the annexation of the Pacific Coast up to the Alaska boundary. Already, anticipating that the Americans would get the land south of the Columbia, Fort Vancouver had been built on the river's northern bank, but now even this seemed imperilled, and in

1842 James Douglas went on an expedition to discover a suitable alternative site. He found it on the southern tip of Vancouver Island; the post he established there and called Fort Camosun eventually became Victoria.

When the Oregon Boundary Treaty was signed in 1846 the international boundary was far north of the Columbia River, at the 49th parallel, and in 1849 Douglas—now in charge of the company's Pacific Coast district—moved its headquarters north to Victoria. To prevent American encroachment, the British government decided that a more regular administration was needed, and in the same year Vancouver Island became a crown colony, leased to the Hudson's Bay Company. The Colonial Office sent a governor, Richard Blanshard, but Douglas got rid of him by non-cooperation, and in 1851 was himself appointed governor while remaining the Hudson Bay Company's chief factor. Despite murmurs from the few settlers who reached the island, Douglas ran it as a fur-trading outpost rather than a regular colony. Then, in 1857, the discovery of gold on the Fraser River dramatically changed the situation.

News of gold on the Fraser, reaching San Francisco in spring 1858, set off a rush from the depleted California fields. Twenty thousand people crowded into Victoria, hitherto a settlement with a few hundred white inhabitants. The miners crossed the Gulf of Georgia to the mainland in unseaworthy craft, and led by some of the worst Californian desperadoes, began to clash with the Indians. The situation offered an open temptation for American intervention unless decisive British action were taken.

Douglas took it. His governor's commission extended only to Vancouver Island and the Queen Charlottes. On the mainland he was merely the representative of a fur-trading company. But he issued technically illegal proclamations imposing regulations on the entry of miners, he used visiting naval ships and their marines to make a show of force, and by the time the Colonial Office turned British Columbia into a crown colony and appointed him governor, the danger was contained. Douglas went on to create towns like New Westminster and Fort Langley, and establish the beginning of a road network up the Fraser and into the Cariboo.

Douglas's decisive acts were suited for crises such as the gold rush. But when the West Coast colonies began to acquire a settled population interested in self-government, the governor showed an inflexibility that led men like Amor De Cosmos, editor of the *British Colonist* in Victoria, to criticize him bitterly. In 1864, bowing to the changing winds, Douglas resigned his governorship. He lived on in Victoria, the city he had created, until his death in 1877, and saw the British Columbia he had preserved from the Americans become a part of Canada. His thoughts on this event are unrecorded, yet without his decisive presence in the critical year of 1858, it might never have taken place.

Amor De Cosmos

Amor De Cosmos, it might very well be said, came into being on 17 February 1854, the day the California legislature passed a bill changing the name of a certain William Alexander Smith, born almost thirty years before, in August 1825, at Windsor, Nova Scotia. When he assumed his unusual name, which he claimed projected what he loved most in existence – "order, beauty, the world, the universe" – Smith was a photographer and a speculator in properties in the California mining village of Mud Springs, which also had recently changed its name – to El Dorado. Three years before, he had been clerk in a wholesale grocery warehouse in Halifax, where he had learnt much about democratic politics from the great reformer Joseph Howe. He had crossed the United States overland by wagon train, wintering in Salt Lake City, before in 1852 he came to the gold fields and found that there was more money to be made providing services to the miners, like accurate photographs of claims that could be used in litigation, than by actually digging and panning gold.

In 1858 the news of gold in the Fraser Valley reached San Francisco, and among those who set out to try their fortunes was Amor De Cosmos. Once again, he had no intention of performing hard manual toil, and he settled in Victoria, which became the commercial capital of the gold rush. He seems to have sustained himself by buying and selling properties, but his ambition was to become a radical journalist and politician. Years afterwards, De Cosmos declared, "I am one of those who believe that political hatreds attest the vitality of a State," and when in late 1858 he founded the *British Colonist* in Victoria, in opposition to the autocratic regime of Governor James Douglas, he did not spare denunciation, which he combined with a plea for the kind of responsible government he had seen established in Nova Scotia a decade before. By 1860 he had added a demand for the amalgamation of all the British North American possessions into a single nation, and these two points essentially represented the policy to which De Cosmos dedicated his life.

In the crown colony of Vancouver Island, dominated by the Hudson's Bay Company interests and by the authorita-rian tradition of company rule, De Cosmos did not find his task easy. In 1859 Douglas had tried to suppress the *Colonist* by evoking an English law that required massive sureties for a newspaper to appear; at a public meeting in Victoria the citizens subscribed enough for the necessary bonds, and soon the *Colonist* became a daily instead of a weekly thorn in the side of Douglas and the "Fort Clique," as his followers were called.

Later, in 1860 when De Cosmos tried to gain election to the Legislative Assembly of Vancouver Island, he was twice defeated by election frauds which were allowed to go unremedied; not until 1863 did he eventually enter the assembly and become virtual leader of the opposition. His methods were flamboyant but arresting. Like a more celebrated contemporary, he was often drunk when he spoke, and he frequently became involved in fights with opponents on whose heads he would freely use his heavy walking stick. Once he and another legislator wearied their more numerous opponents into submission by speaking in turn for twenty-six hours on end. By such methods De Cosmos gained and held attention. He was mostly responsible for the union of the colonies of Vancouver Island and British Columbia. When he was unable to persuade the Legislative Council of the united colony to press for confederation with Canada, he turned to the people, raised a great agitation in Victoria, and organized the famous Yale Convention of 1868, where popularly chosen delegates from all over the colony supported union with the dominion.

At last, in 1871, all that De Cosmos had striven for was achieved, including responsible government, provided for under the terms of Confederation. From this point his political life began to lose direction. He had been a natural leader in opposition, an excellent political guerrilla, but as second premier of British Columbia in 1872 he ran an unimaginative government which ended when rioters invaded the assembly and De Cosmos resigned. Similarly, in the eleven years he served as member of the House of Commons, De Cosmos showed little constructive imagination and spent most of his time defending provincial interests. He rarely displayed a wider vision, but when he did it was in a way that shocked his Victoria fellow citizens, for in 1882 he made in the House of Commons a speech calling for Canada's future independence. "I was born a British subject. . . . I do not wish to die without all the rights, privileges and immunities of the citizen of a nation." The Victorians defeated him in the next election, 1882, and De Cosmos retired into private life, becoming steadily more eccentric, until shortly before his death in 1897 he was declared insane. By this time he was almost forgotten, and it was left for an old enemy, J.S. Helmcken, to protest at the meagre funeral given to "a public man, a pioneer, who 'has stood behind the gun.' "

John Sebastian Helmcken

John Sebastian Helmcken was the first man to practise European medicine on the Pacific Coast of Canada; he was also one of the most prominent figures in the early political history of Vancouver Island and British Columbia. Helmcken was born in London in 1824 to a family of German extraction; his father was a sugar-factory worker and later the keeper of a tavern, which his mother continued after she became a widow. John Helmcken started work at thirteen as errand boy to a local physician, to whom he was later articled as a medical pupil. He attended Guy's Hospital in 1844, became a licensed apothecary in 1847, and in 1848 a member of the Royal College of Surgeons, which allowed him to practise medically.

Already, in fact, he had been employed as surgeon on the Hudson's Bay Company's ship, the *Prince Rupert*, on its 1847 voyage to York Factory, and in 1848-49 he took a similar appointment on the *Malacca*, bound for Bombay and Canton. Finally, in 1849 he received a regular appointment as surgeon to the company and sailed for Vancouver Island, reaching Victoria in the spring of 1850, spending a short period as surgeon and magistrate at Fort Rupert, and before the end of the year becoming company surgeon at Victoria, a post he retained until 1885.

From this point Helmcken was in the thick of the changing life of the British Pacific Coast possessions. In 1852 he became *de facto* a member of the ruling elite by marrying James Douglas's daughter Cecilia, and when a legislative assembly was created for Vancouver Island he was elected to it and chosen as speaker, a position he held until the union of Vancouver Island and British Columbia in 1866. Helmcken was conservative by nature, and his links with the company and with Douglas personally made the democratic element in the colony suspect him of blindly supporting the establishment. But in fact Helmcken was a man of independent judgement, not liable to be cowed by either side. When the two colonies were united he was glad to be relieved of the speaker's office and become an ordinary member of the Legislative Council so that he might play his part in the debate over the entry of British Columbia into Confederation that developed in the years after 1866.

Helmcken has often been represented as opposed to Confederation and inclined to prefer annexation to the United States, but that oversimplifies his position. He was never opposed to Confederation as such, but he approached it cautiously and doubted whether union with Canada could be made effective without a railway connection, which, knowing what he did of the British Columbian mountains, he did not at first believe feasible. If Confederation was in fact impracticable, then Helmcken believed annexation might be inevitable, but that was as far as he ever went. However, he tended to reason out his thoughts in public, and so misunderstandings arose. In the end he gave full support to union with Canada and was chosen as one of the delegates who went to Ottawa in 1870 to arrange the terms of entry into Confederation with the dominion government.

Unlike other early British Columbian politicians prominent in the Confederation debate, Helmcken did not go on to high office in either the province or the dominion. His ambitions did not lie in a political direction; indeed he had too ironical a view of life to be truly ambitious in any way. He had unwillingly assumed a public responsibility by standing for election in 1855 when there were few people in the colony to take public office, but once British Columbia's future seemed decided he retired completely from political life, devoting himself to his medical practice and to such public matters of local interest as organizing hospitals in Victoria and establishing the British Columbia Medical Society and the British Columbia Medical Council. He was a familiar figure in Victoria at the turn of the century, vividly described in Emily Carr's memoirs, and he continued to practise until 1910, when he was eighty-six. He died in 1920, at ninety-six, and his house, built in 1852 and the oldest surviving house in Victoria, became a museum. His *Reminiscences* were finally published in 1975; they reveal the man and the life of his times through a highly whimsical eye.

Matthew Baillie Begbie

Sir Matthew Baillie Begbie has gone down in the folklore of western Canada as the "hanging judge" of British Columbia; there is even an apocryphal tale that on one occasion, when a hangman could not be found, he applied the noose himself. The truth about Begbie is somewhat less grim than the legends but equally extraordinary.

When the call came to Begbie to abandon his law practice in London and leave for the distant Pacific coast of North America, he was a man of talent whose expectations had never materialized. He had been born in 1819 either en route to the Indian Ocean or on the island of Mauritius to which his father, Colonel T. S. Begbie of the Forty-fourth Foot, had been posted. He was educated at St. Peter's College, Cambridge, where he became an M.A. in 1844, the same year that he was called to the bar at Lincoln's Inn. He travelled in Europe, became fluent in French and Italian, and then settled down to make a career as a lawyer. He had the appearance and the manner. He was tall – six foot four; he was handsome, with his bold eyes and his dark Van Dyck beard; and he dressed dashingly (but perhaps too eccentrically to inspire trust in Victorian clients) in a great black cloak and a wide-brimmed soft black hat. Certainly, success did not come to him in England either in law or – according to the legend – in love, and when he received the offer to become a judge in remote British Columbia, he accepted a task for which, as it turned out, his flamboyant character admirably suited him.

The task was to impose British law with the aid of a few constables on some tens of thousands of miners accustomed to the violence and vigilante law of the Californian gold fields. Many of them were fervently anti-British Americans, willing to create incidents that might be the excuse for United States intervention north of the 49th parallel. Begbie decided that he could only succeed by carrying the law in all its dignity into the heart of the mining country, and so he became a hard-travelling judge, riding from camp to camp and setting up his court in any store or saloon that happened to be convenient, but always presiding with strict legality and inspiring awe by the sheer contrast between his powdered wig and scarlet judge's robes, and the rough garb of the miners who filled the courts.

Begbie was fearless, using all the advantages of his physical presence as well as his legal office, and conducting his trials with a grim humour that has been preserved in the mythology of the Far West. There were times when he would keep a jury that wished to acquit an obviously guilty man secluded for long periods to temper their stubbornness. Sometimes the juries had more staying power even than Begbie, and then he would express his opinion of them with biting sarcasm. When one such jury acquitted a mugger, Begbie dismissed the prisoner with the remark: "The jurymen say you are not guilty, but with that I do not agree. It is now my duty to set you free and I warn you not to pursue your evil ways, but if you ever again should be so inclined, I hope you select your victim from the men who have acquitted you."

In fact Begbie did not, by the standards of the time, sentence many men to hanging, though he often used the threat of the gallows. His inclination to appear quickly at any trouble spot – and to administer the law strictly when he did – created an entirely different atmosphere from that of the California gold fields. Between them, Begbie and the Irish chief of police, Chartres Brew, kept in check the natural tendency to violence of British Columbia's early population of itinerant fortune hunters. On one famous occasion Begbie arrived at Wild Horse Creek when a riotous situation was developing. "Boys," shouted Begbie as he addressed the mob of excited and armed miners, "if there is any shooting in Kootenay, there will be hanging in Kootenay." There was no shooting.

Begbie became chief justice of British Columbia in 1866 and retained the position until his death in 1894 at the age of seventy-five. As a judge he was always the autocrat, yet there are many stories of his kindness outside the courtroom, and he was a man of whimsical courtesy, celebrated for the great parties he would give in his last years in Victoria, when he would have his servants tie bunches of cherries on the ornamental trees for his guests to pick when they wandered among the sunlit English borders as the band played and as Sir Matthew exerted his majesty charm.

John Robson

The leaders of the battle for constitutional reform and Confederation in far western Canada were almost all Upper Canadians or Maritimers who found their way to the region during or after the gold rush of 1858. The British, who originally made their homes on Vancouver Island under the aegis of the Hudson's Bay Company, tended to be more conservative politically and also to be less receptive to the ideas of union with the central Canadian provinces.

Thus, if the leading protagonist of reform on Vancouver Island was the Nova Scotian, Amor De Cosmos, his mainland counterpart in the newer colony of British Columbia was the Upper Canadian, John Robson, a man of equally fiery temperament and strong convictions.

John Robson was born in 1824 in the lumber town of Perth in the Ottawa Valley. He was educated at Perth grammar school and dabbled in journalism before, in 1859, he was attracted to British Columbia by the news of the gold rush. Robson settled in New Westminster, the raw shacktown that was capital of the new colony. Already the first impetus of the gold rush had slackened, and Robson, like many others, found it hard to keep alive in an area where the supply of labour–as in all gold rushes–quickly exceeded the demand. He survived by various kinds of manual work until by 1861 he had gathered enough money to start the first newspaper in the mainland colony, the *British Columbian.*

Robson followed the line De Cosmos had pioneered in Vancouver Island's *British Colonist*–hard-hitting criticism of the existing regime accompanied by equally strong demands for constitutional government. Robson's task was more difficult than that of De Cosmos, since while there was a legislative assembly and a semblance of democratic government on Vancouver Island, on the mainland the only elective institution was the New Westminster Municipal Council–and Governor James Douglas ruled merely with the advice of an appointed executive council. There were other grievances; for example, the colonial officers of British Columbia mostly lived out of the colony in the pleasant setting of Victoria and came to the mainland as seldom as possible. Such grievances Robson pursued in the *British Columbian* without fear of person, for he published one feature relating to Matthew Baillie Begbie which the judge regarded as in contempt and for which he imprisoned Robson.

Robson's imprisonment was rather like Henry David Thoreau's. He spent two days in the New Westminster jail against Thoreau's one day in Concord lockup. He made the best of the experience by writing a famous editorial in his cell. "Fellow colonists, we greet you from our dungeon," he declaimed. "Startled by the wild shrieks of a dying maniac on one hand, and the clanking of the murderer's chains on the other, while the foul and scant atmosphere of our cell, loaded with noxious effluvia from the filthy dens occupied by lunatics, renders life almost intolerable, our readers will overlook any incoherency or want of collected thoughts in our writings."

Robson's journalism made him a popular figure– "Honest John" –among the discontented British Columbians. He was elected to the New Westminster Council in 1864 and became its chairman. When the two Pacific colonies were united into British Columbia, he was elected to the Legislative Council in 1867. In 1868 he was present with De Cosmos at the Yale convention in favour of Confederation, and when the capital of British Columbia was moved from New Westminster to Victoria, he moved with it, taking over in 1869 the editorship of the *Colonist*, which De Cosmos had founded. After Confederation he served from 1871-75 in the provincial legislative assembly, resigned to spend four years as paymaster and commissary for the CPR surveys in the British Columbian mountains, and in 1879 went back to New Westminster, editing the *British Columbian* again and speculating in land, among other places at Coal Harbour, where he profited greatly by the establishment of the CPR terminus at Vancouver.

Meanwhile, in 1882 Robson was re-elected to the assembly, became provincial secretary in 1883, and in 1889 premier of British Columbia. During his period in office he carried out some notable legislation protecting the resources of British Columbia and in particular checking the spread of American economic influence. Robson was not unfriendly to tycoons; he merely preferred them to be native.

His rule and his life came to an end abruptly in 1892 when he went to London to consult with the imperial authorities about a scheme he had devised for importing Scottish crofters to develop a British Columbian deep sea fishing industry. He caught his finger in the door of a cab, blood poisoning followed, and Honest John was dead within three days.

William Barker

Billy Barker survives in the collective memory as a legend rather than a person, as a type figure of the thousands of men of all classes, races, and ages, who in the 1860s were drawn by a golden magnet to the Cariboo region in the high plateaus of British Columbia, where he gave his name to the famous settlement of Barkerville, for a brief period the most populous community in North America west of Chicago.

Barker was a Cornishman, born round about 1820; as a first occupation he became one of the potters who worked with the white clay of the duchy. Some time in his thirties Billy tired of the everlasting round of the potter's wheel, but Cornishmen are notably amphibious, and Billy found little difficulty in changing from clay to salt water and becoming a seaman. As a seaman he went from ship to ship until he found himself in the crew of a whaler that docked at Victoria in the critical summer of 1858, when the tiny outpost of the British Empire was afflicted with gold fever. Billy, and a fair proportion of his fellow crewmen, jumped ship and headed for the rich diggings of the Fraser Canyon.

Panning the sand bars of the Fraser, Billy Barker was one of those who always "made wages" without getting rich. As the bars of the Fraser were worked out, the prospectors began to drift northward. In 1860 Doc Keithley made the first strike in the Cariboo region on the stream that became known as Keithley Creek. Billy Barker was one of the survivors of the Fraser Valley rush who, before Colonel Moody's Royal Engineers made the Cariboo Road, packed their way northward over the hard trails – one of the anonymous, shabby, weather-burnt legion who went like lemmings, possessed by a single mania, and unnoticed until fortune chose to light on them.

Billy Barker, as it turned out, was one of fortune's unlikely choices, yet there was persistence as well as luck in the strike that brought him fame and temporary riches. Williams Creek, the best known gold-bearing stream of Cariboo, was named not for Billy Barker but for "Dutch" William Dietz, its original discoverer. Here a whole series of miners became wealthy and celebrated. Cariboo Cameron was one of them; he eventually took his beloved wife out of the country, embalmed in whisky in a lead coffin. Billy

Barker was another, obsessed with the idea that far under the present creek bed some primeval stream had once run over the bedrock. Dismissed as a fool by his neighbours, he had dug fifty feet down without striking pay dirt, and then, on 21 August 1862, he hit a narrow rock ledge and came out with a thousand dollars' worth of nuggets for his first day's work.

Billy Barker, the nondescript Cornishman, became a local hero overnight. Indeed, it was the first time anyone had ever noticed him, and to this period we owe the description of him as "a man of less than average height, stout, with heavy body, slightly bowed legs," and a face "partially hidden by a bushy black beard, plentifully streaked with gray." Billy and his partners took $600,000 out of their claims, a sum worth several times its equivalent today. A town of four thousand people rose up around his shack and grew as the years went by; named Barkerville in his honour, it survived the other early settlements of Williams Creek – Richfield and Camerontown – and in recent years has been resurrected as a tourist attraction. For Billy Barker it was the place where he could relax after the day's toil and do his dance among the German hurdy-gurdy girls as he chanted his somewhat inaccurate little song:

> I'm English Bill,
> Never worked, never will.
> Get away, girls,
> Or I'll tousle your curls.

One girl was not frightened away. Billy left the Cariboo a rich man with his share of the claim's proceeds, but married to an extravagant woman who helped him spend his fortune almost as quickly as he made it. For Billy there was an easy solution – to return to Cariboo for more of the same. But fortune did not smile again, and though he wandered for decades in the mountains of Cariboo and farther north, he never made another rich strike, and in 1892 he died, destitute, in the Old Men's Home in Victoria.

William Duncan

William Duncan was perhaps the most remarkable of the many missionaries who came to the Pacific Coast in the nineteenth century. He was born in 1832 at Bishop's Burton, near Beverley in Yorkshire, and after a grammar school education he began working with a wholesale leather merchant. He was successful in the trade and might have made a good businessman, but he was greatly influenced by the evangelical movement, which penetrated the Church of England in the early Victorian era, and decided that he had a duty to spread the gospel among pagan peoples. He was trained at Highbury College and appointed a lay missionary. Although his missionary career was to last sixty years, Duncan never sought to be ordained as a priest and refused several times in later years when ordination was urged upon him.

In 1856 he was sent to Vancouver Island under the auspices of the Church Missionary Society. Captain James Prevost, one of the naval commanders stationed on the Coast, was closely associated with the CMS; it was he who sponsored Duncan's appointment and designated Fort Simpson, where the Tsimshian had gathered in a large village near the Hudson's Bay post, as the place where his mission should begin. James Douglas, governor of Vancouver Island and the Hudson's Bay Company's chief factor, was less than enthusiastic. There was little love between fur traders and missionaries, and Douglas did not want to risk the life of an inexperienced religious teacher among the often violent northern peoples of the Coast. But Duncan was set on going to Fort Simpson, and Prevost insisted that it was CMS policy to establish missionaries away from white settlements–like Victoria–so that they could teach in a setting as little contaminated as possible by alien elements.

Douglas finally gave in and Duncan reached Fort Simpson in 1857. For almost a year he stayed in the fort, learning the Tsimshian language and emerging at the end of this period to preach his sermons in the great long houses of the Indian chiefs. Duncan was often insulted, threatened with violence and death, and forced to witness the demoralization of the Tsimshian at a time when both alcohol and alien diseases were rotting them physically and beginning to destroy their social structure. But he endured and made converts of powerful chiefs. Yet it seemed impossible, while converts and pagans remained together, to prevent the former from backsliding. Duncan decided that isolation was the only answer and he led his followers back to the site of one of their former winter villages, at a place called Metlakatla near Prince Rupert. There he proceeded to create a model Christian community.

Duncan was a strong-willed man who established a personal ascendancy over his followers that was enhanced by good fortune, for the people he led to Metlakatla escaped the smallpox epidemic that killed thousands of Indians on the Coast later in 1862, and many of the survivors came from Fort Simpson to join him. He did his best to turn his followers into good Victorian workingmen, dressing them in English clothes, putting them in houses resembling English cottages, and creating a native police force. To save his parishioners from the demoralizing proximity of the Hudson's Bay post at Fort Simpson, he set up a store, bought a trading schooner, and established a salmon cannery, a sawmill, and workshops to make rope and nets. And, of course, he founded a school and built an immense wooden church to hold a thousand people.

Metlakatla was a prosperous community, and if the Indians were forced to abandon many old customs, Duncan seemed to give them other things that filled their lives. He retained control for twenty-five years, and several ordained missionaries worked with him before they branched out to set up their own missions in the Queen Charlotte Islands and on the Nass River. But Duncan's relations with the church hierarchy became steadily worse, particularly as he refused to allow the Indian converts to receive Holy Communion, which he felt bore too close a resemblance to their ritual cannibalism. When Bishop Ridley appeared on the scene in the 1880s with CMS authority to take over the mission, Duncan resisted. There were fights in the British Columbia courts, which awarded the site of the mission to the bishop, and finally, in 1887, Duncan departed to set up a new mission on Annette Island in Alaska. Most of the Indians sided with Duncan, and eight hundred–a large part of the Tsimshian people–accompanied him to create yet another successful industrial mission village, New Metlakatla, where he died in 1918.

Duncan in his own way was a good man. Yet he was one of those who did much to destroy the way of life of the Coast Indians by branding their customs as pagan and robbing them of a reason to continue their great artistic tradition.

David Oppenheimer

Oppenheimer Park in Vancouver is a rough rectangle of half-dead grass, mostly occupied by baseball ovals and situated on a decaying edge of the city's Chinatown, surrounded by cheap rooming houses, seedy stores, and an old church taken over by the Buddhists. It seems a scanty monument to any man, and particularly to David Oppenheimer, the early mayor of Vancouver to whom the city owes its splendid Stanley Park.

David Oppenheimer was one of a family of five German Jewish brothers who migrated from Bavaria to New York in 1848, when David himself was only fourteen. The next year gold was found in California, and the Oppenheimer brothers joined the westward trek, and wisely avoiding the attempt to gain a fortune by digging gold, became small-scale merchants in San Francisco. The brothers were moderately successful, but towards the end of the 1850s they realized that the early boom in California was coming to an end, and when the first news of gold on the Fraser River reached their ears in the spring of 1858, they decided to try their fortunes in the new colony of British Columbia.

The Oppenheimers were part of a considerable mercantile movement, for if Vancouver Island and British Columbia remained politically British, their economic links ran southward until the completion of the Canadian Pacific Railway, and it was migrants from California (not all Americans) who appeared at the end of the 1850s to build their San Francisco-style warehouses in Victoria and to challenge the moribund monopoly of the Hudson's Bay Company.

Most of these merchants in the early days stayed in Victoria or moved to New Westminster, but the Oppenheimers were more adventurous and went immediately to Fort Yale, a strategic place at the base of the Fraser Canyon where the miners left the river boats to trek overland to the upriver bars. Those who had not outfitted themselves in Victoria were likely to do so in Yale, and the dry goods business which the Oppenheimers established there was quickly successful. When the rush went north to Cariboo and the new town of Barkerville rose in the wilderness, Oppenheimer Bros. was one of the first firms to move there; some idea of the extent of their business can be gained from the fact that

when Barkerville burned down in 1868, their loss was estimated at $100,000.

The Oppenheimers also established a branch in Victoria, but it was in the 1880s that David Oppenheimer's sense of commercial opportunity was most dramatically illustrated, for as soon as he heard that Coal Harbour, instead of Port Moody, was being considered as the western terminus for the Canadian Pacific Railway, he moved in with his brother Isaac, acquired land where downtown Vancouver now stands, and established a wholesale grocery warehouse.

Vancouver seemed to David Oppenheimer the end of the commercial road, and now he turned much of his attention from business to public service. He gave away real estate for schools and parks. He contributed to Jewish causes, but he was also a founder of the YMCA's Vancouver branch. It was as Vancouver's second mayor, serving from 1887 to 1892, that Oppenheimer made his abiding mark on the region. He was resolved to turn Vancouver from a raw settlement among the stumps into a city that would be worthy of its magnificent setting. He built sidewalks, constructed bridges, and founded the Vancouver Street Railway and the Vancouver Transport Company, which in 1890-91 built the first electric interurban railway in Canada. He created the Vancouver Board of Trade and resolutely publicized the city's attractions, to which he notably added. It was during his period as mayor that Vancouver, having leased the military reservation of Coal Peninsula from the federal government for a dollar a year, decided to turn it into a park that would uniquely combine gardens, sea walks, and natural forest. In September 1888 it was opened by the governor general of Canada, Lord Stanley, and with a gesture unusual in those imperial days, dedicated for the enjoyment of people of all races, colours, and creeds. It was named after Stanley, but David Oppenheimer – who died in 1897 – is remembered by the people of Vancouver as the man who established one of the finest of the world's parks and ensured that it should be inalienable.

Kootenay Brown

John George Brown, legendary through the southern Rockies as Kootenay Brown, was perhaps the best Canadian example of the type known in the United States as "mountain men," for he learned to live as well as any Indian off the land of the cordillera and the western prairies. But by origin he was an Anglo-Irish gentleman, born in 1839 and educated according to his station.

Brown joined the British Army and served in India as a subaltern in the First Battalion of the Eighth Regiment of Infantry. After a year he resigned his commission, and hearing of the fortunes that were being made in the gold fields, he reached British Columbia in time to take part in the rush to Cariboo in 1862. When he failed there as a prospector, he decided to find other ways to make the land support him and for two years wandered as a trapper through the mountains and plateaus of central British Columbia, building up a knowledge of the ways of the land that later would stand him in good stead.

Arriving at Boston Bar to buy stores in 1864, Brown heard of the discovery of gold at Wild Horse Creek in the Kootenay area of British Columbia. He went there, found that all the good claims had been staked, and enrolled as a constable in the police force organized by Chartres Brew. One of his assignments was to arrest a counterfeiter and organize a posse which rounded up the man's partners to appear in Judge Begbie's court. However, the only reward Brown got was a reduction in pay during one of the economy drives to which the fledgling government of British Columbia was periodically forced by the fluctuating economy of a colony based on mining, and he resigned to wander prospecting across the Rockies until he reached the Medicine Hat area. There he and his companion were attacked by Blackfoot and escaped with difficulty. Brown had an arrow in his back, and after pulling it out he rode for days to Fort Edmonton and then to Duck Creek, where he remained for a time with Gabriel Dumont's band of Métis hunters.

Going on to Fort Garry, Brown bought goods to set himself up as an Indian trader, and after wandering for a couple of years in the Canadian prairies, he moved down into

Dakota and became a pony express rider carrying United States mail until he was ambushed by the Sioux, who robbed and stripped him. He escaped by diving into a lake and hiding in the reed beds, afterwards walking naked to the nearest military post, where he decided to abandon his dangerous mail route and become a scout for the American army. Even this turned out to be perilous work, for he nearly died when he was lost in a blizzard for three days, but he carried on until 1874 as an irregular employee of the army, acting not only as scout but also as a mail carrier and interpreter, for by now he had acquired a knowledge of the principal Indian languages.

In 1874 he began to feel increasingly unsympathetic to the policy followed by the Americans in their Indian wars. He moved back into Canadian territory and built his first cabin at what was then called Kootenay Lake, in the eastern foothills of the Rockies; it later became Waterton Lake but retained its original name long enough for it to become attached to Brown as his nickname. Henceforward he was Kootenay Brown.

For some time he earned a living as a wandering commercial buffalo hunter, travelling with bands of Canadian Métis, working indiscriminately in Canadian and American territory, and playing his part in bringing an end to the old West by destroying the great herds; when the buffalo hunting grew thin, he hunted wolves as an alternative. He finally left American territory in 1877 after–in a fit of anger–he had killed a man named Louis Ell in Montana. He was acquitted of the charge but decided to move finally to Canada, where he stayed the rest of his life. He set up a store in partnership with a former whisky trader named Fred Kanouse on Lower Waterton Lake, where he traded with the Indians.

Later, Kootenay Brown served as a scout in the Rocky Mountain Rangers during the North-West Rebellion of 1885, but he took no part in the actual fighting against the Métis rebels. In later years, as travellers and settlers appeared in the southern Rockies, his services as a guide were often in demand, and his company was valued by the Fort Macleod ranchers for the tales he told about the gold rushes and the buffalo hunts and his encounters with Indians in the legendary days of the untamed prairies. In 1910 his role as a pioneer was recognized when the area in which his cabin stood was turned into Waterton National Park and he was appointed the first superintendent, which he remained until his death in 1916.

Peter Vasil'evich Verigin

Peter Verigin was the first leader of the Doukhobor sect in Canada; his followers called this man of massive presence Peter the Lordly. Peter, the son of a rich peasant, was born in 1859 at Slavyanka, a Doukhobor settlement in the Russian Caucasus. The Doukhobors are a Russian sect who reject the Orthodox church and regard God as immanent in all men, from which they deduce the need for pacificism, since to harm other men is to harm God. They live by an oral tradition called the Living Book, expressed in psalms and hymns which they sing with remarkable power, and they have accepted the religious authority of a series of leaders in whom the spirit of Christ is regarded as being incarnate. When Peter Verigin was born, the leader was a woman, Lukeria Kalmikova, and in his boyhood she trained him as her successor. However, when Lukeria died in 1886 the sect was divided over the question of the succession, and only one section – known as the Large Party – accepted Peter when the Doukhobors met early in 1887 to choose the new leader. He was immediately arrested and sent to exile in Siberia, not because a crime had been proved against him but because the Small Party had warned the tsarist authorities that he was plotting resistance.

It was not the first time the Doukhobors had been persecuted. In 1802 they were exiled to the Crimea, and in 1841 to the Caucasus. They had prospered in the Caucasus and their religious observance had grown lax. In Siberia, Peter Verigin began to think of calling his people back to the way of righteousness; and in the instructions he sent them he was greatly influenced by disciples of Leo Tolstoy, who were his fellow exiles. He told his followers to abstain from eating meat, to give up alcohol and tobacco, and finally, to burn all their arms and refuse military service. This they did in 1895 and immediately were subjected to a cruel persecution by the tsarist authorities. Leo Tolstoy was able to spread the news in the world press, and eventually the tsar was persuaded to allow the Doukhobors to leave Russia. The first party went to Cyprus, but the climate was unsatisfactory, and eventually, through the intervention of Prince Kropotkin[10] and Professor James Mavor of Toronto, arrangements were made for 7,500 to come to Canada.

They arrived in 1898 and 1899. Peter Verigin was not allowed to leave Siberia and join his people until 1902.

The Doukhobors settled in villages in Saskatchewan, under an understanding with the minister of the interior, Clifford Sifton, that they could own land communally without registering homesteads as individuals and that they need not take an oath of allegiance. At first everything went well and Verigin strengthened the communal organization, introducing flour mills and other industries, and centralizing purchasing. When Clifford Sifton resigned, the new minister reneged on the original understanding, insisting on individual registration of homesteads and an oath of allegiance. The Doukhobors refused, and most of the lands they had cleared and broken were confiscated and given to non-Doukhobor homesteaders.

This injustice merely fanned Doukhobor zeal, and six thousand members of the sect accompanied Peter Verigin when, in 1908, he took up options on land in British Columbia and created the Christian Community of Universal Brotherhood. It was the biggest intentional community in Canadian history, with thousands of acres of orchards and wheat lands, a jam factory, lumber mills and brick works, aimed at making the community as far as possible self-sufficient. Life was spartan, and men who worked outside had to turn their wages over to the common pool to pay off the debts the community carried. Even in British Columbia there was trouble with the authorities – over the registration of deaths and births, which Doukhobors did not think necessary, and over education, since Verigin and his followers considered that Canadian state education was aimed at encouraging militarism. There were also internal disputes. The radical Sons of Freedom appeared. Some Doukhobors broke away to become individual farmers or businessmen. But on the whole Peter Verigin controlled his community efficiently – if at times somewhat oppressively – and it seemed in good condition when he was killed in a still unexplained explosion on 29 October 1924, travelling on a train in the mountains near Grand Forks. Without his guiding hand it quickly disintegrated, and it vanished completely in 1938 when the creditors foreclosed.

Peter
Veregin.

Simon Gun-an-Noot

The most peaceful of all outlaws in Canadian history must have been Simon Gun-an-Noot, who in June 1906 vanished to avoid a charge of murder and for thirteen years evaded his pursuers without harming any of them as they hunted him through the wilderness of northern British Columbia. In the end he survived to live openly in the world as a free man.

Simon Gun-an-Noot was a Gitksan Indian from the Skeena River country, born early in the 1870s and generally known among whites as Simon Johnson. He was one of the Indians who seemed to bridge fairly well the gap between his own culture and that of the strangers who had filtered into the local frontier town of Hazelton to set up trading posts, packing outfits, and a Mounted Police detachment. Simon was a good trapper and hunter who during the winter travelled with his dog team far into the hinterland. He often went to Vancouver or Victoria to sell his furs, and with the proceeds he stocked a little store on the edge of the Indian village of Kispiox. Despite his commercial activities, he was something of a loner, living with his wife and child on a fairly isolated holding, where he had a log house and kept cows and horses.

On 18 June 1906 Simon called in at a tavern near Hazelton and quarrelled with a drunken half-breed packer and illegal whisky trader named Alex McIntosh. The next morning McIntosh was found shot dead, and so, in another spot, was a certain Max Leclair. There was nothing to link the murders except that they took place the same night, and nothing–except his quarrel with McIntosh–to link Simon with either. Nevertheless, a local coroner's jury returned a verdict accusing him of McIntosh's murder and recording strong suspicions that he was involved with his brother-in-law, Peter Hi-ma-dan, in Leclair's death.

Who committed the murders was never established, and if Simon and Peter immediately decamped, it was no sign of guilt; the jury's verdict had given them a taste of what they might expect from white justice, and they did not wait to continue the experiment. Instead, with their wives and children and Simon's father, Na-Gun, they set off into the wilderness around the headwaters of the Skeena, Nass, and Stikine rivers. All of them, even the women, were used to the rigours of hunting and knew the necessary skills. Simon, a physically tough man in his thirties, had been trapping in this country since boyhood, and in addition to his knowledge of the country, the party could draw on the contents of the caches he had established to provide for the winter hunting.

It was not one winter or one year that Simon Gun-an-Noot and his companions survived in the bush. There were thirteen years in all. Some members of the band died and other outlaws joined them. They survived partly through Simon Gun-an-Noot's wilderness skills but partly also because of the solidarity of the Indians of the Skeena. This was one of the last regions to be penetrated by white men; the Indians there never made a treaty, and in many areas they successfully resisted the encroachment of white hunters and loggers. For them Simon became a symbol of their own independence, and while he remained in the bush, wandering with his little company of friends and relatives from camp to camp, there were always Indians ready to sell his furs and buy him supplies. Usually there was a little surplus of cash which Simon put away until the day he would decide to re-enter the world and fight his case.

This he finally did in June 1919, when he appeared at the Mounted Police post in Hazelton with a lawyer who had become interested in his case. The trial took place in Vancouver and Simon Gun-an-Noot was acquitted. The scanty evidence in the case had evaporated as witnesses died or lost their memory, and Simon walked out of the court a free man. He had successfully evaded every expedition sent to track him down. Often he had followed his pursuers and could have ambushed them; he always refrained, and so far as we know he never killed a man.

Simon Gun-an-Noot died in 1933, when his heart failed as he was tending his trap line. He was buried in the depths of the wilderness that had so long hidden him from injustice.

John Rae

There was a certain appropriateness to the fact that the Canadian explorer, John Rae, should have found the clues that led to the solution of Sir John Franklin's fate, for Rae was the man who learnt and adapted the skills of survival in the Arctic of which Franklin and his men were so tragically unaware. Franklin went by ship, and Rae by small boat; Franklin depended on the supplies he himself transported into the Arctic, and Rae learnt to live – like the northern Indians and the Eskimo – off the land. Both were born outside Canada and its northland, but Franklin remained an alien until he died there, while Rae became naturalized by his very methods of dealing with the environment. After the 1850s it was Rae's style of exploration that became the model for Arctic journeys.

Like so many of the Hudson's Bay Company's employees, John Rae was an Orkneyman, born in 1813 near Stromness. In boyhood he became a skilful boatman and fisherman, skills that stood him in good stead during his later Arctic travels. He studied medicine in Edinburgh, and on qualifying in 1833, he was accepted as surgeon by the Hudson's Bay Company. In 1835 he became physician and clerk at Moose Factory and he continued in that post for ten years. He took to the country like a duck to water, spending his spare time wandering over the tundra and the northern woodland, trapping and shooting. He was said to be able to travel fifty miles a day on foot. The novelist, R.M. Ballantyne, remembered him as "full of animal spirits" with "a fine intellectual countenance."

It was perhaps for these qualities that in 1846 Sir George Simpson picked Rae to lead an expedition that would survey the unknown coast of the Arctic Sea from Boothia Isthmus to Fury and Hecla Strait. Rae gathered a company of thirteen men, a rough bunch of Orkneymen and half-breeds, Indians and Eskimos, all with skills that would be useful in the barren lands; he was resolved to make the wilderness feed him rather than starve him and he took only four months' supplies, intending to gain the rest by hunting and fishing. He was entirely successful, charting six hundred miles of hitherto unexplored coastline, proving that Boothia was a peninsula and not an island, as had been thought, and

coming back with a full team of healthy men.

By the time Rae returned from this first journey it had already become evident that Sir John Franklin and his expedition were lost, and the search for them was already under way. Sir John Richardson, a former associate of Franklin, undertook an overland quest, and Rae, with his recent experience, seemed an appropriate second-in-command. Together, in 1848-49, they followed the coastline from the Mackenzie to the Coppermine River but found no clues, and when Rae tried to reach Victoria Island by boat the ice frustrated him. Again, however, his method of travel proved more efficient in terms of mobility and more economical in men than the elaborate organization of the naval explorers.

Rae was now put in charge of the company's Mackenzie district, but in 1850 he was asked by the imperial government to make another search by boat and land. Setting out from Fort Confidence down the Coppermine River with two men and two dog sleighs, he stayed out the whole winter, travelled more than five thousand miles, discovered seven hundred miles of new coastline, including Cambridge Bay, and got to within forty miles of the place where Franklin's ships were abandoned. The only clues he found were two bits of wood that might have come from the ships.

Two years afterwards, in 1853, Rae set out on his fourth journey, with some Eskimo companions. He proved that King William Land was an island, spent the winter in an Eskimo camp on Repulse Bay, and in the spring heard of white men having starved to death in the area. Rae never found the bodies of the men, but he did acquire relics of Franklin which gave little doubt of his fate, and he gathered further accounts suggesting that before the end some of Franklin's men had turned cannibal.

Rae returned with his news in 1854 and was given the award of £10,000 for the discovery of Franklin's fate; it was left for others later to find the spots where the men had died. Rae was attacked for his suggestion that cannibalism took place, though Dickens defended him.

It was Rae's last Arctic journey. He retired from the Hudson's Bay Company in 1856 and after some years of surveying in the prairies moved to Hamilton and then to England, where he died in 1893. Not only had he discovered and mapped thousands of miles of Arctic coastline. He had revolutionized northern exploration by his method of travelling with groups of men adept at wilderness skills and small enough in number to live off the land.

Robert Campbell

Like John Rae, Robert Campbell carried on into the mid-nineteenth century the tradition of exploration that one associates with earlier fur traders like Samuel Hearne and Alexander Mackenzie, David Thompson and Simon Fraser. But while Rae's most important explorations were directed towards the shores of the Arctic Sea, Campbell's travels were almost entirely by inland water and principally in and around the area which is now the Yukon Territory.

Campbell was born in 1808, son of a Perthshire sheep farmer, and joined the Hudson's Bay Company's service in 1831. Because of his sheep-herding experience, he was first assigned to an experimental sheep farm which the company had established in the Red River Settlement, and his first task was to travel down through Indian territory to Kentucky, where he bought the 1,475 sheep needed to stock the farm. The drive back was disastrous; the sheep succumbed to various infections on the way, and by the time Campbell reached Red River only 250 of them survived; the idea of the farm was abandoned, leaving Campbell free to enter the fur trade proper.

In 1835 he was sent to Fort Liard in the Mackenzie district and began his explorations of the region. Two years later he established a post at Dease Lake in what is now British Columbia and discovered the source of the Stikine River, down which he travelled in the hope of inducing the Indians who lived along it to trade with his company rather than with the Russians in Alaska. Abandoning the Dease Lake post in 1839 because of the lack of game to feed his men, Campbell took over Fort Halkett at the junction of the Smith and Liard rivers. In 1840 he travelled up the north branch of the Liard and discovered Frances Lake, where in 1843 he built the first trading post in the Yukon region. He explored the Pelly, built Fort Selkirk on its banks in 1848, and in 1851, on a journey which took him via the Porcupine River to the Mackenzie, established that the Pelly was the upper course of the Yukon. On the way he found stone age Indians who had never heard of white men and were unaware of the uses of metal.

Trading in the Yukon area, the Hudson's Bay Company became rivals of the powerful Tlingit peoples of the Alaskan coast, who served as middlemen between the Russian-American Company and the interior tribes. One group of Tlingit, the Chilkat, marched inland and burned down Fort Selkirk, without harming Campbell or the other residents. It was after this disaster that Campbell made his first trip outside the North West in twenty years, when he travelled in winter, mostly on snowshoes, three thousand miles to the Hudson's Bay headquarters at Lachine in Quebec.

He returned in 1854 to take charge of Fort Liard and in 1856 was appointed chief trader in charge of Athabasca, stationed at Fort Chipewyan. There in 1860 he married Eleanora Sterling, who had travelled all the way from Scotland to join him, and established a family. Campbell rose to the rank of chief factor in 1867, but in 1871 he was dismissed from the company's service because he persisted in disregarding the regulations concerning the routes by which furs must be transported. Perhaps it was a good time to go, for Canada had taken over the territorial domains of the Hudson's Bay Company, and the kind of fur trade in which Campbell and his kind had been so venturesome and had explored so much new territory was already nearing its end.

Yet, though he was now sixty-three, Campbell did not retire into inactivity. Returning to the farming life he had abandoned almost forty years before, he acquired a ranch in the wooded hill country of Riding Mountain in Manitoba, and there he lived until his death in 1894, working in his last years on an autobiography that has never been published.

William Carpenter Bompas

For four decades Bishop Bompas was one of the best-known figures of the Canadian North, travelling thousands of miles over that taxing country in the days when dog sleighs in winter and canoes in the brief summer were the only means of transport. There were dozens of other priests, Oblate Catholics as well as Anglicans, whose record was probably as arduous as that of Bompas, and he would have been the last man to claim any more credit than the rest, for he had great humility, but he caught the public imagination of his times, and his record serves as an example of what it meant to be a missionary priest in the Canadian North before the airplane and the snowmobile simplified arctic and subarctic travel.

Bompas was an Englishman, born in London in 1834. He took rather a long time deciding on his vocation, and not until 1865, at the age of thirty-one, was he ordained. Having heard that a sick priest on the Yukon needed relieving, Bompas volunteered for the task, but at the end of his long journey he found the man already recovered, and he himself was assigned to Fort Simpson on the Mackenzie River.

It was a vast parish, many thousands of square miles in extent, and the potential parishioners included not only fur traders but also Indians of several tribes, and Eskimos. For a Londoner with no experience of the wilderness, Bompas showed himself physically and mentally extremely adaptable, travelling untiringly from camp to camp, acting at times the roles of doctor and teacher as well as priest, and patiently learning the languages of the people he visited and recording them, so that he prepared a *Beaver Primer* in the early days of his mission and a *Cree Primer* later on. On the way he encountered plenty of adventures, not all of which were the normal hazards of travel over barren lands and down rapid-strewn rivers. Sometimes he would meet people who had never seen white men before, and at least once he was threatened with death by a band of Eskimo who thought he would bring them ill fortune.

It soon became obvious to the church in England, which controlled the missions, that the Far North was a diocese in itself, and when they wanted to find a suitable man for the see, Bishop Machray of Rupert's Land recommended Bompas for his knowledge and zeal.

Bompas heard of his appointment on a trip he was making down the Peel River to the Yukon, hundreds of miles from his base at Fort Simpson, and he set out immediately, taking several months in those days before railway or even roads existed in the West, to travel the two thousand miles to Winnipeg. When he got there he pleaded with Machray to withdraw the promotion. He had no ambitions for ecclesiastical preferment; all he wanted was to carry on his work among the Indian peoples he had come to love. Machray refused to intervene, since he regarded Bompas as the only possible candidate, and sent him to England. There his protests were equally unavailing and he was duly consecrated by the Archbishop of Canterbury as first bishop of Athabasca.

His elevation did not really make very much difference to Bompas. Other priests came into the territory whom he had to advise and oversee. There were churches to be founded, and schools as well in a region where education depended on the missionaries. But Bompas continued his journeys through the tundra and the northern woodlands, closely observing the manners and customs of the Indians and also the natural history of the region. Out of these observations he wrote two books still worth reading for their vignettes of the Canadian North before Canadians became aware of it: *History of the Diocese of Mackenzie River* (1888) and *Northern Lights on the Bible* (1893).

The diocese of Athabasca was a vast region, covering the present Northwest and Yukon territories and the northern parts of the prairie provinces, and in 1884 Bompas divided the territory, keeping the northern half, which became the diocese of Mackenzie River. By 1891 a new element appeared in the country. The first gold miners began to work on the Yukon, and this influx of white men created problems which led Bompas to a further subdivision; he created a diocese of Selkirk, with its headquarters at Cariboo Crossing, and moved there himself so that during the Klondike rush he dealt with the large masses of white transients as well as the scattered nomad Indians he knew so well. Bompas was equal to the task, became popular among the prospectors, and remained bishop of Selkirk until he died in 1906 at Cariboo Crossing in the North that was now a home he never wished to leave.

Wilfred Thomason Grenfell

Like Norman Bethune in recent years, Wilfred Thomason Grenfell was a doctor who caught the world's imagination with something resembling Bethune's combination of devotion, hard work, courage, and (in earnest of the fact that we are all human and therefore fallible) more than a little vanity. The monument to Grenfell's devotion–in a region that only became Canadian in 1949–is immense, for he literally changed the character of life in Labrador and western Newfoundland.

Wilfred Grenfell was born near Chester in England in 1865, received an elite education at Marlborough College, studied for four years at the London Hospital, was given his licence to practise medicine in 1886, and went on to take his M.D. at Oxford in 1889. Already, as a student, he had fallen under the influence of the late Victorian popular evangelist, Dwight Moody, and had organized a Christian sports club in the slums of the East End of London in the hope of lessening the workers' dependence on drink. But his real interest lay in the deep sea fishermen whose perilous life had stirred his imagination during his Cheshire childhood, and in 1890 he rejected the idea of an ordinary practice to become medical officer to the Mission to Deep Sea Fishermen in the North Atlantic.

Since many English vessels fished the banks of Newfoundland, the mission's interest extended into those waters, and its members soon became aware of the poor conditions under which the Labrador and Newfoundland fishermen lived and worked. In 1892 Grenfell was sent out on an investigatory journey. He found the condition of the resident fishermen of Labrador particularly bad. They were half-starved, they had virtually no medical assistance, and they had little or no religious life. When Grenfell returned to England the Labrador Mission was founded, and Grenfell became its superintendent, going back in 1893 to devote the rest of his life to Labrador and Newfoundland.

Grenfell concentrated on practicalities rather than pieties and set about filling the immediate physical needs of Labrador people, which were better medical facilities and an improvement in the way and level of life, without which medical aid would be no more than a palliative. He established the first hospital, at Battle Harbour, in 1893, and over the years he provided four more hospitals, as well as seven nursing stations and three orphanages.

But he also tried to attack the evils of the system that kept the fishermen in poverty and in a kind of bondage. The merchants operated a truck system by which they supplied a fisherman or trapper with the goods and equipment he needed for his season's work, in exchange for which he undertook to barter his catch at their stores. Usually the fishermen were in debt, and the merchants encouraged them to increase that debt by accepting alcohol. Thus poverty and drink–in Labrador–went together.

Grenfell sought to end the dependence on the merchants by establishing co-operatives, the first of which was founded in 1905, and he also set up agricultural centres to provide locally grown food, and industrial centres to provide alternative means of income. He sponsored the introduction of reindeer into Newfoundland in 1907. He established social clubs for seamen and fishermen. The result was a network of benevolent institutions stretching along the Labrador coast and the opposite coast of Newfoundland, which brought a gradual but steady improvement in the lives of the fishermen and other inhabitants.

Every year Grenfell made an arduous voyage of inspection along the Labrador coast, but he also found time to do an extraordinary amount of writing, and much of the money for his mission was raised by the sale of his very popular books, which included not only accounts of the mission's work but also novels and short stories that still have an interest for their details of Labrador life two generations ago, and two volumes of autobiography, *A Labrador Doctor* (1919) and *Forty Years for Labrador* (1932). Grenfell finally retired from his work in 1935 but continued to lecture, almost to his death in 1940, to raise funds for the International Grenfell Foundation that carried on his work.

Our 'reciprocity' is subject to no
amendments. Xmas.1911.
To W. Mackenzie King from Wilfred Grenfell

Joseph-Elzéar Bernier

Most of the maritime explorers of Canada's shores and waters were British naval officers. One of the few Canadians who distinguished themselves in this field was Joseph-Elzéar Bernier, whose voyages in the early part of this century effectively asserted for the first time Canada's claim to the great Arctic archipelago, of which sovereignty had been transferred to the dominion by Britain in 1881.

Bernier was born at L'Islet in Quebec on New Year's Day 1852 and went to sea with his father, Captain Thomas Bernier, when he was twelve; at the age of seventeen he was already the master of a brigantine. For years he sailed the Atlantic, making 269 crossings in all, and became an expert and resourceful seaman, but it was the still unexplored regions of the Arctic that haunted his mind, and he longed for the opportunity to sail among the unknown white islands.

When he had tired of navigating ships on the Atlantic route, Bernier took up life on shore for a period. From 1887 to 1893 he was dockmaster of the Lorne graving dock at Lauzon, for a period he managed the Dominion Ice Company, and then he served as governor of the prison in Quebec. But all through these land-bound years he made plans to explore the Arctic, and he developed the sector theory of Arctic sovereignty, which holds that a country facing the North Pole should possess the seas and islands within a triangle whose base is its northern coast and whose sides are longitudinal lines from each end of the base with the pole as apex.

Bernier spent several years trying to persuade the Canadian government to send him on an exploration voyage into the Arctic archipelago. When that seemed to fail, he went on lecture tours in the vain attempt to raise the money for outfitting a private expedition. Finally, in 1904, he was appointed captain of the *Arctic*, a three-masted steamer which the Department of Marine and Fisheries had acquired for Arctic patrols. The voyage he made was with a patrol commanded by Major Moodie of the Royal North-West Mounted Police, but on later voyages Bernier commanded both the vessel and the patrol. By 1910 he had discovered most of the Canadian islands up to the 80th parallel and left documents of possession on them. But he

was not content with such formal gestures. Each time he returned south he urged on the government and the public the importance of the North to Canada and the need to take more than nominal possession, and his urgings were undoubtedly responsible for an increase in the Mounted Police posts scattered through the Arctic archipelago. In 1910 he attempted the North-West Passage, but he was frustrated by the massive ice floes which barred his westward access off Melville Island.

One of his men having reported the presence of gold on Baffin Island in 1910, Bernier left the government service and led two private expeditions to the island on the *Minnie Maud* between 1910 and 1913; no gold was found, but much of Baffin Island and Melville Peninsula were explored and charted for the first time. Bernier then returned to the government service and continued his explorations of the Arctic islands until 1925. He carried out in all twelve voyages, and at the age of seventy-three was still discovering uncharted territory. At the age of seventy-five he returned to more familiar waters and plotted the route through Hudson's Bay by which grain ships could travel in the summer months, carrying grain from Churchill to the ports of Europe.

Bernier died in 1934 at Lévis, leaving his autobiography, *Master Mariner and Arctic Explorer*, to be published after his death, in 1939.

Vilhjalmur Stefansson

Vilhjalmur Stefansson carried to its logical conclusion John Rae's method of exploration by living off the land, since he showed that the best way to understand the Canadian Arctic in all its aspects was not merely to live by fishing and hunting game but actually to share the lives of the Eskimo themselves, whose hunting culture was extraordinarily well adapted to its special environment.

Stefansson was born in the Icelandic settlement of Gimli on Lake Winnipeg in 1879. Two years later his family moved to North Dakota, and Stefansson was educated at the University of North Dakota and then at Harvard, later going on to his ancestral country of Iceland to study anthropology. His first opportunity for field work occurred when he was appointed anthropologist to the Anglo-American Arctic expedition led by Leffingwell and Mikkelson.

Stefansson arranged to meet the expedition at Herschel Island in the Beaufort Sea, but when he arrived there he found that it had been trapped by the ice at Flaxman Island off the coast of Alaska, about two hundred miles away, and could not keep the rendezvous. He turned disappointment into opportunity by travelling and living with the Eskimo of Herschel Island and the neighbouring coast. When the winter ended, Stefansson made his way to Flaxman Island, only to discover that the expedition was about to return to the United States. He decided to stay on among the Eskimo and finally made his way out of the North by crossing the mountains from the Mackenzie Valley and making his way to Fort Yukon. The year among the Eskimo had convinced him that Europeans could live in the Arctic for long periods by adopting the native way of life.

Accordingly, in 1908 he set out with the Canadian zoologist, Rudolph M. Anderson, to travel for an extended period among the Eskimo of Coronation Gulf and the surrounding islands. In all, he spent four years living among these peoples and becoming expert in the hunting of seal, polar bear, and the caribou of the barren land. It was during this expedition that he discovered the famous Copper (or "blond") Eskimo of Victoria Island; he was convinced they were descended from the Norsemen who had colonized Greenland. In *My Life with the Eskimo* (1913) and later in *Hunters of the Great North* (1922), Stefansson described the life of the Eskimo, as he observed it on these expeditions, with an intimacy unprecedented in previous accounts of the Canadian North.

In 1913 Stefansson returned on an expedition organized by the Canadian government to locate hitherto undiscovered islands in the Arctic archipelago. The expedition lasted until 1918. It began with an accident that might have been fatal without Stefansson's experience in Arctic living, for his ship, the *Karluk*, was crushed in the ice and sank in the Siberian Sea. Stefansson left Anderson, again his companion, to survey the northern coast between Alaska and Coronation Gulf. He himself set off with two companions across the ice to Banks Island and then explored the seas northeast of Prince Patrick Island, discovering Borden, Brock, Meighen, and Loughheed islands, the last uncharted territories of the north. In *The Friendly Arctic* (1921) Stefansson described this expedition, which came to an end when he was stricken with typhoid fever on Herschel Island.

It was his last voyage, but for the rest of his life–which extended more than forty years until his death in 1962–he followed his interest in the Far North, writing books on exploration and an autobiography, *Discovery*, which appeared after his death, in 1964.

Wop May

Around Wilfrid Reid May, as around all the famous air aces, there has always hung the ambiguous aura of daring and death; he risked much and killed often, and there was an especially macabre touch to his literally infantile nickname of "Wop," which appears to have been an adult interpretation of a little girl playmate's attempt to say "Wilfrid," and which clung incongruously to him until his death.

Wop May was born in Carberry, Manitoba, not long before the turn of the century, in time to enlist in the Canadian forces in 1916. He served first in the infantry, fighting the slogging muddy battles of Flanders until he decided to join the Royal Flying Corps. Chance then led him to a dramatic encounter with history. On 21 April 1918 he flew on his first combat flight, and the adversary who sighted him was the celebrated Red Baron, Freiherr Manfred von Richthofen, who had destroyed one Belgian and seventy-nine British planes over the trenches of Picardy. May's guns jammed when von Richthofen attacked, and he turned in flight, with the Red Baron hot in pursuit. But this time there was another Canadian pilot, A. Roy Brown, flying close enough to attack the Red Baron on the flank, and he gunned von Richthofen to the earth. Wop May went on to imitate the Red Baron's record, and before the war ended he had brought down eighteen German planes.

May was one of the aces who survived, with the problem ahead of adjusting to a normal world after the high conflicts of the skies. Canada had in those days a role ready-made for such potential misfits – the unexplored and untravelled northland. Wop May, returning from the wars in 1919, set up his own enterprise, May Airplanes Limited in Edmonton, and for a while he earned a living by barnstorming trick flights, as when he flew ten feet above an Edmonton baseball diamond to allow the mayor to deliver the first ball in history to be pitched from the air.

Slowly the North opened up, and May followed the receding frontiers as a bush pilot, teaching other men his skills, but also using them himself. He founded Commercial Airways in partnership with Vic Horner, another air ace, and in January 1929 the two men flew in through a blizzard to Fort Vermilion, the first winter flight of its kind, to deliver an antitoxin that saved the community from an epidemic. In December of the same year May made communications history with the first mail flight up the Mackenzie Valley to Aklavik. In 1930 he made the first nonstop flight from Edmonton to Winnipeg; his average speed was a mere 112 miles an hour!

Perhaps May's most sensational assignment, in terms of the Canadian myth of the North, occurred in 1932 when Albert Johnson, the so-called Mad Trapper of Rat River, was being hunted for the killing of a Mounted Policeman. May ferried in supplies, scanned the tundra from the air until Johnson was located, and then, after the Mad Trapper was killed in the final gunfight, he flew back a dangerously wounded constable and saved his life.

History caught up on Wop May, as it did on most of the bush pilots who did not die in flight. He founded Canadian Airways Limited in 1936, but the firm was absorbed by Canadian Pacific Airlines in 1942, and May ended prosaically as manager of CP Air's Calgary repair depot. The modern corporation had sucked into its system the daring and enterprise of the individualist pioneers. Perhaps, in May's last years, his greatest satisfaction came from organizing first aid crews during World War II to be dropped by parachute when pilots crashed in the northern wilderness. He died in 1952.

Henry Asbjorn Larsen

Above the beach at English Bay in Vancouver, next to the Maritime Museum, stands an A-shaped structure of wood and glass, and within it, protected from the elements it once dramatically defied, is preserved a sturdy, schooner-rigged wooden ship, so small and snub-prowed that its history at first sight seems incredible. For this is the *St. Roch*, the second ship to sail the legendary North-West Passage, the first to sail it both ways, the first to sail it in a single season.

The earliest of all conquests of the North-West Passage was made by the Norwegian, Roald Amundsen, and it took him three years, from 1903 to 1906, to nose his ship, the *Gjoa*, through the complex of frozen straits, gulfs, and channels between Hudson Strait and the Beaufort Sea. After Amundsen's achievement more than thirty years elapsed before another captain successfully challenged the passage; then it was a fellow countryman, at least by birth, for Henry Asbjorn Larsen was born in Norway in 1899 near the mouth of Oslo Fjord.

Even as a boy, Henry Larsen was fascinated by the accounts he read of the great polar explorers, especially Amundsen, Nansen, and the great Icelandic Canadian, Vilhjalmur Stefansson. There were seamen in Larsen's family, as in most Norwegian families, and when he was fifteen he sailed on a lumber ship captained by his uncle. He worked on a number of sailing ships through World War I, and then in 1919 signed on his first steamer, the *Vinstra*, as boatswain. The next year he graduated from navigation school and then spent two years of compulsory service in the Norwegian navy. Afterwards he sailed as mate on several freighters. It was not until 1924 that he reached the Arctic seas on a two-masted schooner, *The Maid of Orleans*, later renamed *The Old Maid*. He spent two years in the Arctic, where he encountered the Eskimo, whom he liked at first sight, and the RCMP. He was confirmed in his desire to become an Arctic explorer, and he formed a shrewd opinion that one way to do it was –strangely enough– by becoming a Mounted Policeman.

Accordingly, in 1927 Larsen took out Canadian citizenship and in 1928 he joined the RCMP, which needed a navigator for its new patrol ship, the *St. Roch*, built in the shipyards of North Vancouver and about to be launched. So the *St. Roch* sailed with Henry Larsen as master, though, such being the conventions of RCMP promotion, he ranked as a mere constable.

The first years of the *St. Roch*'s service, and Larsen's as well, were relatively uneventful. For eleven years he followed the routine of patrolling the western Arctic, supplying the northern outposts and providing a floating detachment available for emergency service. Larsen was certainly voyaging constantly in his beloved Arctic, but the opportunity did not present itself for the feats of exploration he longed to achieve until the outbreak of World War II. Then the Canadian government again became concerned to assert its sovereignty over the Arctic seas, and it was decided that the one way to do so would be to send a Canadian ship through the North-West Passage.

Larsen – now promoted to the rank of sergeant – was ordered to leave from Vancouver with supplies for eighteen months, to visit the northern outposts, and then to attempt sailing the *St. Roch* through the passage from west to east, the opposite direction to Amundsen's voyage, with the aim of reaching Halifax. The *St. Roch* sailed on 21 June 1940. Conditions were bad and the ship had to spend two winters in the ice before it reached Halifax in the autumn of 1942. Then it was decided to fit the *St. Roch* with a more powerful engine for the return trip, but owing to the wartime commitments of the Halifax shipyards, this could not be done in time for a return in 1943. In July 1944 the ship was finally ready to sail; and this time, taking a more northerly route than Amundsen's, through Lancaster Sound and Barrow Strait, and encountering unusually favourable ice conditions, it reached Vancouver in an amazing eighty-six days.

Larsen stayed with the RCMP until 1961, making his slow way upward to the rank of superintendent, which he reached in 1953. He retired in 1961 and died in Vancouver in 1964, the last of the great Arctic travellers.

Susanna Moodie

Susanna Moodie was one of the brilliant children of the London merchant, Thomas Strickland, who in the manner of Jane Austen's businessmen had become a country squire, owner of Reydon Hall at Bungay in Suffolk. One of her sisters, Agnes Strickland, became a popular biographer in Victorian England. Another was the Canadian writer, Catharine Parr Traill, whose biography follows. Her brother, Samuel Strickland, was a vivid memoirist of Upper Canadian pioneer life. Indeed, if it were not for the three Stricklands–Susanna, Catharine, and Samuel–our knowledge of how Canadians lived in the earlier nineteenth century would be far narrower and less detailed than it is.

Susanna Strickland and her sisters had already begun to write in the amateurish way of pre-Victorian young ladies when after their father's death they discovered that their literary efforts could contribute, with no breach of the genteel rules of behaviour, to the finances of an impoverished family. Susanna had a sharp and somewhat ironic mind, and the half-pay officer she married in 1831, Lieutenant John Moodie of the Fusiliers, was a man of intellectual rather than practical bent. In 1832, attracted by offers of land for former officers in Upper Canada, they set off across the Atlantic in a sailing boat that lay becalmed for weeks off Newfoundland. Samuel Strickland, Susanna's brother, had already gone to Upper Canada in 1825 in the employ of the Canada Company.

Susanna and her husband first settled on a farm near Cobourg, but Moodie's ineptness in practical matters, and Susanna's conventional rigidities, made them a ready prey for their neighbours, who resented Susanna's English airs and graces. Two years later they were glad to move to the real backwoods in Douro Township, north of Peterborough, where Samuel Strickland and the Traills were already settled. Here they cleared land and established a farm successfully, though they never became reconciled to pioneer life. It was something of a relief when after serving against William Lyon Mackenzie's rebels in 1837, Moodie was rewarded with the appointment of sheriff of Hastings County. In 1839 he and Susanna moved to Belleville, and in this Loyalist town, where some at least of the British gentilities

had been reconstructed, they lived until John Moodie's death in 1869. Then Susanna moved to Toronto, where she died in 1885.

Susanna Moodie's activities as a writer in Canada first became evident in the *Literary Garland and British North America Magazine*, the most important pre-Confederation Canadian literary journal, which began publication in Montreal in 1838 and printed the works of the Moodies, Catharine Parr Traill, Anna Jameson,[11] John Richardson, and most of the other contemporary writers of any significance. From 1839 to 1851, Susanna wrote regularly for the *Garland*, contributing serial fiction, short stories and verse, and some of the chapters of her best-known book, *Roughing It in the Bush*, which rather harshly described her adventures at Cobourg and in Douro Township, and appeared in 1852. A somewhat softer view of Canadian life was advanced in *Life in the Clearings*, which appeared in the following year.

Susanna Moodie contributed to the short-lived Belleville *Victoria Magazine* (1847-48) and published a number of novels, some sensational and some didactic, which appeared before she became silent as a writer in the mid-1860s. None of them is of lasting interest, and Susanna Moodie owes the deep mark she had made on the Canadian imagination solely to her two pioneer narratives, *Roughing It in the Bush* and *Life in the Clearings*, which not only provide sharp documentary glimpses of Upper Canadian life in the 1830s and 1840s, but also, less deliberately, offer us invaluable character sketches of representatives of at least one of the classic types of early Canadian, the refugees from the Napoleonic wars.

Catharine Parr Traill

Catharine Parr Traill, Susanna Moodie's elder sister, was born in 1802, before the Strickland family left London for Bungay. She was the first of the Stricklands to take to writing and to achieve publication. Her book of stories for children, *The Blind Highland Piper*, was published in 1818 when she was barely sixteen, and by the time she was twenty she had published a children's story whose popularity long outlasted her departure from England: *Little Downy, or, The History of a Field Mouse: A Moral Tale*.

Little Downy projected an interest in natural history which lasted through Catharine Parr Strickland's life and which stood her in good stead when in 1832, after her marriage to Lieutenant Thomas Traill, an officer on half-pay, she immediately set out for Upper Canada.

After a harrowing journey, during which Catharine contracted cholera in Toronto and barely survived, the Traills reached Cobourg a week before the Moodies (who had gone by a different boat) and immediately set out to join Samuel Strickland in Douro County. It was a lucky decision, for it saved them the dispiriting experiences with unsympathetic neighbours that the Moodies endured.

Apart from that, Catharine was of a more adaptable, practical and inquiring nature than Susanna, and her first book, compiled from letters written home to England, and published in 1835 as *The Backwoods of Canada*, is a very wise and engaging book, in no way understressing the hardships genteel English people may encounter in the backwoods areas, but filled with information about how to make life comfortable, which gives an invaluable picture of pioneer Upper Canada. A sequel, *The Female Emigrant's Guide* (1855) was more deliberately practical in intent but is equally fascinating as a document of our social history.

Like her sister, Catharine Parr Traill contributed to the *Literary Garland* and wrote more children's stories after she reached Canada, including *The Canadian Crusoes* (1852) and *Lady Mary and Her Nurse: A Peep into the Canadian Forest* (1856). But she found her great role as a popular naturalist, identifying and describing the plants of Upper Canada. *Rambles in the Canadian Forest* appeared in 1859, *Canadian Wild Flowers* in 1869, and her most ambitious work, *Studies of Plant Life in Canada; or Gleanings from Forest, Lake, and Plain*, in 1885. The last two books, illustrated by very fine lithographs of paintings by her niece Agnes FitzGibbon (Susanna Moodie's daughter), are classics of Canadian botany. Unlike her sister Susanna, Catharine Parr Traill continued writing almost to the end of her very long life, and in her last decade two final volumes of gleanings from her work appeared: *Pearls and Pebbles: or The Notes of an Old Naturalist* (1894) and *Cot and Cradle Stories* (1895), both edited by Mary Agnes FitzGibbon, who was Catharine's grandniece and also the granddaughter of the James FitzGibbon to whom Laura Secord delivered her historic message in 1813; Upper Canada was then a small world and its historic figures were constantly intermingling. She died at Lakefield, Ontario, in 1899.

Like Susanna Moodie's books, Catharine Parr Traill's narratives of life in Canada before Confederation survive because of their continuing vitality on a number of levels: as landscapes of a country at the point of losing its pristine wildness; as records of the pioneer way of life told by the kind of people who experience it most painfully yet are able to tell it most vividly; and as –with the works of John Richardson and Anna Jameson and a very few other writers–the beginnings of what would in the end become our distinctive Canadian literature.

Charles Mair

Charles Mair, one of the few Canadian poets to be propelled into the midst of dramatic historical events, was born in 1838, an Upper Canadian, and at heart he remained one for the rest of his long life. He came from Lanark, a small town near Ottawa where his family was engaged in lumbering. He spent two periods at Queen's University, studying for a medical degree which he never took. During his student years he began to write poetry and in 1868 published *Dreamland and Other Poems*, which attracted a favourable attention that was not entirely unjustified, since–despite a general sentimentality of approach–Mair did perceive and render natural scenes with a vivid directness unusual among early Canadian poets.

In 1868 Mair went to Ottawa as a journalist; there he met Captain George T. Denison and a number of other young men who combined imperialist and nationalist sentiments and founded the Canada First movement. One of the aims of Canada First was to establish the control over the North West which its members regarded as essential for a strong Canada, and they were deeply interested in developments on the Red River at the end of the 1860s. Already, in 1868, in anticipation of taking over Rupert's Land from the Hudson's Bay Company, the Canadian government began building a road from Lake Superior to the Red River, and Mair obtained employment as paymaster for the operation. At the same time he served as correspondent for the Toronto *Globe* and made himself so unpopular by his published remarks about Red River women that one of them horse-whipped him publicly. Mair's misfortunes did not end with this adventure. He became closely associated with Dr. John Schultz, leader of the extreme Canadian faction on the Red River, whose niece he married, and when the discontented Métis established their provisional government over the territory in 1869, Mair was one of those who, under Schultz, offered armed resistance. He was captured by the Métis militia and threatened by Riel with execution, but he escaped and found his way through the United States back to Ontario, where he and Schultz embarked on an inflammatory propaganda among the Orangemen to prevent any compromise between the dominion government and Riel.

After the rebellion, Mair returned to the North West and set up a general store at Portage la Prairie. In 1878, he moved on to the Saskatchewan country, settling in Prince Albert where he speculated in real estate. As events built up towards the North-West Rebellion, Mair developed a sympathy for the Métis sense of grievance and warned Sir John A. Macdonald of the consequences of continued failure to satisfy them. Seeing that his warnings were unheeded, he left Prince Albert in 1884, though in 1885 he served in General Middleton's expedition, which suppressed the rebellion. Afterwards he returned to Prince Albert and in 1886 published his second important work, the massive verse play called *Tecumseh*, dealing with the War of 1812 and presenting the Indian leader, whose name it bears, as a symbol of Canadian defiance of American domination. It was a cumbersome work, but here and there the experiences of Mair's years in the West shone through in splendid passages describing the prairies before the settlers and the railway came.

Like the Indians and the Métis, Mair himself became something of an Ishmael in the new West, trading as far as Kamloops and never succeeding, until in 1898, when he was sixty, Clifford Sifton found him a post in the immigration service. There Mair remained for the next twenty-three years, retiring at the age of eighty-three with still six years of living ahead. The one event of moment in this long final career was the journey Mair made in 1899 as one of the party under David Laird which negotiated the treaty with the Indians of the Peace and Mackenzie rivers.

Mair's literary achievements were slight in quantity and uneven in quality, but they are important in the record of Canadian writing, most of all because Mair was one of the first poets to see Canada as a man who belonged to the land, a native in feeling as well as birth, rather than, like most of his contemporaries, as a colonial imprisoned in his garrison society.

Charles G. D. Roberts

Charles George Douglas Roberts was the first Canadian poet with any claim to real originality or to an importance in the wider world of English-speaking literatures. There were several kinds of appropriateness to this fact; Roberts came from a Loyalist clan that had links with both Oxford and New England, and he was born in the Atlantic region of Canada which provided the first Canadian literature in English and, indeed, in French as well, if we remember seventeenth century Marc Lescarbot at Port Royal.

Charles G.D. Roberts was born near Fredericton in 1860, the son of Canon George Goodridge Roberts. His brother, Theodore Goodridge Roberts, was a poet of minor stature, and his cousin was Bliss Carman. Roberts himself combined, as many Canadians have since done, the vocation of poetry with the occupation of teaching. He taught in a small school in Chatham, was made principal of the York Street school in Fredericton in his early twenties and then, after a short unhappy stint editing the *Week* for Goldwin Smith in Toronto, became at the age of twenty-five professor of English at King's College in Windsor, Nova Scotia, where he remained until 1895. At this point he abandoned teaching for good.

By this time Roberts had already published several books, including his most important collections of poems. *Orion, and Other Poems*, published in 1880, had shown that Canada had a poet as capable as any English versifier in the traditional tones and forms, and it made Roberts something of a leader among the younger men who were now emerging and who later became known as the Confederation Poets: Archibald Lampman, Duncan Campbell Scott, and the poet's cousin, Bliss Carman. The other two early books of verse, *In Divers Tones* (1886), which included the famous "The Tantramar Revisited," and *Songs of the Common Day* (1893), were important in a different way. Here Roberts was applying his highly developed techniques to present for the first time a vision of the Canadian landscape and Canadian country life seen as they were, and not–as in the work of most earlier Canadian writers–as modified English settings. With Roberts and his contemporaries, Canadian poetry began to move away from colonialism.

Liberated from teaching, Roberts set out to follow the calling of full-time professional writer, embarking on fiction, history, and miscellaneous journalism to provide the living that allowed him to write poetry. He moved to New York in 1897, stayed there a decade, and then spent four years wandering abroad before he settled in England in 1911. When World War I began in 1914 he was already fifty-four and too old for active service, but he was accepted for training functions; he transferred from the British to the Canadian forces, and eventually, having reached the rank of major, he was taken out of ordinary military activities to write part of the official Canadian history of the war. After the war he remained in England until 1925, when he returned to Canada and lived in Toronto until his death in 1943.

Roberts's output in these years was voluminous, including more than twenty collections of stories about wild animals, as well as historical novels and a number of romantic works–like *The Heart of the Ancient Wood* (1900) and *In the Morning of Time* (1919)– concerning the efforts of men to reconcile themselves with the world of nature. Such books today read like attempts, unsuccessful because of their sentimentality, to anticipate very modern ecological concerns by means of outdated fictional forms.

Among Roberts's prose it is only the best of his stories about wild animals that are likely to survive, particularly those in such volumes as *Kindred of the Wild* (1902), *The Watchers of the Trails* (1904), and *Neighbours Unknown* (1911), largely because they give an inward authenticity to the lives of animals rather than portraying them as human beings in pelts. Roberts was a pioneer in this peculiarly Canadian genre, as he was in the writing of poetry contemporary in intent and sometimes in achievement.

Archibald Lampman

There was a Keatsian quality not only to the poetry but also to the life of Archibald Lampman, for while the other three Confederation Poets lived long lives, Lampman died early, at the age of thirty-eight. Yet there was time enough for him to develop a strongly individual voice, and Lampman's position among Canadian poets has risen in recent years, largely because his misgivings about the society of his time arouse sympathetic echoes in modern minds.

In external terms, Lampman's life was remarkably uneventful, largely owing to chronic ill health, which he often laughed off as "hypochondria" but which culminated in the heart disease that caused his early death. He was born in 1861—the son of an Anglican clergyman—in the village of Morpeth in western Ontario. When he was six his parents moved into the Rice Lake district, and he was educated at Cobourg and Port Hope, finally going on to Trinity College in Toronto, where he graduated in 1882.

It was while he was still an undergraduate that the publication of Charles G.D. Roberts's *Orion* (1880) convinced Lampman that at last the time had come when Canadians could write poetry as good as that of British poets yet true to their Canadian experience and environment. He himself was already writing, and contributing poetry and essays to the Trinity College undergraduate magazine *Rouge et Noir*.

After leaving Trinity College, Lampman taught for a year at Orangeville, Ontario, and then found employment in the financial section of the post office at Ottawa, a position he held for the rest of his life, with one slight promotion. In the early years Lampman found life in Ottawa congenial. The weight and hours of work were relatively slight, so he had time to devote to his poetry, which he tended to work at meticulously, polishing and repolishing. Ottawa in the 1880s was still a small town, with rural surroundings in which he could walk and observe nature, and nearby wildernesses in which he could go on camping holidays. There were even sympathetic friends with like interests, such as Duncan Campbell Scott, who was already there when Lampman arrived, and another poet, Wilfred Campbell, a former clergyman who arrived in 1891 to take up a civil service career. The three of them collaborated in a literary column in the Toronto *Globe*, and the esteem with which Lampman was held in the capital is shown by the fact that in 1895 he was elected to the Royal Society of Canada, not yet the exclusive province of academics it has since become.

Lampman's poems found early acceptance, and he was soon contributing not only to Canadian journals but also to American magazines like the *Atlantic Monthly*, *Harper's*, and *Scribner's*. His first collection of poems, *Among the Millet* (1888), was published at his own expense, but it was comparatively successful. His next book, *Lyrics of Earth* (1893), was brought out by a Boston publisher. The last book Lampman himself prepared was *Alcyone*, and this was in the process of publication in 1899 when he died.

After Lampman's death, Duncan Campbell Scott, his literary executor, published in 1900 a collected edition, *Poems*, with a memoir, and then, many years later in 1943, he brought out Lampman's unfinished narrative poem of Dollard's last fight in *At the Long Sault and Other Poems*.

At the Long Sault, on which Lampman was working at the time of his death, shows the poet breaking out into far more irregular and experimental verse than he had used during his earlier career. This attempt to handle a tale of action in verse that is formally appropriate came at the end of a development that began with some of the most sensitive nature poetry ever written in Canada—poems like "Among the Timothy," "Heat," "Solitude," and "A Sunset at Les Éboulements." But owing to an incompletely explained combination of circumstances— certainly including mounting ill health and growing dissatisfaction with his work, as well as a loss of faith due to the influence of Darwinian concepts—Lampman also began to write a sardonic and despairing kind of verse, typified in his great poem of urban malaise, "The City of the End of Things." In this later phase Lampman was very much a man between two worlds; if he had lived longer he might have been a philosophic and narrative poet of stature, similar to E.J. Pratt in the next generation.

Duncan Campbell Scott

Of the group of men born in the 1860s who became known as the Confederation Poets (Roberts, Lampman, Carman, and Scott), Duncan Campbell Scott may well have been the best and he was certainly the most original both in subject matter and in technical experimentation.

Scott was born in Ottawa in 1862; his father was a Methodist circuit rider in rural Ontario and western Quebec. Duncan Scott was educated at public schools in Ottawa, and later at Stanstead College in Quebec. His parents had ambitions for him, without the cash to support them; they wanted him to become a doctor, but money was tight, and at the age of seventeen Scott became a clerk in the Indian Branch (predecessor of the Department of Indian Affairs) in Ottawa.

It was thought of as a temporary post, but Scott found the work so engrossing that he stayed on. It could never be said of him as of his friend Archibald Lampman that life in the civil service sapped his life as a poet. On the contrary, Scott carried on the two sides of his life with equal vigour and made one side feed the other. While he rose steadily through the service to the ranks of chief clerk, accountant, and finally deputy superintendent-general of Indian Affairs, and did not think of retiring until 1932 (when he was seventy), he treasured for use in his poetry the experiences his work afforded him – the long and arduous journeys into the wilderness where he came into contact with Indians, Métis, loggers, and trappers.

In boyhood, Scott had been interested in painting, music, and writing, and the first two interests later became evident in his poetry, which is very evocative in a visual way and also consciously musical in its sound patterns. Nevertheless, Scott did not begin to consider poetry seriously as a vocation until he met his fellow civil servant, Archibald Lampman, in 1883. Lampman, who had just been fired to emulation by the publication of Charles G.D. Roberts's *Orion* in 1880, transmitted his enthusiasm to his new friend and started Scott on the career of poetry writing which did not end until he published his last book, *The Circle of Affection*, in 1947, the year of his death.

Lampman and Scott formed a very close, mutually-encouraging friendship that lasted until the former's death in 1899, and for a while between 1892 and 1893 they collaborated in a regular literary column for the Toronto *Globe*, entitled "At the Mermaid Tavern."

Scott did not publish his first work of verse, *The Magic House*, until 1893, and afterwards his books appeared at fairly lengthy intervals, but his writing career was so long that in the end he built up a respectable list of poems. It was in his second volume, *Labour and the Angel*, published in 1898, that he included the first of his memorable poems of Indian life, though the best known of all his works in this genre– "The Forsaken," describing an old woman left to die by her people– appeared later in *New World Lyrics* (1905).

Scott wrote two very different kinds of poems. There were his rather conventional Tennysonian lyrics, which are sonorous and mood provoking but unexperimental; and there are the poems of the wilderness in which Scott strives for a vivid authenticity and achieves it by breaking away from Victorian conventions to use hard images and often harsh words. More than the other poets of his day, Scott anticipated the poets of the 1930s who took Canadian poetry out of the past and into modern times.

Scott was also a vivid fiction writer, as such books of ironic little stories as *In the Village of Viger* (1896) and *The Witching of Elspie* show. He wrote one play and spent much time editing and preparing for publication the poems of his friend Lampman. He was editor with Pelham Edgar of the famous "Makers of Canada" series of biographies, in which he wrote a life of John Graves Simcoe. He died, after a long and productive retirement, at Ottawa in 1947.

Ralph Connor

There are many writers who have become so familiar under their pen names that we rarely think of their original names. Few people pause to remember Mark Twain as Samuel Clemens or George Orwell as Eric Blair, and the same applies to the novelist who was so popular among Canadians in the early part of this century as Ralph Connor.

In his rather busy nonliterary life, Ralph Connor was Charles William Gordon, born of Highland ancestry in Glengarry County of Upper Canada in 1860. Gordon was educated at the University of Toronto, the University of Edinburgh, and finally at Knox College in Toronto, after which he was ordained a Presbyterian minister in 1890.

Gordon's first assignment was to Banff in Alberta, where he was put in charge of a mission covering a considerable area that embraced not only mining communities in the Rockies and logging camps in the foothills but also remote pioneer settlements in the prairies. In 1894 Gordon was transferred to Winnipeg as pastor of St. Stephen's Church, and there he remained until his death in 1937, except for a period during World War I when he served as chaplain to the Forty-third Highlanders and later as senior Protestant chaplain to the Canadian forces.

When he returned from the war, Gordon was a man of standing in the Presbyterian church. He became its moderator in 1922 and spent most of his time in office touring Canada to recruit support for the merger of the Presbyterians and the Methodists, which resulted in the formation of the United Church of Canada in 1924. Gordon attempted the reconciliatory role in social matters as well by serving as chairman of the Manitoba Board of Industry, set up in 1920 to try and head off industrial disputes in the years immediately following the Winnipeg general strike.

Although in no way a revolutionary, Gordon believed that being a Christian involved exercising a social conscience. The novels he wrote in his literary persona as Ralph Connor always had as their primary content a kind of confident and muscular Christianity that seemed to Connor and his readers appropriate to the growing new dominion, but the note of criticism was never muted where social misery was observed. Novels like *The Foreigner* (1909) dealing with the plight of unskilled immigrants in Winnipeg, *To Him That Hath* (1921) based on Gordon's experiences at the Manitoba Board of Industry, and *The Arm of Gold* (1932) which exposes the manipulations of international financiers, are manifestations of the kind of social conscience that appeared in many forms among prairie clergymen during this period; other ministers like J.S. Woodsworth and Salem Bland were more explicit in their social statements but no more sincere in their concern than Connor.

But the books just mentioned were neither the best nor the most popular of Connor's novels. He turned to writing in 1897 when a church magazine, the *Westminster*, invited him to write sketches about his missionary work in the Rockies. The nom-de-plume "Ralph Connor" was first used on this occasion through an editor's error; Gordon had asked for the sketches to be signed "Cannor," from the words Canadian North which were part of the name of his mission. The editor wrote down "Connor" and added "Ralph," and so a famous literary name was created.

The most popular novels written under this name fall into two categories. There are the books about the rough pioneer West and the problems of being a preaching and practising Christian there, such as *Black Rock* (1898) and *The Sky Pilot* (1899), and there are those in which Connor turns to the scenes of his early experiences and writes of the Scottish people of eastern Ontario– novels like *The Man from Glengarry* (1901) and *Glengarry School Days* (1902).

Connor wrote in all twenty-five novels as well as an autobiography. His books tend to be sensational and emotional, and at their worst are little more than fictional tracts presenting the triumph of the good (ministers, doctors, and Mounties) over the bad (gamblers, bootleggers and pimps); at their best they show a masterly ear for dialect and a sense of local colour that helps readers envisage with some faithfulness to reality the lives of Glengarry lumbermen, miners in the Selkirks, and poor immigrants in Winnipeg.

Stephen Leacock

Stephen Leacock was what Thomas Carlyle would have called a "Professor of the Dismal Science"–the dismal science being political science, which Leacock taught for more than thirty years. Perhaps it was the very dismalness of his everyday occupation that turned him by reaction into one of the world's best-known humorists, whose wit retained its quality even when translated into languages so remote from Leacock's own English as Japanese and Gujarati.

Stephen Butler Leacock was born in Hampshire in 1869 and came to Canada with his parents when he was six. He was educated at Upper Canada College and the University of Toronto, and took his doctorate of philosophy at the University of Chicago in 1903. In the same year he became a lecturer in economics and political science at McGill University, was appointed professor and head of the department in 1908, and continued in that role until his retirement in 1936. He wrote a basic handbook in his speciality–*Elements of Political Science*–which was published in 1906, and political science led him into the neighbouring subject of history, in which he wrote six astonishingly lifeless books that are now almost forgotten, except for one that is remembered mainly as a Leacockian curiosity. Entitled *Canada–The Foundations of its Future*, it was brought out in 1941 not by an ordinary publishing house but by a firm of distillers, the House of Seagram, a touch which leads one naturally into considering Leacock the humorist who loved to create such incongruous situations, but in literary fantasy rather than real life.

It was with his humorous writing that Leacock gained his international repute and achieved translation into so many languages, and to this day the critics are divided as to whether he should be classed as a satirist intending to expose men's faults or a humorist merely intending to amuse.

Some of Leacock's earlier books–like his first, *Literary Lapses*, which appeared in 1910, and *Nonsense Novels* which followed it–might well be classed as self-deprecating fun. But already, in *Sunshine Sketches of a Little Town* (1912) there is an edge that cuts down to the heart of Canadian pretensions; *Sunshine Sketches*, perhaps Leacock's best-known work, tells of the deceptions and self-deceptions that keep the wheels of society turning in the imaginary town of Mari-

posa, modelled on the real Ontario town of Orillia, where Leacock had his summer home. Setting out to define his own work, Leacock remarked rather late in his career, in *Humour and Humanity* (1937), that "humour may be defined as the kindly contemplation of the incongruities of life, and the artistic expression thereof." Perhaps "the kindly contemplation" does predominate in *Sunshine Sketches*, though there are times even in that book when the clouds of satire threaten to darken the landscape, but when we come to *Arcadian Adventures with the Idle Rich* (1914), the principal rival among Leacock's works to *Sunshine Sketches*, the satire of the social order–and the indignation that inspires it–are too evident to be ignored.

Altogether Leacock published more than thirty books that inhabit the area between humour and satire, most of them collections of shorter pieces which he had contributed to a great variety of Canadian, American, and British periodicals. Almost every book has some satirical content–attacking institutions, prejudices, and illusions. Almost every one projects the self-deprecating irony which Leacock chose as his personal tone, at least in his writing. And if he remains one of the most popular Canadian writers, with many books still in print half a century after they first appeared, it is probably because of his power to arouse laughter rather than anger; the foibles humour records are always with us, while the social evils that satirists attack are never permanent. Leacock died in 1944, writing almost to the end.

Lucy Maud Montgomery

The best of children's books, because they hover in an area of awakening understanding, are those which one can read again after growing up, and *Anne of Green Gables*, written by a lady who preferred to be known for literary purposes as L.M. Montgomery, is certainly one of these. Unfortunately L.M. Montgomery was not always at her best, and though she wrote many other books, it is now only because of this one idyll of youth on Prince Edward Island that we remember her.

Lucy Maud Montgomery was born in 1874 at Clifton on Prince Edward Island. Her mother died when she was young, and she was brought up on her grandparents' farm at Cavendish in a very typical Prince Edward Island red-earth agricultural countryside with the beaches and the rocky shore not too far away. As a child she began to write verses and even published a poem in a local Prince Edward Island newspaper, but it was not until she was training as a teacher at Prince of Wales College in Charlottetown that she actually sold a piece of writing–a short story, for which she received five dollars.

Lucy Maud did not immediately take up the teaching for which she was trained. She went on for a spell to Dalhousie University and in 1901 joined the staff of the evening *Echo* in Halifax. While she worked as a journalist, and later when she returned to Cavendish to teach and look after her sick grandmother, she continued to write and to publish short stories and poems, mainly in American periodicals. It was mostly formula writing of the kind bought in mass by the popular magazines of the time, and Lucy Maud did not strike a really original vein until she hit upon the idea for *Anne of Green Gables*.

It arose out of the routine of periodical writing in which she had become involved. She was invited in 1904 to write a serial for a juvenile magazine. Casting around for a plot, she came upon a newspaper clipping she had put aside, which bore the heading: "Elderly couple apply to orphan asylum for boy; by mistake a girl is sent to them." The situation immediately appealed to her, doubtless because she herself had been an orphan, and instead of wasting it on a serial she decided to make it into a book. The result was *Anne of Green Gables*, one of those limpid and joyful visions of childhood, set in an unspoilt world, that haunt the memory and become–as *Anne of Green Gables* did–a part of the nation's mythology.

Anne of Green Gables was a book very much of its Edwardian time; though its appeal continues in a lost paradise way, it is hard to imagine its being written with such conviction after World War I had shifted our view of the human future. It was also an unrepeatable book, and although Lucy Maud Montgomery wrote seven other books about Anne, and other books for girls, which sold widely, none of the others had the peculiar intensity of appeal that still lingers in *Anne of Green Gables*.

In 1911 Lucy Maud Montgomery married a Presbyterian clergyman, the Reverend Ewen MacDonald, by whom she had two children and with whom she moved to Norval, Ontario. But marriage did not interfere with her continued production of books (*Anne of Ingleside* appeared in 1939, thirty-one years after *Anne of Green Gables*), which were translated into many languages, or with her faithfulness to Prince Edward Island as a fictional setting. She died in Toronto in 1942. The house at Cavendish where she lived with her grandparents is preserved as a national monument.

Nellie McClung

Nellie Letitia Mooney, who as Nellie McClung became one of the most famous Canadian women of her time, was born in 1873 at Chatsworth, Ontario. Her farmer father was drawn by the promise of free land in the West, and in 1880 the family settled near the village of Millford in the Souris Valley, about thirty miles from Brandon, Manitoba.

The rest of Nellie Mooney's life was spent in western Canada. She attended the Winnipeg Normal School and in 1893, at the age of sixteen, began to teach in a one-room school near Manitou. In 1898 she withdrew from teaching to marry Robert Wesley McClung, a young Manitou druggist who later in life became an insurance agent.

It was almost ten years later that Nellie McClung's life began to veer away from the normal existence of a woman in a prairie small town. She became a writer and an activist in many of the directions opened by the rapid social changes taking place in Canada during the early twentieth century.

In 1907 she became involved in the Women's Christian Temperance Union and remained an advocate of prohibition for the rest of her life. Shortly afterwards she began to work for women's rights, and when she and her husband moved to Winnipeg, she joined the Political Equality League, which she continued to work for in Edmonton when her husband was transferred there in 1914. In these two causes she developed into an eloquent and aggressive orator –known as "the Holy Terror" and acting on the motto: "Never retract, never explain, never apologize." Her flamboyant platform style gained her great popularity, and she travelled far over western Canada on her speaking tours.

In the meantime, she had established a position for herself as a popular writer, which gave support to her social activities. Today her novels seem sentimental and even sanctimonious, though the writing is often lively, but they appealed intensely to the reading public of their time, and her first publication, *Sowing Seeds in Danny*, went into seventeen editions and sold a hundred thousand copies. Altogether, in the intervals of a busy public life, she published seventeen books–novels, short stories, essays; perhaps the most interesting to a modern reader are her two autobiographical volumes, *Clearing in the West* (1935) and *The Stream Runs Fast* (1945), which apart from telling of the causes in which she worked so hard, often convey with considerable vividness the character of prairie society in its formative years.

Nellie McClung's involvement in social and political causes did not come to an end until her old age. The agitation for women's votes, in which she took an active part, was successful in Alberta where the necessary changes to the franchise were made in 1916. In 1921 Nellie herself was elected as a Liberal to the Alberta legislature, where she served until 1926. With Emily Murphy, the first woman magistrate in the British Empire, and three other prairie women, she carried on the famous Persons Case. This referred to the clause in the British North America Act relating to appointments to the Senate, which used the word "persons." In 1927 McClung and her associates petitioned the Supreme Court for an interpretation that the term could include women. The court's decision was adverse, but an appeal to the Privy Council in London was successful, and in 1929 the Senate was eventually opened to women. In 1921 Nellie McClung was the first woman chosen as a delegate to a world Methodist conference, held in London. She was the first woman member of the CBC Board of Governors in 1936, and in 1938 she was appointed to the Canadian delegation to the League of Nations and served briefly on the league's committee for social legislation.

In 1943 she retired to Victoria, and there she died in 1951.

Grey Owl

Among the creations of Archibald Stansfeld Belaney were not only his books but also the personality who wrote them, the half-Indian Grey Owl, or Wa-sha-quon-asin, who appeared on the lecture platforms of North America and Britain in Indian garb and span a romantic story of himself out of which the truth does not seem even yet to have been completely disentangled. In recent years a number of writers have attempted to present the real man behind the myth, and probably Lovat Dickson in *Wilderness Man, The Strange Story of Grey Owl*, (1973) came nearest to the truth, but there still remain many areas of doubt, many points in Grey Owl's career that seem to admit more than one interpretation.

Archibald Stansfeld Belaney was born in England in 1888. His father, George Belaney had wandered a great deal and in Florida had married Katherine Cox, who was Archibald's mother. Later her son claimed that she had Indian blood, and based on this theory the claim he made at times to be partly Apache, but there is no reason to believe that she was other than English, since according to Lovat Dickson she left England in the company of George Belaney and her sister Elizabeth, who was George's mistress, and married him after Elizabeth's death. Whatever the truth of this may be, the couple returned to England a few months before Archibald's birth.

His father and mother having parted, young Archibald was brought up by two aunts, a solitary boy, deeply interested in natural history and in taming wild animals, captivated by dreams of the Wild West and of Indians, which he never outgrew; his later life was an attempt to fulfil these childhood longings.

In 1906 at the age of seventeen Belaney went to Canada, worked for a time in Toronto and in 1907 headed into northern Ontario where he became a guide and trapper and associated with the local Ojibwa Indians. In 1910 he took a girl from one of the local bands as his wife, but it is not certain how far the band accepted him, and the union appears to have been somewhat intermittent, since Belaney frequently went away.

Soon after the outbreak of World War I, Belaney volunteered for service, and in France he was wounded in the foot.

Convalescing in England he married a childhood friend, Constance Holmes, but she appears to have been opposed to accompanying him to Canada, and he returned on his own, going back to live in northern Ontario, which he found vastly changed by indiscriminate logging and trapping since he had first gone there in 1907.

In 1925 Belanay took as his common law wife a beautiful Ojibwa girl named Anahareo. By now he had adopted the name of Grey Owl and had begun to dress like the Indians, to live in their style and to pass himself off as a Métis. He and Anahareo went to Temiscouta county in Quebec where they began to breed beaver for restocking the wilderness waterways, and in 1929 Grey Owl began to lecture and to write magazine articles on conservation. His activities aroused the interest of the Department of the Interior, and in 1931 he was employed by them as a ranger, first at Riding Mountain National Park in Manitoba and later on at Prince Albert National Park in the northern woodlands of Saskatchewan, where he built the cabin in which he lived the remaining years of his life.

There were not many of them left, and the life which Grey Owl crammed into them was hardly that of the wilderness hermit. In 1931 he published his first book, *The Men of the Last Frontier*, with which his public myth began. The idea which the book created of an Indian working to preserve the ways of the wild appealed to the sentimental nostalgia of North Americans and Europeans alike, and Grey Owl became almost immediately a transcontinental celebrity. His evocative descriptions of Canadian woodlands, his apparent success in taming beavers, his eloquent pleas for conservation all combined to make instant best sellers of his remaining books: *Pilgrims of the Wild* (1935), *The Adventures of Sajo and her Beaver People* (1935), *Tales of an Empty Cabin* (1936), and *The Tree* (1937).

The writing of these books was interspersed with exhausting, self-advertizing lecture tours in North America and England. He died, prematurely, in 1938. To dismiss Grey Owl as a poseur, which he undoubtedly was, would be an oversimplification of a complex man who was retarded in a world of boyhood fantasy and yet who also had a sincere concern for conservation and was one of the true pioneers of the modern environmental movement. He acted a role, but he acted it well.

Pauline Johnson

Unlike Grey Owl, Pauline Johnson was by race and tradition a true Indian. Her father, George Henry Martin Johnson, was the Mohawk chief of the Six Nations, the Iroquois who had remained faithful to their alliance with the British and emigrated to Canada with the Loyalists at the end of the War of Independence. Her mother, Emily Howells, was an English woman from Bristol.

Born in 1862 on the Six Nations Reserve near Brantford in Upper Canada, Emily Pauline Johnson received the Mohawk name of Tekahionwake. She was educated at Brantford Model School and encouraged at home to read copiously; she acquired a wide acquaintance with the more sentimental type of Victorian verse, which certainly influenced her own writing.

This began early. She published her first poems in a New York magazine when she was twelve, and by her early twenties her lyrics were appearing widely in Canada, Britain, and the United States.

But it was not until the age of thirty that she began to acquire the special reputation we associate with the name of Pauline Johnson. In that year she was invited to give a reading at an author's night of the Young Liberal Club in Toronto. She so impressed the audience with her dramatic rendering of verses giving a romanticized view of Indian traditions that she was invited to give a second performance, for which she wrote her most celebrated single poem, "The Song My Paddle Sings."

Afterwards, Frank Yeigh, president of the Young Liberal Club, suggested that he should arrange a series of recitals. Pauline agreed, and dressed in a somewhat theatrical version of Indian garb, which she would alternate with elaborately sequinned evening gowns, she set off to perform under her Indian name of Tekahionwake. A first series of recitals in Ontario cities and towns was an immediate success, and in 1894 Pauline Johnson set off for an equally successful tour in England, where her striking appearance and the passion with which she read her poems created a deep impression on audiences accustomed to melodramatic and sentimental theatrical performances.

A first volume of her poems, *The White Wampum*, appeared in London in 1895. They tended to extol the virtues of Indians and often condemned the white man for his destruction of the native way of life, but they were very conventionally written and find a place among the romantic verse of the Victorian age rather than among the true literature of the Indian peoples. It was Pauline's stage personality that brought her success.

Returning to Canada, she started on a long career of public appearances, based on what was really a very small production in terms of poetry, for only one other book was published during this period – *Canadian Born*, which appeared in 1903. From 1894 to 1903 Pauline did a long series of Canadian tours, during which, in Winnipeg, she met Walter McRaye and formed a lasting romantic relationship with him. In 1903 she went a second time to England and returned for another four years of tours in Canada. In all, she crossed the country nineteen times. The audiences always came.

In 1907 she retired from the recital circuit and went to live in Vancouver, where she wrote stories for popular magazines and worked with Chief Joseph Capilano on a series of stories illustrating the traditions of the Squamish tribe; it was published in 1911 as *Legends of Vancouver* and still sells in the city. In 1913 she published two volumes of rather sentimental stories, *The Moccasin Maker* and *The Shagganappi*. She died in Vancouver in the same year.

Pauline Johnson was not a great or even a good poet. At best she was a facile versifier, but her style of writing and her romantic stage presence appealed to the audiences of the time, and in hindsight she seems less important for what she herself created than for what her career tells us about the popular taste of Canada in the Laurier era.

Frederick Philip Grove

There are novelists so dedicated to the art of fiction that they present the public with fake accounts of their own lives, and sometimes they live out the lie to the end. Frederick Philip Grove, the earliest important novelist of the Canadian prairies, was one such man. The first authenticated record of Grove's presence in Canada dates from 1912 when he began teaching in Manitoba. In a so-called autobiography—*In Search of Myself*—published in 1946, Grove claimed he had been born of rich Swedish parents in Russia in 1871 and had come to North America in 1892, after which he had had many strange adventures before reaching Manitoba. The facts were notably different, as the Canadian critic, Douglas A. Spettigue, found when he went to Europe to turn up biographical evidence relating to Grove. What Spettigue did find—and document convincingly—was that Grove was born in 1879, not 1871, in East Prussia of relatively poor parents, not in Russia of rich ones, and that his original name was Felix Paul Greve. Under this name he enjoyed a minor but interesting literary career in Europe. Greve wrote two novels, translated Oscar Wilde and other English writers into German, was the friend of André Gide and Stefan George, and finally, after being imprisoned for fraud, vanished from Germany without a trace about 1910. There are still no clues as to what happened to him before he surfaced into recordable history again by becoming F. P. Grove, the Manitoba school teacher.

Grove began to teach at Heskett and later became principal at Gladstone High School. His wife, whom he had married in 1914, taught at another school at Falmouth, thirty miles north. At weekends Grove would visit her, travelling by bicycle in summer and by horse and sleigh in winter, and during the weekday evenings he began to write again, recording the impressions of these journeys which became the basis of the two books with which he returned to publishing: *Over Prairie Trails* (1922) and *The Turn of the Year* (1923). These books of essays, evoking the harsh but beautiful setting of prairie life—and the struggle of the life itself—are the books by Grove which can be read with the least doubt. They are unambitious, they show his sensitivity to environment and to human predicament, and they do not present the often unsuccessful struggle to compress a melodramatic vision of prairie life into the confines of a novel, which frequently spoils his other books.

Not that those books can be dismissed. They show a man with great powers, great sympathies, a vast sense of tragedy, and above all a deeply pessimistic view of the fate of man when he pits himself against the forces of nature. Yet Grove's prose is often too uncouth to express the power of his feelings, and his plots are always clumsy. Writing, in fact, seemed to become more and more of an agony as he grew older. He liberated himself from teaching in 1929 by becoming editor of the short-lived Graphic Press in Ottawa and about a year later moved to a farm near Simcoe, but he was always troubled by the problems that arose from writing immense first versions of his novels, which he would then struggle for years to reduce to a size publishers would even consider.

The books Grove did finally make acceptable for the publishers include *Settlers of the Marsh* (1925), *Our Daily Bread* (1928), *The Yoke of Life* (1930), *Fruits of the Earth* (1933), and *The Master of the Mill* (1944), an impressive epic of the change from a nonmechanical to a machine-dominated world, told in the history of a mill and its owners. But many of Grove's books were not published during his life, and some remain unpublished even now. The patchy nature of his success turned him from a naturally proud into a bitterly arrogant man whose relations with publishers were explosive. He suffered a paralytic stroke in 1945 and died in 1948. His *Letters*, published in 1976, reveal a vain and irritable personality which one hopes was not the better side of Grove's nature.

Paul Kane

Paul Kane was the Canadian equivalent of George Catlin, the painter of American Indians at the point of fatal contact with the white man's culture, and of the two men Kane may well have been the better artist.

Paul Kane was born in County Cork, Ireland, in 1810. His father was a former artilleryman, born in Lancashire, who migrated to Upper Canada in 1819 and settled in York as a wine and spirit merchant. How Kane got his education is uncertain, but it is known that Thomas Drury, the art teacher at Upper Canada College, was aware of his talents and gave him painting lessons. Early in the 1830s Kane became a sign painter and then moved to Cobourg where he worked as a decorative painter in a furniture factory and began to paint portraits in a rather primitive manner.

In 1836 Kane went to the United States and wandered around for five years as an itinerant portraitist. Then, on the advice of American painters he encountered, he sailed to Europe in 1841 and stayed there, mainly in Italy and London, until the spring of 1843. During that time he met George Catlin, and Catlin's remarks about the artist's duty to record the vanishing cultures of the American Indians while there was yet time obviously impressed him. He sailed back to the United States, painted portraits for a year in Mobile, Alabama, and about the end of 1844 returned to Toronto, resolved to begin his task of recording in paint the Indians of British North America and their way of life.

Kane's first season among the Indians began in June 1845, when he set off with a gun and artist's materials, bound for the Pacific coast of what was not yet Canada. He found his whole summer taken up by work among the Ojibwa and other Indians around the Great Lakes, and towards the end of the season encountered a Hudson's Bay trader in Sault Ste. Marie who dissuaded him from proceeding farther west until he had gained the approval of the Hudson's Bay Company and its "little emperor," Sir George Simpson. Kane wisely accepted the advice and in the autumn travelled to Lachine. Simpson was interested. Kane received permission to travel with the company's spring fur brigades and–even more important–he was promised hospitality at Hudson's Bay Company posts.

Kane made his own way to Fort William and there he joined the brigade, taking part in the Métis buffalo hunt from Fort Garry and proceeding across the prairies to the North Saskatchewan, Fort Pitt, and Fort Edmonton. Thence he crossed the Rockies with the fur traders and reached the upper course of the Columbia, which he followed to Fort Vancouver at its mouth, in the region which–when he reached it late in 1846–had just become the Oregon Territory of the United States. Kane spent some time among the local Indians, making extraordinarily vivid oil sketches, and then went north to Fort Victoria on Vancouver Island, which was soon to become the western headquarters of the Hudson's Bay Company. Here he found people from the northern tribes, such as the Haida, who had come south to trade, and he prepared many sketches on Vancouver Island and in the Puget Sound area before returning to Fort Vancouver at the end of June and starting the journey back through the region of the Walla Walla and Nez Percé Indians. He reached Fort Edmonton in December and spent the winter there attending and sketching Cree ceremonials. In May he left Edmonton and reached Toronto in October 1848.

Apart from a later trip to the Red River Settlement in 1849, Kane never returned to the West. He remained in Toronto, working his seven hundred sketches into grandiose canvases in which the colour and life that still survive in the earlier versions were almost entirely lost. The canvases are deliberate compositions; the sketches are records so immediate that they retain their freshness of impact over more than a century. Later Kane turned his diaries into a book, which is still a classic among the travel narratives of the Canadian past, *Wanderings of an Artist among the Indians of North America*, published in 1859.

In his later years Kane slowly grew blind and was embittered by neglect. He died in Toronto, suddenly, in 1871.

Cornelius Krieghoff

Cornelius Krieghoff, most famous of all Canadian *genre* painters, was born in 1815 in Amsterdam, the son of a German coffee house waiter who had artistic ambitions and taught his son what he knew about music and painting, for which arts young Cornelius showed a distinct aptitude. The family moved to Düsseldorf, and for two years Cornelius went to study painting in Schweinfurt. Then, in 1837, at the age of twenty-two, he set off for the United States, which in those days seemed to many Germans a land of liberty in comparison with the petty tyrannies of their own small principalities. There he enlisted in the American army and, his talents being recognized, served as an early war artist, with the rank of corporal, in the campaigns against the Seminole Indians. He was discharged in 1840, married a French-Canadian girl in New York, and headed for Canada, where his brother was already established in Toronto.

Although he set up as a professional painter in Toronto and later in Montreal, Krieghoff at first had little success. He exhibited at the Toronto Society of Artists in 1847 but apparently attracted few buyers and was forced at times to earn a living as a house painter.

Fortunes changed when Krieghoff moved to Quebec in 1853, where he found patrons and customers among the English officers of the garrison and the local merchants; even the governor general, Lord Elgin, was one of his visitors. He worked as a portrait painter, but his real success was in *genre* painting, where he adapted to a new environment a style already well established in the Rhineland when he left it in 1837. For a decade he travelled around the villages of Quebec, observing the life, attending the festivals, and when he returned to his studio turning them into the colourful and somewhat sentimental tableaux which are especially associated with his name and which modern forgers have found so easy to copy.

During this period Krieghoff shared the house of an auctioneer, John Budden, and Budden appears to have acted with skill as his agent and dealer. Krieghoff was extraordinarily prolific. Between 1853 and 1862, it has been estimated, he painted at least seven hundred canvases that can reasonably be authenticated. The number of dubious Krieghoffs in private collections and public galleries would considerably swell the number.

Krieghoff left for Chicago in 1862 or later, and little is known of his life from that time until his death in 1872, except that he appears to have painted very little in his final years.

Krieghoff was not a great painter, by Canadian or any other standards; there were many far better *genre* painters in Holland and Flanders, and even Germany. Yet his craft was competent enough to carry his themes, and he was one of the first painters to record the French-Canadian way of life in the early nineteenth century, among the habitants and also among the townspeople. Admittedly he looked at it from the outside, with the eye of a stranger; but a sharp stranger's eye is often more perceptive than the eye of a native, and although he presented the French Canadians as they may not wish to have been shown, he also presented them as they were seen by others. Yet in the last analysis, his paintings are a traveller's record expressed in an alien idiom. As sociological records they are part of Canadian visual history; as art they are irremovably in the Germanic tradition.

William Notman

If this book has a predecessor in the history of Canadian publishing, it is *Portraits of British Americans*, whose three volumes appeared in Montreal between 1865 and 1868. The text was by the biographer John Fennings Taylor and the photographs were by the greatest of early Canadian photographers, William Notman.

Notman was a Scot, born in Paisley in 1826; his father was an artist who made a living designing paisley shawls. William himself wanted to be an artist, but his father persuaded him of the precariousness of the occupation, and eventually he went into the wholesale dry goods business, strongly established among the textile mills of Paisley.

When Notman came to Canada in 1856 it was to join an import house in Montreal. He had already learnt the daguerreotype process in Scotland, and during the slack winter season he came to an agreement with his employer by which he could absent himself from the business to set up a photographic studio, and if it did not succeed would be taken back.

The studio – or "gallery," in the favoured terminology of the day – was established at Bleury Street in Montreal in November 1856 and was a success, largely because Notman was not content to be a good portraitist. He recognized not only the wide public interest in the stereoscope at that time but also the appeal of topical events, and during the building of Robert Stephenson's great tubular railway bridge over the St. Lawrence at Montreal, which was completed in 1859, Notman produced a remarkable series of stereographs that established his name.

When the Prince of Wales (later Edward VII) toured Canada in 1860, Notman was active in photographing the visit and also in compiling a series of six hundred photographs, which the Canadian government presented to the prince. As a result of this presentation, Notman became in 1861 a photographer to the queen; he won his first gold medal at the International Exhibition of 1862 in London.

Fashionable photographers' "galleries" in the mid-nineteenth century were rather like the studios of fashionable painters – places to which foreign travellers and the local gentility would pay visits to admire the works exhibited and buy the elegant volumes of photographic prints, as well as to be photographed.

Photography, in fact, became big business in the Victorian age. Notman and his sons – William and Charles – as well as their employees all took photographs that bore the Notman name. Notman began to open branch studios, the first in Ottawa in 1867, followed by others in Halifax and Toronto, and a second Montreal studio in 1878. He extended his activities to the United States, where the Notman Photographic Company eventually had studios in seven different towns and cities, and he founded the Centennial Photographic Company which operated a monopoly on taking photographs at the Philadelphia Centennial Exhibition in 1876.

The Notman studios were well known not only for their portraits and the superb landscape studies which Notman and his sons travelled to take across Canada as transport became available (they were among the earliest photographers to follow the Canadian Pacific through the Rockies to the Pacific), but also for their famous composites – group studies made of figures separately photographed, pasted on a painted background, and then photographed again.

Apart from his own photographs and those taken in his studios, Notman bought many negatives from other photographers. The Notman Archive in the McCord Museum of Montreal, assembled by the family, contains no less than 400,000 prints and negatives, and often it is hard to tell whether photographs were taken by William Notman himself or merely acquired. He died in Montreal and his sons carried on the business for many years.

Tom Thomson

When we think of the Group of Seven and the birth of a true Canadian school of painting, it is Tom Thomson we are likely to remember first, and especially those two great paintings, brilliant in colour and concept alike, *The West Wind* and *The Jack Pine*, both painted in 1917, the last year of Thomson's short life. Yet though he knew its members and influenced them, Thomson was not actually a member of the group; if he had lived longer it would have been undoubtedly a Group of Eight.

Thomas John Thomson was born in 1877 at Claremont, Ontario. When he was a small child his father took up a farm at Leith, near Owen Sound, so that Georgian Bay was the scene of Thomson's childhood, and there, in his teens, he became an expert boatman. Tom felt no urge to become a farmer like his father; his education was scanty in formal terms, and he started his working life as an apprentice machinist at Owen Sound. Very soon he tired of that work, and then for a time he went to a business college in Chatham, until he realized that he felt no greater urge towards the office desk than he had towards the work bench.

Meanwhile two of Tom Thomson's brothers had moved restlessly westward and settled eventually in Seattle, where Tom joined them in 1901. Over the years, in a desultory way, he had been teaching himself drawing and painting, and when he found a job as draftsman for a firm of photo-engravers, he not only found the work congenial but realized that he had started on his true life's work.

Four years later, in 1905, Tom Thomson returned to Toronto; in 1911 he joined the commercial art firm of Grip Limited. Among the other artists whom Grip employed were at least three men who had a considerable influence on the remainder of Tom's life; Arthur Lismer and J. E. H. MacDonald, both later to be members of the Group of Seven, encouraged him to work more ambitiously and to take up oil painting, and Tom McLean, an artist now otherwise forgotten, told him of the beautiful northern country of the Shield, centring on Algonquin Park.

Thomson went to Algonquin Park for the first time in the summer of 1912 and was fascinated by the wildness and colour of the landscape. In the spring of 1913 his painting, *A Northern Lake,* based on sketches made during his summer tour, was bought by the Government of Ontario and attracted his first patrons, particularly Dr. James MacCallum, who encouraged and financially assisted Thomson for the rest of his life.

By May 1913 Thomson was able to give up his job and to become a truly professional artist, living by his brush and working in winter, first in the small shack he inhabited behind the Studio Building in Toronto, and then in the Studio Building itself. There he shared a studio with another new painter friend, A. Y. Jackson. In the summers Thomson would go to Canoe Lake in Algonquin Park, and there he would paint and from time to time work as a forest ranger.

Three years of brilliant productivity followed, for all of Thomson's important canvases were painted between 1914 and the summer of 1917, when in July he disappeared on Canoe Lake. His craft was found, and later his floating body. That Thomson, an expert canoeist and a good swimmer, could have drowned accidentally seemed unthinkable, and a mystery still hangs over his death. Murder has always been considered a possibility, but although at least one highly likely candidate for the role of murderer has been offered by investigators of the mystery, the final clues that might tell how Thomson actually died have always been missing. It can be said for certain, however, that Tom Thomson's death in 1917 cut short the most promising career in the whole history of Canadian art.

Alexander Young Jackson

It is left for biographers to resurrect A. Y. Jackson's Christian names. To his admirers he was always "A. Y." For decades, when he finally died in 1974 at the age of ninety-two, he had been the dean of Canadian painting, but his greatest days had been over for almost forty years; after the 1930s he added nothing to the Canadian tradition or to his own work in terms of new kinds of vision.

Jackson was born in Montreal in 1882, and having shown an early flair for drawing, he was apprenticed to a lithographer at the age of twelve. Shortly afterwards he decided that he wanted to become a painter and began taking evening classes, at the period almost the only kind of art instruction available in Montreal.

Jackson went on to Chicago, where the opportunities were somewhat broader, and eventually moved on to Paris, where he studied at the art academies, which were open to all comers provided they paid a small fee, and spent much time wandering through the galleries and absorbing the art of Europe. It is perhaps significant that this was the period of Art Nouveau, of Gauguin, of the cult of vibrant primary colours and dark sinuous outlines–characteristics which were to be repeated in Jackson's own painting not long afterwards.

Jackson returned from Europe excited by the painting he had seen being done there, but also with a nudging feeling that a way of interpreting the Canadian landscape should be developed, as authentic and vibrant as that which the Impressionists had found in France, but true to the land itself.

Montreal was not the place for such an attitude to flourish; the best Montreal painters were oriented towards Europe and tended like James Wilson Morrice[12] (perhaps the greatest of all Canadian painters) to live abroad and become absorbed into the School of Paris. Jackson eventually moved to Toronto in 1913, persuaded by J. E. H. MacDonald and other painters with whom he eventually formed the Group of Seven. In 1914 he moved into the legendary Studio Building, and there he shared a studio with Tom Thomson–at least, during the winters when Thomson was not painting in the woodlands of northern Ontario. It was Thomson who introduced Jackson to his favourite painting region, in and around Algonquin Park, and who influenced him profoundly in the few years–before Thomson's death in 1917–when they worked beside each other. From this time Jackson began to paint the earliest of the paintings by which he is now best known, such as *Terre Sauvage* (1913) and the *Red Maple* (1914).

It was not until 1920 that the Group of Seven assumed a formal shape with the first exhibition of seven friends who had come to believe that Canadian art must set out to project the true character of the land, without being merely representational as many earlier landscapists had been. A Canadian style was needed, and they believed they had discovered it. The original Group of Seven, who took part in that historic show, were A. Y. Jackson, Arthur Lismer, F. H. Varley, Lawren Harris, J. E. H. MacDonald, Frank H. Johnston, and Franklin Carmichael; missing was Tom Thomson, who had been the forerunner and inspirer of them all.

The first reaction of many Canadians to the Group of Seven– like the first reaction of Parisians to the Impressionists or the first reaction of Londoners to James McNeill Whistler–was one of surprise at what they saw as the crude colouring and tortured outlines of the paintings. But soon art lovers began to recognize that these canvases were intrinsically true, if not factual, representations of the land. Not that it mattered greatly to Jackson, who had an almost fanatical devotion to his craft, regardless of success, and for decades travelled over the country, producing paintings of the Arctic and of Quebec every bit as vibrant as those he had done in northern Ontario.

By the later 1930s Jackson and his fellow artists were accepted by Canadians; their work fitted the growing trend of artistic and literary nationalism. But by this time, ironically, Jackson had really ceased to develop, and during his last years he tended to paint according to formulas he had established in his younger days. He kept up his Toronto studio until 1955, then moved to Manotick near Ottawa, and when he died had lived for years on the premises of the McMichael Collection at Kleinburg, Ontario. He died there in 1974. His best late work was in prose rather than paint–his autobiography, *A Painter's Country* (1958).

Emily Carr

Few artists, even in Canada, can have waited so long for recognition as Emily Carr. She had developed a name in her native Victoria as an eccentric aging woman, keeping a ramshackle boarding house, breeding sheep dogs for sale, making pottery for tourists, and wandering the streets with an entourage of exotic pets long before she gained even modest recognition as a painter or a writer. There was no serious exhibition of her paintings until she was fifty-six, and her first book was not published until she was seventy, four years before her death. Yet now we would be conscious of a great gap in Canadian art and Canadian writing if Emily Carr's works were not there.

In volumes like *The Book of Small* (1942), *The House of All Sorts* (1944), and *Growing Pains* (1946), Emily Carr recorded vividly in her final years the circumstances of her life in Victoria, which began in 1871, the year British Columbia entered Confederation, and ended in 1945. Her mother died when she was twelve, her father when she was fourteen; she was left to the mercies of a pietistic and detested elder sister until she broke free to study art, which she did first in San Francisco. She returned to Victoria in 1895 and began to visit the Indian villages along the British Columbia coast, sketching their people and their vanishing totemic art, and attempting to transfer to whatever surface of paper, cardboard, or canvas might be available the feeling of the dense primeval rain forests of the Pacific coast.

Later Emily Carr went to England, where she saw Queen Victoria's funeral and studied at the Westminster School of Art. She returned to Canada in 1904, and in 1910 went to Paris for what in those days was an almost obligatory painter's graduation, a stint at the famous Académie Colarossi. All she learnt on these European trips, which she detested, were a few techniques; the general concepts of painting that were offered seemed to have little relation to the kind of personal visions she wished to endue with form.

It was after she returned to British Columbia in 1911 that – recognizing she could make no living by painting – Emily Carr was forced into keeping her lodging house and inventing other expedients to make money. For fifteen years she had little leisure or energy for painting, though she went as often as she could in the summers to work in the Indian villages of the coastal islands and along the Skeena and Nass rivers.

It was, in a way that they probably never understood, the Indians who opened Emily Carr's path to recognition, for in 1927, working in northern British Columbia, the ethnologist Marius Barbeau heard from them of the eccentric white woman who painted in the villages. On his way back through Vancouver, Barbeau called on Emily Carr and was so impressed by her paintings that he introduced her to Eric Brown, then director of the National Gallery. That year Brown arranged her first major exhibition in Ottawa. The public recognition and the appreciation of her fellow artists, especially of the Group of Seven, encouraged Emily Carr, and she returned with vigour to her painting, producing the splendid last works in which she finally realized her vision of the northern forests.

In 1937 she learnt that she was suffering from heart disease and would have to conserve her energy. She put an end to the arduous trips she was still making in her early sixties to the remote northern Indian villages, and took to writing. There were so many experiences with the Indians that she wanted to recall, and when she put these together in her first book, *Klee Wyck*, and published it in 1941, she was immediately recognized as a writer of great originality and awarded the Governor General's Gold Medal. Later, in the books mentioned at the beginning of this entry, she returned to telling of her childhood and womanhood in a natural and vivid prose that makes her a classic autobiographer. In her writing, as in her painting, Emily Carr's vision was intense and personal; she would have made a good sister for William Blake.

George Monro Grant

Only one book by George Grant is still reprinted and read. It is the travel narrative, *Ocean to Ocean* which he wrote after he had gone as Sandford Fleming's secretary on a journey in 1872 from the Great Lakes to the Pacific coast, searching out the route for a transcontinental railway that would have to wait a good many years for completion. And at first sight there seems a major irony that this celebrated churchman and university administrator should be remembered by an adventurous recollection of a single interlude in a long and useful life, rather than by the works–forgotten except by scholars–that more faithfully represent his daily preoccupations: books like *New Year Sermons, Our Five Foreign Missions*, and *The Religions of the World*. Yet, in fact, Grant was large enough in personality to contain within himself both the adventurer and the pillar of society. We remember Principal Grant more than we remember other religious leaders and academic functionaries because he had a visionary streak that most of his kind lacked, and his visionary streak embraced the future of Canada.

Grant was born of good Scottish stock in 1835 at Albion Mines in Nova Scotia. He was educated at Thomas McCulloch's famous Pictou Academy before going on to Glasgow University. In 1860 he was ordained minister in the Church of Scotland, but he never committed himself to the sharply defined partisan attitudes which then broke up the Presbyterians into warring factions. As minister of St. Matthew's Church in Halifax he strove towards a reunion; and in 1875, when he was moderator of the Church of Scotland in Canada, all the various groups reunited in the Presbyterian Church of Canada, of which he became moderator in 1899.

Long before that, Grant had moved from the active pastorate into the realm of education. In 1877 he became principal of Queen's University and showed himself to be a remarkable organizer who charmed up endowments and placed the institution on a sound financial basis. Grant remained principal of Queen's until his death in 1902, but this did not mean that his attention was any more restricted to university administration than it had been to parochial responsibilities in earlier days. His imagination was stirred by the federation of Canada, and his long journey with Sandford Fleming had convinced him of the "great future" which he believed belonged to the Canadian people and of which he tried to make them aware, not only in *Ocean to Ocean* but also in the series of descriptive accounts of various parts of the country that he published in 1882 under the title of *Picturesque Canada*. In 1883 Grant went on a second journey with Sandford Fleming, during which they surveyed the route through the Kicking Horse Pass by which the Canadian Pacific Railway would eventually find its way through the Rockies.

Yet though Grant was inspired by the physical magnitude of Canada and also by the surge of national feeling Confederation seemed to release, he was not in the modern sense a Canadian nationalist. He was, rather, an imperial federalist, seeing Canada's future unfolding until it became an equal partner within the British Empire, assuming all the responsibilities such a position would involve. He was a founding member in 1884 of the Canadian branch of the Imperial Federation League, and he followed the league's policy of opposing reciprocity treaties with the United States on the grounds that they would lead to economic and eventually political subordination. He defended his position in lectures which were later published, like *Imperial Federation* (1890) and *Advantages of Imperial Federation* (1891), and here he adopted a tone of political optimism contrasting strongly with Goldwin Smith's pessimistic assumption that Canada would be unable to resist the geographical and economic forces propelling it towards union with the United States. Grant, indeed, devoted a whole pamphlet to refuting the arguments against the dominion's long-term viability, which Smith had put forward in *Canada and the Canadian Question*.

Grant was a founding member of the Royal Society of Canada and became its president in 1901. To this, as to everything he did, he brought the earnest conscientiousness which once led him to tell Sir John A. Macdonald that he would always support him when he was in the right–to which a rueful Sir John is said to have made the classic answer: "What I need is men who'll support me when I'm in the wrong!"

Goldwin Smith

Goldwin Smith was a regius professor of history at Oxford who became a Canadian journalist; an advocate of Canadian independence who ended by accepting the inevitability of American annexation. Controversial and contradictory by nature, Smith was nevertheless one of the most brilliant intellectuals and men of letters in nineteenth century Canada.

He was born at Reading, England, in 1823, a doctor's son, and gained admission to Eton. From there he went on to Magdalen College at Oxford. His brilliance was recognized and an academic career immediately opened to him. He became Stowell law professor at Oxford in 1846; in 1854 he was secretary to the royal commission investigating Oxford University; in 1858 he became regius professor of history.

But there was a touch of the intellectual adventurer in Smith that tempted him away from the quiet quadrangles of Oxford colleges. In England he began to dabble in journalism, writing for the *Saturday Review* and the London *Daily News*, where he strongly advocated that Britain divest herself of her colonies. In 1864 he went to the United States in a delegation of sympathizers with the northern cause, and in 1868 he accepted an invitation from Cornell University to become professor of English and constitutional history.

Then in 1871 he abandoned the academic life completely and came to Toronto, where he lived the rest of his life. He had money and wed money, marrying the widow of William Henry Boulton and becoming squire of that famous Toronto pseudo-manor house, The Grange. From interest rather than need he became a prolific journalist, contributing articles and often cash to publications like the *Canadian Monthly*, the *Nation*, the *Week*, and finally, at the end of his life, the *Farmer's Sun*, as well as to his own paper, the *Bystander*, which appeared intermittently between 1880 and 1890.

Although he wrote many books of literary criticism (on Jane Austen, Cowper, Shakespeare) and history (especially Irish and American), it was political polemics that most interested Goldwin Smith, and perhaps his greatest importance in the history of our culture lies in the eloquence with which he debated some of our central national issues, such as imperialism and independence, and Canada's relations to Britain and the United States.

Smith's interest in the problems aroused by imperialism was already evident in some of the articles he wrote in England, but it was when he reached Canada that he became deeply involved, first through his association with the Canada First party. He became president of the National Club, which the Canada Firsters established, and in 1874 delivered an address in which he attacked the ideas of imperial federation that was becoming fashionable and declared that Canada must be independent.

But Smith did not long remain in alliance with Canada First. He was essentially a pragmatist repelled by what he regarded as idealistic extremes, which made him antagonistic to the movements for Irish home rule and women's rights. And he moved steadily away from the advocacy of Canadian independence to support of the idea of a commercial union with the United States, and finally to the conclusion that a separate and independent Canada was in the long run unfeasible and that absorption in the American federation was inevitable and would probably be beneficial.

This point of view Smith developed most strongly in his best-known book, which earned him more enemies than friends, *Canada and the Canadian Question* (1891). An intensely pessimistic book for a nationalist to read, it shows how all Canada's regions are continuations of American regions and maintains that their economic and political problems will be solved by union with their counterparts south of the border. The French–English conflict Smith regarded as insoluble in Canada as it existed; the French-speaking element would lose importance in the great federation of Anglo-Saxons resulting from union with the Americans, and the problem would then solve itself by the assimilation of the francophones. More than eighty years afterwards, *Canada and the Canadian Question* remains the most brilliant of all the books that have spoken for continental union.

Smith died in Toronto in 1910, having devoted much of his final years to criticism of Christian doctrine in the light of evolutionary theory.

Harold Adams Innis

By profession Harold Adams Innis was an economist, but his mind moved widely over the disciplines, and by the end of his comparatively short life he had profoundly influenced Canadian historical thought and produced theories regarding modern mass communication which were to have a worldwide effect. He had a highly originative mind, and other men became more famous by developing his insights.

Innis was born in 1894 near Otterville in Ontario. He was educated at McMaster University and the University of Toronto, graduating in 1916 and immediately enlisting in the Canadian army. He was wounded in France in 1917 and discharged from the army. He returned to his studies, finally taking his Ph.D. in economics at the University of Chicago in 1920. Then he was appointed lecturer in economics at the University of Toronto.

One side of Innis was the typical academic career man. He became head of the Department of Economics at Toronto in 1937 and dean of Graduate Studies in 1947, after which he held both positions until his death in 1952. He was president in turn of the Canadian Political Science Association, the Royal Society of Canada, and the American Economic Association. He served on the Nova Scotia Royal Commission of Economic Inquiry in 1934, on the Manitoba Royal Commission on Adult Education in 1946, and on the federal Royal Commission on Transport between 1948 and 1951.

Most academics would regard that as sufficient achievement. Innis paralleled it with the career as a seminal scholar for which he is now remembered. He began to study the history of the Canadian economy, and he discovered that in the process he was learning more and more about the origins of Canadian society, Canadian culture, and the very political shape of Canada. His doctoral thesis had concerned the creation of the Canadian Pacific Railway, and in due course he developed out of this his first book, *A History of the Canadian Pacific Railway* (1923). It was no mere factual history, though that was included. It was also a study of the relationship between the development of forms of transport and the shape taken by a nation. The route of the Canadian Pacific had been determined generations before when the fur trad-

ers discovered and developed their east-west routes by water and portage, and provided the geographical pattern on which Canada developed from a loose fur-trading empire into a colony, and finally – by the time Innis wrote his book – into a nation fumbling for its identity.

Innis worked backward in time for the subjects of his two other classics of Canadian historical interpretation, *The Fur Trade in Canada: An Introduction to Canadian Economic History* (1930) and *The Cod Fisheries: The History of an International Economy* (1940). In the first he showed how the fur industry – Canada's second great staple – was tied geographically to the St. Lawrence – Great Lakes system, and in the second he took the first great staple in historical terms and showed how the cod fishery brought Canada into an international market and hence into the conflicting spheres of English and American economic influence. The effect of such books on leading Canadian historians in our time, like D. G. Creighton and A. R. M. Lower, was profound. Neither would have written as he did if Innis had not been there as a pioneer.

During the brief years of his post-World War II career, Innis turned from transportation to the related theme of mass communications and their dominant influence on human institutions and cultures. *Empire and Communications* (1950), *The Bias of Communications* (1951), and *Changing Concepts of Time* (1952) are classics in their field, but they failed to reach a wide audience because, ironically, Innis's densely written prose made him difficult to read – a poor communicator. His ideas, however, were not condemned to oblivion; Marshall McLuhan was later to offer them to the public in a more popular form. Innis died in 1952 in Toronto, and D. G. Creighton, his most important disciple, wrote in 1957 a biographical tribute: *Harold Adams Innis: Portrait of a Scholar*.

Robert Laird Borden

Circumstances sometimes propel the least likely men into positions of political power, especially in times of crisis, as the case of Robert L. Borden demonstrates. Borden guided Canada as prime minister from 1911 to 1920. It was the Conservative interregnum between long Liberal reigns by Laurier and Mackenzie King, but it was also the period of World War I and of notable Canadian progress towards political independence.

Borden–born in 1854 at Grand Pré, Nova Scotia, and a lawyer by profession–was an honest man with much personal dignity, but he lacked the charismatic appeal of predecessors like Macdonald and Laurier, and only the extraordinary misfortunes that descended on the Conservative party after Macdonald's death allowed him to become its leader, almost by default. Death or misfortune had removed five successive Tory prime ministers in the five years between 1891 and 1896, and the party was drained of energy and leadership by the time Borden was elected to the House of Commons in 1896, the year of Laurier's great Liberal victory.

Apart from their parliamentary misfortunes, the Conservatives were demoralized by internal disputes arising from issues like the Manitoba Schools Act, over which brilliant men like D'Alton McCarthy had left the party, and by accusations of corruption which became more serious as Canadian politics began to turn away from the free and easy patronage that had been customary in the days before Confederation.

The Conservatives began to look for a man of solid worth, above suspicion, to lead them; and Borden, even if he was not particularly brilliant, seemed their best choice at a time when the Liberal party was in a phase of dynamic renewal under men like Laurier and Sifton. In 1901, when Sir Charles Tupper resigned, Borden was chosen party leader. He patiently reshaped the organization and in doing so heightened morale so that in 1911 the Conservatives were ready to take advantage of Laurier's troubles with his own party rebels.

They won the election and Borden became prime minister. Three years later, a man who hated militarism, he found himself guiding Canada through those years of war which were the most difficult period the country had yet endured.

There was not merely the human tragedy, which began almost immediately, for in 1914 Canada automatically entered the war as soon as Britain declared it, and Canadian soldiers were soon dying for the errors of British generals. There was also the bitter disunity that split Canada over the issue of conscription. Laurier and his Liberals had always opposed conscription, and although the 1917 general elections gave Borden a substantial majority in the country as a whole, the people of Quebec were almost unanimously against it. The division between English-speaking and French-speaking Canadians widened into a crevasse of resentment whose bitter memories all the years since 1917 have not entirely wiped away.

Borden imposed conscription unwillingly. Like Mackenzie King in a later war, he saw it as a necessity but a tragic one. He put more heart into the struggle to persuade the imperial authorities that in a war Canada was fighting, Canadian decisions must play their part. He insisted on a separate Canadian command at the front, and his demands for a share in decision making led to the formation of the Imperial War Cabinet. Finally, through his insistence, Canada sat at the peace conference with the same status as the small independent nations; later it became a founding member of the League of Nations and began to play an independent international role. These achievements place Borden among the important Canadian prime ministers.

Exhausted by the efforts and inner conflicts of the war years, Borden retired in 1920 from the prime ministership and from politics in general. But he continued to live in Ottawa, and almost until his death in 1937 he gave advice to political leaders, when they asked, and sometimes represented Canada at international conferences. It had been a fuller and more influential life than Borden could have imagined possible when in 1901 he took over the leadership of a broken party.

Arthur William Currie

Arthur William Currie was a citizen soldier who showed himself more brilliant than most of the professional generals. He also became one of the key figures in the assertion of Canadian independence that was accelerated by the conditions of World War I.

Currie began as an educator, and after a distinguished military career, ended as one. He was born in 1875 in Napperton, Ontario, and educated at the Strathroy Collegiate Institute. In 1893 he migrated to British Columbia and taught there for five years. Then in 1900 he established a real estate and insurance office in Victoria.

In 1897, while still a school teacher, Currie had joined the local militia, and in 1900 he was commissioned. He took an almost academic interest in the study of strategy and tactics, and by 1914 he had risen to the rank of lieutenant-colonel in command of the Fifth Canadian Garrison Artillery.

When war broke out in 1914, Currie was given command of the Vancouver Highland Battalion and went abroad in the first Canadian contingent, which he led in resisting the German assault at St. Julien, near Ypres, in April 1915. Subsequently he was appointed brigadier-general and given command of the Second Canadian Infantry Brigade. Later, promoted to major-general, he commanded the First Canadian Infantry Division in the battle of the Somme and the famous assault on Vimy Ridge in April 1917. Almost immediately afterwards Currie was given the highest rank in the Canadian forces serving abroad when he was appointed to succeed Sir Julian Byng as general officer commanding the Canadian Corps, with the rank of lieutenant-general.

Throughout the war, Currie had to fight campaigns on two fronts: against the German generals and against the British generals. In the field he showed organizing ability and tactical flexibility, and he was one of the few First War generals to retain the respect of his men, with a resultant high morale, though he had his critics who accused him of unnecessarily wasting men's lives. He may have done so; most generals did in trench fighting. Behind the lines he was perpetually involved in a struggle to prevent the British generals and especially the commander-in-chief, Douglas Haig, from destroying the identity of the Canadian forces by distributing their units among the Imperial Corps. In this struggle he had the support of the Canadian prime minister, Sir Robert Borden, and he succeeded in gaining the respect of the British prime minister, Lloyd George, who is said at one time to have considered replacing Haig by Currie as commander-in-chief.

Currie kept his men together as a separate army to the end and rode at the head of them into Mons on the signing of the armistice. Afterwards he commanded the Canadian forces on the Rhine until 1919, when he returned to Canada. He was then promoted to the rank of general and appointed inspector general of the Canadian Militia.

But Currie was a citizen soldier to the end, little interested in the career of a regular peacetime general, and when he was offered one of the highest posts in the teaching profession, that of principal and vice-chancellor of McGill University, he accepted it and fulfilled the role with good judgment until his death in Montreal in 1933.

Arthur Meighen

Arthur Meighen was one of the most brilliant debaters ever to enter the Canadian parliament and perhaps the most eloquent leader of the Conservative party since Sir John Macdonald. But he failed to inspire the confidence of his party or his country, and so his abilities were tragically wasted.

Meighen was born in 1874, the son of a poor Ottawa Valley farmer. He was educated at the University of Toronto and taught for a year but in 1898 moved west to the prairies and studied law in Winnipeg. He was called to the Manitoba bar in 1903 and began to practise that year in Portage la Prairie, showing himself an excellent courtroom lawyer.

It had become almost a tradition at this period for a brilliant lawyer in western Canada to enter the rather sparsely populated political scene; and as Meighen had not only ability but also strong Tory inclinations, it was natural that when he was elected to Parliament in 1908 it should be as a Conservative. He revealed himself a brilliant debater during the last years of Laurier's Liberal rule, and when the Conservatives returned to power under Borden he became solicitor general in 1913. This was not yet an office with cabinet rank, but in 1917 Meighen did enter the cabinet as secretary of state, and when the Union government was formed later in the same year he became minister of the interior.

It was during this period that Meighen sowed the seeds of his own future defeats by a number of authoritarian measures that he believed were demanded by the wartime emergency. He was responsible for the Wartime Elections Act, which disenfranchised many people likely to oppose conscription, an issue in the 1917 election. At the same time he incurred the resentment of the Quebecois by describing them publicly as "a backward people." And after the war, in 1919, when he was acting minister of justice, he antagonized labour by his obvious partiality towards the employers during the Winnipeg general strike.

When Sir Robert Borden resigned in 1920, he recommended that Meighen should follow him as leader of what was still nominally the Union government, and so Meighen became prime minister, though many Conservatives were doubtful of his ability to carry the country with him and though many Liberals who had remained within the wartime coalition both distrusted Meighen and were an... return to party politics. Even before Meighen decided a general election in 1921, there had been defections fr the ranks, particularly over the continued imposition tariffs, a policy Meighen was inflexible and unwise to defend during the election.

The result was a crushing defeat for the Conservatives. who came third at the polls with fifty seats, even trailir newly formed Progressive party. Meighen lost his ov though he was returned in an early by-election. He ag proved his quality as an opposition debater, but in 1925 elections he was still unable to gain a majority, though Mackenzie King was forced to operate a minority government with the help of the Progressives.

When opportunity did come to Meighen, it took a derisory form. In 1926 evidence was uncovered of graft in the customs department, and King went to the governor general with the request to dissolve Parliament. Instead, with dubious constitutionality, Lord Byng called on Meighen to form a cabinet. Injudiciously, Meighen agreed. He was defeated within three months by an alliance of Liberals and Progressives. In the subsequent election the Conservatives lost decisively, and in 1927 Meighen resigned the party leadership.

He returned to the practice of law and in 1932 accepted appointment to the Senate. In 1941 he was induced to re-enter active politics and resume the leadership of the Conservative party, but when he gave up his seat in the Senate he was defeated in a by-election, and he departed from political life to enter commerce in Toronto, where he died in 1960. Meighen had ability and more integrity than most politicians, but he suffered from an intellectual pride that made him unable to read other men's minds, and so he never made the allowances that in politics lead to success. Time and again his inflexibility guaranteed his defeat.

William Lyon Mackenzie King

Sir John A. Macdonald ruled Canada for many years through a combination of political astuteness and charisma. Mackenzie King, who ruled Canada longer than Sir John or any other Canadian prime minister, had virtually no charisma. He was a rather dowdy, unimpressive bachelor with a curious inner life, but he possessed in abundance the power to recognize and use opportunity, and men who appeared far more brilliant rarely succeeded in out-manoeuvring him.

William Lyon Mackenzie King was born in 1874 in Berlin, Ontario, which forty years later, in World War I, was renamed Kitchener. He owed the full splendour of his name to the fact that his mother was the daughter of the Upper Canadian rebel, William Lyon Mackenzie. King treasured the link, and since he was a practising spiritualist, he believed that both his grandfather and his mother regularly guided his political course through signs and other communications. This, however, King kept mostly to himself and his diaries, which since his death have been revealing how far in his inner self he was from the dull political technician he appeared at first sight.

King's education began at the University of Toronto and continued through postgraduate work at Harvard. His scholarship was brilliant enough to impress Sir William Mulock, appointed Canada's first minister of labour in 1900; Mulock chose King as his deputy minister, a remarkable first step into the civil service for a man of twenty-six.

King also impressed Sir Wilfrid Laurier, who persuaded him to go into politics and stand for Parliament as a Liberal. Elected in 1908, King was appointed minister of labour in 1909 but lost his seat when Laurier was defeated in 1911. He spent his period out of Parliament as labour adviser to the Rockefeller Foundation but remained faithful to Laurier during the difficult war years when the Liberals were in political limbo, with the result that when Laurier died in 1919 he succeeded him as party leader and became prime minister in 1921.

Throughout King's early years as prime minister of Canada he was energetic in defining the extent of Canada's independence within the commonwealth. During the Chanak crisis of 1922 he refused to send Canadian troops to assist Britain in her dispute with Turkey. Later in the decade he was active in the imperial conferences that led to the Statute of Westminster, by which Britain conceded the autonomy of dominions.

Of more immediate importance to Canadian domestic politics was the role he played in the Constitutional Crisis of 1926. A customs scandal had blown up, and King asked the governor general, Lord Byng, to dissolve Parliament. Instead, Byng called on the Conservative leader, Arthur Meighen, to form a government, which King soon defeated with the help of the Progressives. King then went to the country on the issue of the unconstitutionality of the governor general's refusal to accept the prime minister's advice, and thus he established a further stage in Canada's autonomy. To that autonomy he gave final form in 1939 when he insisted that Canada declare war on Germany independently of Great Britain.

King was defeated in 1930 by the Conservatives under R. B. Bennett, but this worked to his advantage since he was out of power during the most difficult years of the depression and so was able to return triumphantly in 1935. The depression relaxed more through a change in world economic trends than from any palliatives the Liberals applied, and the onset of war in 1939 ended the unemployment that crippled the country. King continued as prime minister throughout the war years. He had pledged in 1939 that there would be no conscription for overseas service, but in 1942 political pressures forced him to hold a national referendum, with predictable results: a vast majority of English Canadians in favour and a vast majority of French Canadians opposed. The bitterness between the two founding peoples that had arisen in World War I was repeated.

But in the end, by sheer political astuteness, King weathered this as he had weathered other political storms, and after the war he regained the Liberal political lead in Quebec so that when he resigned in 1948 he was able to hand over both the prime ministership and the party leadership to a Quebecois, Louis St. Laurent. King, prime minister for a total of twenty-two years, had been in office longer than any other prime minister of a commonwealth nation. He died, still a bachelor, in 1950.

John Wesley Dafoe

John W. Dafoe was one of the great journalists of our country and one of the few Canadians to have played an influential role in political life over a long period without being elected to any kind of parliament.

He emerged out of the old farming and lumbering society of the Ottawa Valley; his father had to follow both occupations to make a living. John Wesley Dafoe–his very name significant of the Methodist family background–was born in 1866 at Combermere and educated at Arnprior; at the age of seventeen he began his long journalistic career as a cub reporter for the *Montreal Star*. At eighteen he was that paper's parliamentary correspondent in Ottawa and at nineteen he became editor of the *Ottawa Evening Journal*. Realizing he had less experience than he needed for such a post, he resigned the following year–1886–to join the *Manitoba Free Press*, where he stayed for the next six years.

By the time Dafoe reached Winnipeg he had been converted from his family's Orange Toryism to Liberalism, largely through listening to one of Edward Blake's more carefully reasoned speeches, and a Liberal he remained the rest of his life. This made the *Manitoba Free Press*, which Clifford Sifton had given a Liberal viewpoint, a congenial haven for Dafoe, and after he went away in 1892 to work almost a decade for various Montreal papers, he was glad in 1901 to accept Sifton's offer of the editorship of the *Free Press*, a post he retained–through the paper's metamorphosis into the *Winnipeg Free Press* in 1931–until his death in 1944.

Dafoe set out to make the *Free Press* a Liberal paper similar to the *Manchester Guardian* in England; he succeeded in making it one of the best and most powerful papers in North America. In the process he became influential not only as a vigorous (though sometimes rather turgid) editorialist but also as an adviser of politicians, so that he was close to Laurier and Mackenzie King as well as to Sifton.

Dafoe's contract with Sifton allowed him total editorial independence, and there were times when this led to a sharp difference between the policies the two men advocated. In the national dispute during 1911 over a reciprocity treaty with the United States, for example, Dafoe supported Laurier while Sifton sharply opposed him.

Dafoe's great weakness as a guide of public opinion was his failure to recognize the threat of American domination over Canada. He had a long-standing distrust of Britain, which he dated from the failure of British delegates in the Alaska boundary negotiations of 1903 to gain terms sufficiently favourable to Canada; he once said that disappointment over this issue was "the real beginning of nationalism in Canada." He constantly advocated the increase of Canadian autonomy within the Empire, particularly admiring Sir Robert Borden's insistence on Canadian rights during World War I, and acting as Mackenzie King's unofficial adviser during the Imperial Conference of 1923. He envisaged the Empire as an extremely loose collection of independent states (which it has in fact become) and he placed real reliance on Canada's role in the League of Nations and on support for collective security, to which he devoted hundreds of editorials during the anxious years between the two world wars.

At the same time, Dafoe's view of Canada's role on the American continent is amply illustrated in the titles of two of his books: *Canada: An American Nation* (1935) and *Canada Fights: An American Democracy at War* (1941). Dafoe saw Canada's future inextricably linked, economically and politically, with that of the United States, and the prospect did not cause him much anxiety; undoubtedly his imperceptiveness in this respect had its effect on Canadian policies during World War II and immediately afterwards, the period of continental politics. In terms of internal Canadian politics, a great deal of Dafoe's original Conservatism lingered beneath the Liberal overlay; he saw the Winnipeg general strike of 1919 as a Bolshevik plot, and he was a bitter opponent of the CCF, all his life regarding socialism of any kind as necessarily a foe to liberty.

Emily Gowan Murphy

Emily Murphy, one of the most celebrated of Canadian feminists, was born as Emily Gowan Ferguson at Cookstown, Ontario, in 1868. Her grandfather, Ogle Gowan, had been a Tory journalist, editor of the Brockville *Statesman* and the Toronto *Patriot*, a member of the Upper Canadian assembly and for many years grand master of the Orange Association of British America.

Emily Ferguson was educated at the Bishop Strachan School in Toronto, and at the age of nineteen she married Arthur Murphy, the Anglican rector of Chatham, who was also a missionary travelling in the nearby rural areas. In 1904 the family, which now included two daughters, moved west to the Swan River district of Manitoba, where Murphy continued his missionary work, and three years later to Edmonton, where Emily lived the rest of her life.

Emily Murphy was never content with the ordinary life of a clergyman's wife. She possessed a sharp eye and ear, and had inherited from her grandfather a gift for writing, which she first gave expression in the diary she kept in Chatham and afterwards in the prairies, noting down shrewdly and often satirically the events and personalities of small town and frontier life.

It was out of these diaries that she gathered the material for the series of books reflecting on life as she saw it, which she published under the nom-de-plume of Janey Canuck. The first of them, *Janey Canuck Abroad* (1901) was an account, drawn from her journals, of a visit to England and Germany. Many of the attitudes that characterized the more famous Emily Murphy of later years were already evident. She countered English criticism of Canadian frontier crudeness with sharp observations on English snobbery and the English class system in general, and there are some particularly graphic descriptions of London slums in which she stresses how women and children were the prime victims of the dual curses of poverty and drunkenness.

Janey Canuck Abroad was followed in 1910 by *Janey Canuck in the West*, which largely concerned Emily Murphy's life at Swan River, in 1912 by *Open Trails*, and in 1914 by *Seeds of Pine*, sketches of life in Alberta. Her later writing tended to be related to a growing social activism and consisted largely of magazine articles on social issues, published under Emily Murphy's maiden name of Emily Ferguson in journals like *Maclean's*. The principal book she published in this later period was *The Black Candle* (1922), which reflected the campaign she carried on during the 1920s against the illegal drug traffic.

Emily Murphy's principal crusades, however, centred around the manifold issues involved in the establishment of equal rights for women. With Edmonton as her centre, she campaigned for married women's property rights and also for a women's court, in which cases where women were involved could be heard in a sympathetic atmosphere and where women could feel free to testify without embarrassment. In 1916 the Province of Alberta accepted her arguments and set up in Edmonton a women's court, presided over, appropriately, by Emily Murphy herself, who thus became the first woman magistrate in the British Empire.

Lawyers who found her a competent and uncompromising judge attempted to unseat her and Alice Jamieson, who presided over a women's court in Calgary, on the grounds that women had no legal status in matters of right and privilege. When this argument was rejected by the Supreme Court of Alberta, Emily Murphy and other feminists proceeded to claim their rights in the famous Persons Case. This case (described in the profile of Nellie McClung) was finally successful when the Privy Council in 1929 ruled that a "person" eligible for appointment to the Senate could be a woman.

The first woman member, Cairine Wilson, was appointed to the Senate in 1930. It was generally thought that Emily Murphy, who resigned her post as magistrate in 1931, would be the second woman senator, but in 1933 her life and her courageous career were brought suddenly to an end when she died of a heart attack.

Thomas Alexander Crerar

Canadian federal politics turned from the two-party to the three-party pattern not through the appearance of the CCF in the 1930s but through the meteoric emergence in 1920-21 of the Progressive party as a movement representing populist agrarian dissent in both the west of Canada and in Ontario. In the 1921 election the Progressives, with sixty-five seats, emerged as the second strongest party in the House of Commons. By 1926 the party had almost faded away. The reasons for its strange rise and fall are to be found not only in the exceptional political circumstances of the time but also in the personality of the man who dominated and then deserted it at the moment of opportunity, Thomas Alexander Crerar.

Crerar was born in 1876 at Molesworth, Ontario, but his parents moved to a farm in Manitoba on the wave of westward migration, and he was brought up on the prairies and himself farmed there for a while. Becoming involved in the movement to protect farmers' interests by co-operative organization and political action, he acquired a key position in 1907 when he became president of a farmer-owned marketing group, the Grain Growers' Grain Company, later the United Grain Growers.

Crerar was active in the organization of the Canadian Council of Agriculture, formed in 1909-10 to co-ordinate the activity of the various provincial farm bodies, and in the drawing up in 1916 of the council's Farmer's Platform for political action, aimed largely at instituting various well-known agrarian panaceas such as lower tariffs and the nationalization of the railways. In the elections of 1917, however, the Council of Agriculture did not pursue its platform, since the main issue then was the formation of a Union government to conduct World War I with the maximum efficiency, and one of the concessions which Prime Minister Borden made to farmer opinion was the appointment of Crerar – a leading farmer M.P. – to the post of minister of agriculture.

Crerar resigned in 1919 and became leader of a group of twelve farmer M.P.'s who objected to the current government policy of high tariffs and formed themselves in 1920 into the Progressive party, following the example of similar agrarian parties, which had emerged in the American Midwest, and encouraged by the victory of the United Farmers in the 1919 Ontario provincial elections.

The Progressive party was endorsed by the Canadian Council of Agriculture, whose New National Policy, calling for lower tariffs, reciprocity with the United States, and a tough line with the railways, it adopted. Crerar and his associates were probably as surprised as everyone else when the Progressive party came second in the elections with sixty-five seats in the House of Commons, while the Conservatives had only fifty. With a United Farmers' victory in Alberta in the same year and in Manitoba in 1922, it seemed as though the chances of the agrarian groups wielding decisive influence in the country's policies were considerable.

In fact, however, Crerar was a leader without a policy. He was basically a Liberal who wanted quick and drastic reductions in the tariffs to enable farmers to buy machinery cheaply, but otherwise his policies were virtually indistinguishable from those of Mackenzie King, and instead of forming his caucus in the Commons into an effective opposition, he let King buy him off with a concession on railway freight rates and allowed the Conservatives to assume the role of a genuine opposition. Apart from his own lack of a policy, Crerar found himself completely unable to discipline a party, many of whose members were either radical populists or quasi-socialists, and in 1922 he resigned the leadership of the Progressives, pleading that it conflicted with his duties as president of the United Grain Growers. Within five years the Progressive party had broken apart, many of its members – like Crerar – returning to the Liberals and others joining with urban socialists in 1932-33 to form the CCF, a party distant from Crerar's viewpoint.

Crerar remained an influential man because of his position with the United Grain Growers, and when he resigned the presidency of that organization in 1929, Mackenzie King made him minister of railways. When King returned to power in 1935, Crerar went back to the cabinet as a western representative and stayed there in various positions until he was appointed to the Senate in 1945. He died, almost a centenarian, in 1975, after many years of retirement.

Agnes Macphail

Agnes Macphail was not one of the celebrated fighters for women's suffrage in Canada; her campaigns were mainly in other fields – for co-operation and against war, for a better deal for the farmers and against the existing Canadian penal system. In fact, it could be said of Agnes Macphail that she walked into politics as if sexual differences did not exist and always fought as an equal for the issues that moved her, without regard to her own personal situation.

She was born in 1890 in rural Ontario and took her teacher's training course at the Stratford Normal School. She taught always in small country schools, where she became aware of the problems that faced the farmers in a situation where the leading political parties tended to represent always the interests of the manufacturers, the banks, the railways: all those groups and interests which the farmers saw as exploiters of the people who cultivated the earth and provided the country's economic basis.

In 1919 Agnes Macphail became sufficiently concerned about rural problems to begin speaking at public meetings in the farmers' cause, and she became an active member of the United Farmers of Ontario (UFO), a political movement based on the idea of "occupational" representation – that is, that farmers and rural people should elect representatives who would speak for the rural interest and who then might ally themselves with other groups representing the labour interest, rather than becoming involved in what the leaders of the UFO regarded as the corrupt existing parties.

Agnes Macphail impressed the farmers of Ontario with her intelligence, integrity, and energy, and in 1921 she was chosen over several male rivals at the UFO convention for the Southeast Grey constituency to stand as their candidate in that year's federal elections. She was elected and thus became the first woman member of the House of Commons.

She entered Parliament as an independent but immediately joined the Progressive party led by T. A. Crerar, which had gained sixty-five seats and was in fact the second party, with the Conservatives trailing it by fifteen seats. When Crerar and his successor in the Progressive leadership, Robert Forke, failed to make the party an independent force and gave tacit support to Mackenzie King's Liberal government in return for minor concessions, radical populists like Agnes Macphail quickly became restive, and in 1924 she and five Alberta members broke away to form a separate caucus of quasi-socialist farmers' representatives, whom the press called the Ginger Group, a title its members gladly accepted.

As the Progressive party disintegrated, the Ginger Group retained its identity as a small faction of ten or a dozen M.P.'s, working in alliance with J. S. Woodsworth and other labour representatives, and eventually in 1932-33 merging with labour and socialist groups to form the Co-operative Commonwealth Federation (CCF). In these developments Agnes Macphail pursued a rather unattached course, continuing until 1940 to represent her Ontario constituency as an independent but in fact usually voting in Parliament with the CCF.

In 1940, after nineteen years of membership, Agnes Macphail lost her seat in the House of Commons. She now joined the CCF, and in 1943 was elected on the party's ticket to the Ontario legislature, where she continued to sit as a CCF member until 1951.

Apart from her parliamentary activities, Agnes Macphail was an active worker for the Ontario Co-operative Union and spent a great deal of time organizing co-operative stores and marketing agencies in the rural areas of the province. She was a dedicated pacifist, and when she became a Canadian delegate to the League of Nations in Geneva, she was the first woman to be elected to the disarmament committee. She was also active in penal reform and was largely responsible for the 1938 royal commission which investigated the Canadian prisons and brought in a sensational report revealing their gross defects.

Agnes Macphail died in Toronto in 1954, shortly after her retirement from political life.

Richard Bedford Bennett

There are parts of Canada, particularly in the prairies, where the name of R. B. Bennett is still remembered with derision and even hatred, not because he was a worse man than other Canadian political leaders but mainly because he had the misfortune to come into power at a time of national crisis–in the midst of the Great Depression–and had neither the skill nor the strength to solve the nation's problems. Perhaps such worldwide problems were insoluble by any Canadian leader, but Bennett was the man in charge of the country at the time, and he was inevitably blamed.

Richard Bedford Bennett came of old English-Canadian stock. His father's and his mother's families had both arrived from Connecticut before the American Revolution. He was born at Hopewell Hill in New Brunswick in 1870, and he trained first as a teacher but afterwards went on to law school at Dalhousie University and in 1893 was called to the New Brunswick bar. In 1897 he moved to Calgary, where the prospects seemed greener than in the Maritimes. He became a partner of Senator James Lougheed, acted as local counsel for the Canadian Pacific Railway, and invested heavily in hydro power and industry, as well as inheriting a controlling interest in the Eddy match company.

Thus, when Bennett was moving into politics, he was already a wealthy man with interests to defend. His early political career was broken and erratic. He was elected as a Conservative to the legislature of the North-West Territories in 1898 but was defeated when he competed in the first Alberta elections of 1905. He was elected provincially in 1909 but resigned in 1911. He was elected to the House of Commons in 1914 but quarrelled with the prime minister, Borden, and did not seek re-election in 1917. When Meighen became prime minister in 1920, Bennett accepted the post of minister of justice but had to abandon it because he was defeated in a by-election. He did enter the House of Commons in 1925 and was minister of finance in Meighen's brief and disastrous second government in 1926. But scanty as his record may have been, Bennett was chosen as leader of the Conservative party when Meighen resigned in 1927.

In 1930 Bennett campaigned on a programme of high tariffs with imperial preferences and public works that would provide employment and alleviate the evils of the depression. Some of his proposals, such as the Transcanada Highway and the St. Lawrence Seaway, were in fact to be achieved by later governments many years after Bennett's term of office. But though he won the election, the depression continued to run ahead of him, and most of his schemes proved at the time impractical. The United States Senate rejected a seaway treaty, and Bennett postponed other measures year after year, until his government became a byword for stagnation and people in the prairies who could no longer afford gasoline gave the name of "Bennett buggies" to the horse-drawn automobiles often seen on the roads. When Bennett did finally, at the end of 1934, bring forward a series of proposals based on the American New Deal, these were ruled unconstitutional by the courts.

Meanwhile there was a split in the cabinet and in the Conservative caucus, and H. H. Stevens led the malcontents in forming a Reconstructionist party. The division played into the hands of the Liberals, and an impatient country returned Mackenzie King to power in 1935 with 171 seats; so began the long period of Liberal rule that was not broken until the advent of John Diefenbaker as Conservative prime minister in 1957.

Bennett remained as leader of the opposition until 1938, when he retired from politics and went to live on a country estate he had bought near Dorking in England. There he lived out his remaining years, a lonely old bachelor, blamed for a failure that was by no means wholly his fault, and hardly consoled by his elevation to the House of Lords as Viscount Bennett in 1941. He died in 1947.

James Shaver Woodsworth

The political left in Canada has drawn an astonishing number of leaders from the ranks of the clergy. The first leader of a socialist (CCF) government in Canada was the former Baptist minister T. C. Douglas in Saskatchewan, and the first leader of the federal CCF party was the former Methodist minister, J. S. Woodsworth. Both of them reached socialism through a wave of awakening social consciousness that was strong in a number of Canadian churches at the beginning of the present century and was manifested in other ways by writers like Ralph Connor and Salem Bland. James Shaver Woodsworth, like the others, came to his political position through the hard process of realizing that what the church represents may not always accord with one's own conception of how Christianity must adapt itself to modern conditions.

J. S. Woodsworth, as in later years he was almost universally known, was born near Islington, Ontario, in 1874, the son and grandson of Methodist ministers, and in childhood went to Manitoba, where his father became a missionary at Portage la Prairie. He was educated at Wesley College in Winnipeg and Victoria College in Toronto, being ordained as a Methodist minister in 1896. He served as pastor to churches in Winnipeg and Revelstoke, British Columbia, but increasingly he found his own beliefs differing from those he was expected to preach, and in 1907 he proposed to resign from the Methodist ministry but was persuaded to take charge of the All People's Mission in Winnipeg, a post which brought him into contact with the poorest people in the city and especially with the unskilled immigrants who could not gain a living in Canada. In 1908 he published *The Strangers within Our Gates*, a study of their condition that combined scholarship and compassion. In another book, *My Neighbor* (1910), he gave a further view of the lives of the urban poor and stressed the social obligations of Christians.

It was evident that Woodsworth was rapidly moving out of the orbit of formal Christianity, and in 1912 he resigned from the mission to become field secretary of the Canadian Welfare League. Shortly afterwards, in 1916, the three prairie provinces set up a Bureau of Social Research, and Woodsworth was appointed director, only to be dismissed in 1917 for his stand against Canadian participation in World War I and against national registration, which he rightly regarded as the precursor of conscription. He was taken on as preacher at a mission in Gibson's Landing, British Columbia, but again was dismissed, this time for helping to organize a co-operative. He now resigned finally from the Methodist ministry and began to work as a longshoreman in Vancouver.

Yet Woodsworth still retained strong links with the prairies. In 1918 he helped organize the Non-Partisan League–a radical farmers' group–in Alberta. In 1919 he was present in Winnipeg to participate in the general strike. He was among a number of its leaders arrested on a charge of criminal libel, but when one of his associates was acquitted the charges against him were dropped. The experience was a virtual baptism into the labour movement, to which Woodsworth dedicated his life from this time onwards.

In 1921 he was elected to the House of Commons as labour member for Winnipeg North; he retained the seat for the rest of his life. In Parliament, often single-handed, he fought long but frequently successful battles for social reforms, including better working conditions for farmers and industrial workers, and the first federal old age legislation, which he shamed a reluctant government into passing in 1926. With other labour members he formed an alliance with the Ginger Group, the lively left wing that split away from the moribund Progressive party, and the alliance led to the formation of the CCF in 1932. Woodsworth became its first president, and house leader when the party won seven seats in the 1935 election.

All his life Woodsworth remained a convinced pacifist. In 1939 he went against the rest of the House of Commons, and even against the members of his own party, by casting a single vote against Canada's entry into World War II. Yet such was the respect in which he was held that the CCF retained him as president and later honorary president, and his constituents returned him in the next election, though few accepted his antiwar views. In 1940 Woodsworth suffered a severe stroke which caused his retirement from active politics, and in 1942 he died, perhaps the most respected of all Canadian political leaders. If Canada has had a Gandhi, his name was surely Woodsworth.

William Aberhart

Social Credit, as devised by the British engineer Major C. H. Douglas in the early 1920s, was an intricate monetary theory which claimed that the redistribution of purchasing power would lead to the solution of most of the economic injustices within our society. Social Credit, as it has played a part in Canadian federal politics and in the provincial politics of Alberta, British Columbia, and Quebec, has been a much-diluted form of the original doctrine, and in practice the Social Credit governments that have held power for long periods in Alberta and British Columbia have been little more than right-wing populist administrations pursuing relatively conservative economic and social policies.

The first Social Credit government in Canada–and in the world–came into power in Alberta in 1935, and the man who led the Social Crediters to their landslide victory was William Aberhart, already well known in Calgary as "Bible Bill."

Aberhart was born in 1878 in Hibbard, Ontario, and after graduating at Queen's University in 1906, he became a school teacher. He moved to Alberta in 1910, and in 1915 became principal of the Crescent Heights High School in Calgary. Aberhart was a religious enthusiast, a zealous fundamentalist, and in 1918 he established his own quasi-church, the Calgary Prophetic Bible Institute, where he gave regular classes in biblical interpretation. He immediately recognized the value of radio as a means of communicating ideas; during the later 1920s he instituted a "Back to the Bible Hour" on a local radio station, and his influence spread rapidly outward from Calgary as he acquired a regular audience of rural people in all parts of the province.

Social Credit had already begun to gather a following in Alberta even before Aberhart became involved. Major Douglas had come to Canada in 1923. Interviewed by the House of Commons Standing Committee on Banking and Commerce, he made an impression on members of the United Farmers of Alberta, and they were the first to spread Social Credit literature in the province. Aberhart first became actively involved in 1932 when he began to introduce a simplified version of Social Credit into his lectures. It offered a promise at which the depression-ridden country people reached with eagerness. When the United Farmers of Alberta, then the government of the province, refused to incorporate his version of the doctrine in its platform, Aberhart hurriedly organized a Social Credit party and led it to a decisive victory–fifty-six seats out of sixty-three–in the provincial elections of 1935. Aberhart was not a candidate, but one of the successful candidates vacated his seat and Aberhart won the by-election, becoming premier. It was less a vote of confidence in Social Credit, since few of the electors understood even Aberhart's simplification of the theory, than an expression of despair at the failure of other parties to solve the problems of the depression.

Aberhart attempted to put his theories of monetary reform into practice in a number of ways. He promised a $25 monthly dividend to every inhabitant of Alberta; he also attempted to issue a kind of scrip called "prosperity certificates" to serve as a medium of local exchange. But all these measures were disallowed by the federal courts, so that Aberhart was really able to offer only a programme of reform in education and a reasonably efficient administration, which carried him through to the end of the depression and to the point where oil discoveries began to change Alberta's whole economic situation. Aberhart was still the unchallenged premier of Alberta when he died suddenly in Vancouver in 1943. He left a party so strongly entrenched that it would retain power for another quarter of a century.

Notes

1. *Executive Council.* The structure of colonial governments in British North America was based on the imperial government, with the appointed Executive Council fulfilling the functions of a cabinet, and a two-chamber legislature consisting of the Legislative Council and the Legislative Assembly. The Legislative Council in its early form consisted of the officers of the crown plus appointed lay members; in later years it became the usual custom for the lay members to be elected. The Legislative Assembly was elected, on a limited suffrage, and was regarded as having control of money matters, whereas all other legislation had to pass both houses. Occasionally, as in British Columbia, there was no assembly and the only elected representatives were the lay members of the Legislative Council.

2. *Durham Report.* After the rebellions of 1837 in Lower and Upper Canada, John George Lambton, Earl of Durham, commonly known as "Radical Jack" because of his political inclinations, was sent out as governor general and high commissioner to inquire into the causes of the rebellions. He arrived and departed in 1838 and prepared his report in 1839, dying in 1840. The report, which offended the Quebecois by describing them as a people without a history and a culture, recommended the union of the colonies, which took place in 1841, and also responsible government, which was not implemented until 1849.

3. *Double Shuffle.* The Double Shuffle was a manoeuvre based on Sir John A. Macdonald's awareness of loopholes in Canadian parliamentary rules. At the end of July 1858 the Macdonald–Cartier ministry was defeated and a government led by George Brown took its place. According to the rules of the day, the newly appointed ministers had to seek re-election, and while Brown and his associates were out of Parliament, Macdonald and Cartier defeated the new government. Brown asked the governor general to dissolve Parliament; instead, he called on Cartier and Macdonald again. Macdonald then discovered an obscure rule by which a minister could change his post and need not seek re-election, provided it were done within a month. All the min-

isters in the new cabinet therefore took different posts than they had had before their defeat. This happened on the night of 6 August. On the morning of the seventh they availed themselves of the clause to make a second shift – back to their old posts. This was the Double Shuffle, a legal but hardly ethical procedure.

4. *National Policy.* The National Policy, which Sir John A. Macdonald adopted as his platform in March 1878, was a three-pronged programme, embracing protective tariffs to nurture Canadian farming, mining, and manufactures, the completion of the CPR to create a national economy, and the encouragement of immigration to occupy the West and provide markets for Canadian manufacturers.

5. *The Canada Company.* An English company of land speculators that operated from 1824 to 1843, acquiring two million acres in the Guelph region which was opened to colonization. The novelist, John Galt, was its first superintendent and he gave his name to one of the new towns built under the company's aegis.

6. *Rupert's Land.* Named in 1670 after Prince Rupert, uncle of Charles II and first governor of the Hudson's Bay Company, this was the territory of the rivers flowing into Hudson's Bay, granted to the company by its original charter.

7. *Canada First.* This was the first nationalist movement in Canada, founded in 1868 by a group including Charles Mair. Later, temporary supporters included Goldwin Smith and Edward Blake, but the movement had died away by the end of the 1870s.

8. *Bloc Populaire.* The Bloc Populaire, which emerged in 1943 out of Quebecois opposition to conscription, was a loose alliance of nationalists and opponents of Maurice Duplessis, led by Maxime Raymond and André Laurendeau. It had some success in elections during the latter part of World War II but fell apart with the end of hostilities in 1945.

9. *Adrien Arcand.* Arcand (1888-1967) was Canada's only important avowedly fascist leader, editing papers like *Le Goglu* and *Le Patriote* in Montreal, and heading groups like the National Unity Party, which combined anti-Communism and anti-Semitism with Arcand's own brand of Quebec nationalism. Arcand was interned throughout World War II and afterwards failed to regain his following.

10. *Prince Kropotkin, Professor James Mavor.* Prince Peter Kropotkin, the great anarchist, travelled the Canadian prairies in 1895 and saw the Mennonite settlements there. When the Doukhobors had to leave tsarist Russia because of persecution, it was Kropotkin who suggested they come to the Canadian prairies, and his friend James Mavor, professor of political economy at the University of Toronto (and grand-

father of Mavor Moore) set on foot the necessary negotiations with the Canadian government.

11. *Anna Jameson, John Richardson.* Important Upper Canadian writers of the prephotographic era. Anna Jameson was in Canada briefly, from 1836-37, but she wrote one of the most vivid early accounts of the country, *Winter Studies and Summer Rambles in Canada* (1838). Richardson, military historian and novelist, was a native Canadian of Loyalist descent who fought as a boy in the War of 1812, of which he wrote a history. His most important works are his two novels, *Wacousta* (1832) and *The Canadian Brothers* (1840), rather gothic tales of violent action, and his long narrative poem, *Tecumseh* (1828) about the great Indian beside whom he fought against the Americans in 1812.

12. *James Wilson Morrice.* There are many who regard James Wilson Morrice (1865-1924) as the finest Canadian painter. Most of his life, after he first reached Paris in 1890, was lived away from Canada (though he made annual trips home up to 1914 and painted many fine works in Quebec); he died in Tunis. Morrice was accepted in Paris as a painter equal to most of the Europeans of his time; he was the close friend of Henri Matisse and also of Somerset Maugham and Arnold Bennett. Because he lived so much abroad, his influence on Canadian painting and his repute here have never been as great as they deserved.

Picture Credits

Archives Nationales du Québec: p. 99
Archives of Ontario: pp. 23, 27, 205
Archives of Saskatchewan: p. 125
Canadian Pacific: p. 131
City of Edmonton Archives: p. 239
Eaton Archives: p. 71
Glenbow-Alberta Institute: pp. 55, 105, 115, 117, 123, 133,
    137, 139, 141, 163, 203, 249
Hudson's Bay Company Archives: p. 169
National Gallery of Canada: pp. 75, 211
Notman Photographic Archives: pp. 13, 17, 21, 25, 29, 31,
    35, 39, 41, 45, 47, 49, 57, 83, 107, 143, 199, 215
Provincial Archives of Alberta: p. 173
Provincial Archives of British Columbia: pp. 147, 151, 153,
    157, 159, 161, 165, 167, 207, 221
Provincial Archives of Manitoba: pp. 111, 135, 197
Public Archives of Canada:

p. 11, C-1993	p. 89, C-3844	p. 183, C-70771
p. 15, C-31493	p. 91, PA-13027	p. 185, C-7043
p. 19, C-5961	p. 93, C-27360	p. 187, C-22884
p. 33, C-10144	p. 95, PA-47186	p. 189, PA-25944
p. 37, PA-25465	p. 97, C-16657	p. 191, PA-7764
p. 43, C-26415	p. 101, PA-74099	p. 193, C-68854
p. 51, C-20052	p. 103, C-88566	p. 195, C-3187
p. 53, C-14100	p. 109, PA-26321	p. 201, C-11299
p. 59, PA-28973	p. 119, PA-26668	p. 213, C-7571
p. 61, PA-25698	p. 121, C-27663	p. 223, C-37819
p. 63, PA-27030	p. 127, C-1873	p. 227, C-3407
p. 65, PA-25998	p. 129, C-15289	p. 229, PA-27948
p. 67, PA-27943	p. 145, C-9071	p. 231, PA-1370
p. 69, PA-12278	p. 149, PA-25397	p. 233, C-5799
p. 73, PA-57342	p. 155, C-36107	p. 235, C-26989
p. 77, C-17335	p. 171, C-18290	p. 241, C-3509
p. 79, C-21005	p. 175, C-22876	p. 243, C-21562 (Copyright:
p. 81, PA-25433	p. 177, C-6672	Karsh, Ottawa)
p. 85, C-15876	p. 179, C-18138	p. 245, C-7731
p. 87, C-23565	p. 181, C-57591	p. 247, C-55449

RCMP Archives: p. 113
Tom Thomson Memorial Gallery of Fine Art, Owen Sound: p. 217
University of Toronto Archives: p. 225
Winnipeg Free Press: p. 237

A. L. Grove: p. 209
Dr. Naomi Jackson Groves: p. 219

Index

Aberhart, William, 248
Allan, Sir Hugh, 48
Almighty Voice, 138
Archibald, Sir Adams George, 108
Aubert de Gaspé, Philippe-Joseph, 100

Baldwin, Robert, 14
Barker, William, 156
Begbie, Sir Matthew Baillie, 152
Belaney, Archibald Stansfeld. *See* Grey Owl
Bell, Alexander Graham, 76
Bengough, John Wilson, 74
Bennett, Richard Bedford (Viscount Bennett), 244
Bernier, Joseph-Elzéar, 176
Big Bear, 126
Blake, Edward, 62
Bompas, William Carpenter, 172
Borden, Sir Robert Laird, 228
Bourassa, Henri, 92
Bourget, Mgr. Ignace, 84
Brown, George, 42
Brown, Kootenay, 162

Campbell, Robert, 170
Carr, Emily, 220
Cartier, Sir George-Étienne, 34
Cartwright, Sir Richard John, 68
Connor, Ralph (Charles William Gordon), 196
Crerar, Thomas Alexander, 240
Crowfoot, 122
Currie, Sir Arthur William, 230

Dafoe, John Wesley, 236
Davin, Nicholas Flood, 134
Dawson, George Mercer, 142
De Cosmos, Amor, 148
Dewdney, Edgar, 118
Dorion, Sir Antoine-Aimé, 82
Douglas, Sir James, 146
Dumont, Gabriel, 120

Duncan, William, 158

Eaton, Timothy, 70
Edwards, Robert Chambers (Bob Edwards), 136

Fleming, Sir Sandford, 130
Fréchette, Louis-Honoré, 98

Galt, Sir Alexander Tilloch, 38
Gordon, Charles William. *See* Connor, Ralph
Grant, George Monro, 222
Grenfell, Sir Wilfred Thomason, 174
Grey Owl (Archibald Stansfeld Belaney), 204
Groulx, Abbé Lionel-Adolphe, 96
Grove, Frederick Philip, 208
Gun-an-Noot, Simon, 166
Gzowski, Sir Casimir Stanislaus, 28

Helmcken, John Sebastian, 150
Hincks, Sir Francis, 16
Houde, Camillien, 94
Howe, Joseph, 36

Innis, Harold Adams, 226

Jackson, Alexander Young, 218
Johnson, Emily Pauline, 206

Kane, Paul, 210
King, William Lyon Mackenzie, 234
Krieghoff, Cornelius, 212

Lacombe, Albert, 116
Laflamme, Toussaint Antoine Rodolphe, 80
La Fontaine, Sir Louis-Hippolyte, 18
Lampman, Archibald, 192
Larsen, Henry Asbjorn, 182
Laurier, Sir Wilfrid, 64
Leacock, Stephen, 198

McCarthy, D'Alton, 60
McClung, Nellie, 202
Macdonald, Sir John Alexander, 32
Macdonald, John Sandfield, 20
McGee, Thomas D'Arcy, 40
Mackenzie, Alexander, 50
Mackenzie, William Lyon, 10
MacNab, Sir Allan Napier, 12
Macphail, Agnes, 242
Mair, Charles, 188
May, Wilfrid Reid (Wop May), 180
Meighen, Arthur, 232
Mercier, Honoré, 88
Merritt, William Hamilton, 26
Molson, William, 30

Montgomery, Lucy Maud, 200
Moodie, Susanna, 184
Mowat, Sir Oliver, 58
Murphy, Emily Gowan, 238
Murray, Margaret, 72

Nelligan, Émile, 102
Norquay, John, 110
Notman, William, 214

Oppenheimer, David, 160
Otter, Sir William Dillon, 128

Papineau, Louis-Joseph, 78
Piapot, 132
Poundmaker, 124

Rae, John, 168
Riel, Louis, 104
Roberts, Sir Charles G. D., 190
Robson, John, 154
Ryerson, Adolphus Egerton, 22

Saunders, Sir Charles Edward, 144
Scott, Duncan Campbell, 194
Sifton, Sir Clifford, 66
Simpson, Sir George, 24
Smith, Sir Donald Alexander
    (Baron Strathcona and Mount Royal), 52
Smith, Goldwin, 224
Steele, Sir Samuel Benfield, 114
Stefansson, Vilhjalmur, 178
Stephen, Sir George (Baron Mount Stephen), 54
Strathcona, Lord. *See* Smith, Donald Alexander

Taché, Mgr. Alexandre-Antonin, 106
Tarte, Joseph-Israel, 90
Taschereau, Elzéar Alexandre, 86
Thomson, Thomas John (Tom Thomson), 216
Tilley, Sir Samuel Leonard, 44
Traill, Catharine Parr, 186
Tupper, Sir Charles, 46

Van Horne, Sir William Cornelius, 56
Verigin, Peter Vasil'evich, 164

Walsh, James Morrow, 112
Ware, John, 140
Woodsworth, James Shaver, 246

Faces from History

Editorial/Carlotta Lemieux
Design/David Shaw & Associates Ltd.
Typesetting/Howarth & Smith Ltd.
Printing and binding/The Bryant Press Ltd.